Walking Through Social Research is a poignant collection of essays that explores walking as immersion in city life. This rich and compelling collection engages with issues of violence, speculation and vulnerability, showing us how mis-steps, walk-alongs, air walks and walking together reach and reveal urban complexities.

Suzanne Hall, *Director of the Cities Programme, London School of Economics and Political Science, UK*

Bates and Rhys-Taylor offer an exciting collection of essays that take us on a variety of walks across a diversity of cities. This book is a timely contribution to the field of urban studies as it offers multiple reasons of why the practice of walking is essential to researching, knowing and reflecting on urban life. The essays are a pure joy to read as they offer a fine balance between theory, methods and empirical studies. An inspiring and fascinating read.

Monica Degen, *Senior Lecturer in Cultural Sociology, Brunel University London, UK*

Walking Through Social Research

As an ethnographic method walking has a long history, but it has only recently begun to attract focused attention. By walking alongside participants, researchers have been able to observe, experience and make sense of a broad range of everyday practices. At the same time, the idea of talking and walking with participants has enabled research to be informed by the landscapes in which it takes place. By sharing conversations in place, and at the participants' pace, sociologists are beginning to develop both a feel for, and a theoretical understanding of, the transient, embodied and multisensual aspects of walking. The result, as this collection demonstrates, is an understanding of the social world evermore congruent with people's lived experiences of it.

This interdisciplinary collection comprises a unique journey through a variety of walking methodologies. The collection highlights a range of possibilities for enfolding sound, smell, emotion, movement and memory into our accounts, illustrating the sensuousness, skill, pitfalls and rewards of walking as a research practice. Each chapter draws on original empirical research to present ways of walking and to discuss the conceptual, practical and technical issues that walking entails. Alongside feet on the ground, the devices and technologies that make up hybrid research mobilities are brought to attention. This collection is bookended by two short pedestrian essays that take the reader on illustrative urban walks, suggesting routes through the city, as well as ways in which the reader might make their own path through walking methods.

An innovative title, *Walking Through Social Research* will be of interest to undergraduate and postgraduate students, researchers and academics who are interested in Sociology, Geography, Cultural Studies, Urban Studies and Qualitative Research Methods.

Charlotte Bates is a Sociologist at the Cardiff School of Social Sciences, Cardiff University, UK.

Alex Rhys-Taylor is a Sociologist at the Centre for Urban and Community Research, Goldsmiths, University of London, UK.

Routledge Advances in Research Methods

Walking Through Social Research

Edited by
**Charlotte Bates and
Alex Rhys-Taylor**

Routledge
Taylor & Francis Group

LONDON AND NEW YORK

First published 2017 by Routledge

2 Park Square, Milton Park, Abingdon, Oxfordshire OX14 4RN
711 Third Avenue, New York, NY 10017

Routledge is an imprint of the Taylor & Francis Group, an informa business

First issued in paperback 2018

Library of Congress Cataloging in Publication Data
Names: Bates, Charlotte, 1978– editor. | Rhys-Taylor, Alex, editor.
Title: Walking through social research / [edited by] Charlotte Bates and
Alex Rhys-Taylor.
Description: Abingdon, Oxon; New York, NY: Routledge, 2017. |
Series: Routledge advances in research methods; 22 | Includes
bibliographical references and index.
Identifiers: LCCN 2016046575 | ISBN 9781138674042 (hardback)
Subjects: LCSH: Sociology–Methodology. | Cultural geography–
Methodology. | Walking–Social aspects.
Classification: LCC HM511.W35 2017 | DDC 301.01–dc23
LC record available at https://lccn.loc.gov/2016046575

ISBN: 978-1-138-67404-2 (hbk)
ISBN: 978-1-138-39314-1 (pbk)

Typeset in Times New Roman
by Wearset Ltd, Boldon, Tyne and Wear

Contents

Figures

Contributors

Les Back is a Professor of Sociology at Goldsmiths, University of London. His work attempts to create a sensuous or live sociology committed to new modes of sociological writing and representation. His books include: *Academic Diary* (Goldsmiths Press, 2016), *Live Methods*, co-edited with Nirmal Puwar (Wiley-Blackwell, 2012) and *The Art of Listening* (Berg, 2007).

Charlotte Bates is a Lecturer at the Cardiff School of Social Sciences. Her research explores the interconnections between the body, everyday life and place, with a particular focus on illness and disability. She is interested in developing inventive and sensuous ways of doing sociology and her first edited collection, *Video Methods: Social Science Research in Motion* (Routledge, 2015), was published in the Routledge Advances in Research Methods series.

Andrew Clark is a Reader in Sociology at the University of Salford. His research focuses on applied but theoretically informed issues relating to social and spatial inequalities. Recent research has investigated experiences of domestic fire, perceptions of urban regeneration and the neighbourhood experiences of people living with dementia.

Jennifer Gabrys is a Reader in the Department of Sociology at Goldsmiths, University of London, and Principal Investigator on the ERC-funded project, Citizen Sense, which engages with inventive approaches to workshops and walking in order to test and query environmental sensing technology. Jennifer's books include *Program Earth: Environmental Sensing Technology and the Making of a Computational Planet* (University of Minnesota Press, 2016) and *Digital Rubbish: A Natural History of Electronics* (University of Michigan Press, 2011). Her work can be found at citizensense.net and jennifergabrys.net.

Michael Gallagher is a Research Fellow in the Faculty of Education at Manchester Metropolitan University. His research spans human geography and childhood studies, with particular interests in sound, media and experimental methods. His work can be found at www.michaelgallagher.co.uk.

Tom Hall is a Lecturer at the Cardiff School of Social Sciences where he teaches urban sociology and anthropology. His research and writing focus on aspects of city space, local knowledge and the street-level practices of urban care, repair and patrol. He is the author of *Better Times Than This*, an ethnography of youth homelessness (Pluto Press, 2003) and *Footwork*, an account of urban outreach work with rough sleepers and sex workers (Pluto Press, 2017).

Helena Holgersson is a Sociologist and Lecturer in the Department for Cultural Sciences at the University of Gothenburg, Sweden. Her research focuses on urban planning, migration, culture and democracy, and ethnographic methods. Recent publications include 'Post-Political Narratives and Emotions: Dealing with Discursive Displacement in Everyday Life' in *Stories of Cosmopolitan Belonging: Emotion and Location* (Routledge, 2014), and 'Challenging the Hegemonic Gaze on Foot: Walk-Alongs as a Useful Method in Gentrification Research' in *Walking in the European City: Quotidian Mobility and Urban Ethnography* (Routledge, 2014).

Emma Jackson is a Lecturer in the Department of Sociology at Goldsmiths, University of London, researching and teaching on the relationship between class, multiculture and the production of urban space. Prior to this she held an Urban Studies Foundation Fellowship at the University of Glasgow. Emma is co-editor of *Stories of Cosmopolitan Belonging: Emotion and Location* (Routledge, 2014) and co-author of *The Middle Classes and the City: A Study of Paris and London* (Palgrave Macmillan, 2015).

Caroline Knowles is Co-Director of the Centre for Urban and Community Research and Professor of Sociology at Goldsmiths, University of London. She is the author of *Flip-Flop: A Journey through Globalisation's Backroads* (Pluto Press, 2014), and co-author with Douglas Harper of *Hong Kong: Migrant Lives, Landscapes and Journeys* (University of Chicago Press, 2009).

Mike Michael is a Professor at the Department of Sociology, Philosophy and Anthropology at the University of Exeter. His interests have included the relation of everyday life to technoscience, and biotechnological and biomedical innovation and culture. Recent publications include *Innovation and Biomedicine: Ethics, Evidence and Expectation in HIV*, co-authored with Marsha Rosengarten (Palgrave, 2013), and *Actor-Network Theory: Trials, Trails and Translations* (Sage, 2016).

Jonathan Prior is a Lecturer in Human Geography in the School of Geography and Planning at Cardiff University. His research spans environmental and landscape policy making and sonic geography, and he is interested in developing phonographic methods for geographical, social science and arts research. His work can be found at http://12gatestothecity.com.

Alex Rhys-Taylor is a Sociologist at the Centre for Urban and Community Research, Goldsmiths, University of London. His research focuses on the relationship between multisensory experiences of urban spaces and the production of social formations. He is the author of *Food and Multiculture: A Sensory Ethnography of East London* (Bloomsbury, 2017).

Robin James Smith is a Lecturer in Sociology at the Cardiff School of Social Sciences. His research focuses on interaction, mobility practices and the social organisation of public space. He is co-editor with Kevin Hetherington of *Urban Rhythms: Mobilities, Space and Interaction in the Contemporary City* (Wiley-Blackwell, 2013) in the Sociological Review Monograph series.

April Vannini is an Educator and Researcher teaching in the School of Communication and Culture at Royal Roads University. Her research interests are diverse and interdisciplinary but primarily focus on critical communication studies, contemporary cultural studies, and cultural theory and philosophy. Together with Phillip Vannini she is the author of *Wilderness* (Routledge, 2016), published in the Routledge Key Ideas in Geography series.

Phillip Vannini is a Professor in the School of Communication and Culture at Royal Roads University and Canada Research Chair in Public Ethnography. He is a transdisciplinary and multimodal ethnographer who studies subjects as diverse as nature-cultures, mobilities, assemblages and the social aspects of human embodiment. His books include *Non-Representational Methodologies* (Routledge, 2015) and *Off the Grid* (Routledge, 2014).

Finding Our Feet

Charlotte Bates and Alex Rhys-Taylor

There are two key strands in writing about the relationship between walking and social science. These strands reflect schisms running through the related disciplines of anthropology, human geography and sociology, characterised by a divergence around the variable emphasis placed on theoretical meditations and empiricism. Nietzsche's typically aphoristic assertion that "All truly great thoughts are conceived by walking" characterises the first strand. With antecedents in classical Greek philosophy, carried through the Enlightenment revival of humanist practices by Jean Jacques Rousseau to the existential introspection of Søren Kierkegaard and Friedrich Nietzsche, walking has repeatedly been described as central to the production of philosophical knowledge. Therein walking is understood primarily as a meditative practice through which access to rational and meaningful thought is achieved. The practice also has resonances with the Christian tradition of prayer walking, Buddhist walking meditations and the 'temporal mobility' of Australian aborigines, wherein the thoughts and visions that appear to the walker as they pace through the world are attributed a transcendental status, revealing something beyond the immediacy of everyday life. Walks like these are typically long rambles through nature, in which the elements act as both a form of cleansing, and an elicitation device, blowing away the cobwebs of everyday concerns and prompting reflection on 'deeper' truths. These histories and philosophies of walking are illuminated in books such as Rebecca Solnit's *Wanderlust: A History of Walking* (2002) and Frédéric Gros' *A Philosophy of Walking* (2014).

More recently, a second strand of writing on walking has emerged. Rather than emphasising the deductive insights delivered through ambulatory cognition, this strand concerns itself with theorising the world through consideration of the everyday pedestrian practices of others. Early works in this tradition theorise walking as a practice of power and resistance (de Certeau 1984), or an intrinsically social activity, responsive to the movements of others (Goffman 1971). Somewhere between these two strands, we find the work of Walter Benjamin, who, drawing on Baudelaire's *flâneur*, used walking as both a tool to develop and process one's own inner thoughts *and* a way of surveying others and the worlds in which they live, a way of 'botanising on the asphalt'. Renewed interest in the *flâneur*, coupled with the corporeal turn across the social sciences of the late twentieth century, has brought walking to attention as a methodological tool in and of itself. The take up of 'walking as a method' has been especially notable in the field of ethnography. Typified by what sociologist Margarethe Kusenbach (2003) has called the 'go-along', researchers have started to observe, experience and make sense of an array of hitherto overlooked everyday practices by walking alongside participants. Perhaps most importantly, the idea of 'talking whilst walking' (Anderson 2004) has enabled research interviews to be informed, not just by the lives of research participants, but also by the landscapes in which they live. By sharing conversations in place and at the participants' pace, researchers are beginning to more fully appreciate the transient, embodied and multisensual aspects of 'the social'.

This interdisciplinary collection provides a guided route through a variety of walks, exploring the possibilities for conducting research on the move along the way. It highlights a range of possibilities for enfolding sound, smell, emotion, movement and memory into our accounts, illustrating the sensuousness and the skill of walking as research practice. Each chapter draws on original empirical research to present ways of walking and to discuss the conceptual, practical and technical issues that walking entails. Alongside feet on the ground, the devices and technologies that make up hybrid research mobilities are brought to attention, as are the illuminating moments when both walking and research fail, when we stumble. Keeping pace with advances in qualitative research methods, the collection explores walking as both a challenge and an opportunity to expand our attentiveness and move *with* the social world, highlighting the range of possibilities that walking offers for the growth and development of our methodological repertoire.

Wanderers and Walkers

Aligning themselves firmly with the more meditative tradition, many books on walking typically begin with one of an assortment of heroic characters. The poet, the pilgrim, the philosopher, the *flâneur*. Typical of a particular type of wayfaring, these figures represent "the Borrovian or Whitmanesque walker, out for the romance of the way" (Macfarlane 2012, 314). There is of course, another "shadow history" of walking that "involves the tramps, the hobos, the vagrants, the dispossessed, the fugitives, the harmed and the jobless, bodging life together as they 'padded' it down the roads..." (Macfarlane 2012, 316). These walkers deserve our attention, not least for the ways in which their everyday footsteps juxtapose artful wandering with walking as a necessity. Such practices have been captured wonderfully in books such as Tom Hall's *Footwork: Urban Outreach and Hidden Lives* (2017), Emma Jackson's *Young Homeless People and Urban Space: Fixed in Mobility* (2015) and Caroline Knowles' *Flip-Flop: A Journey through Globalisation's Backroads* (2014).

This collection aligns itself more with the latter under-acknowledged tradition of walking as a necessity than it does with the heroic tradition of transcendental hiking. However, the aim of the collection is not simply to foreground the plight of those destined to live life on their feet. Rather, by taking a series of conspicuously prosaic walking practices, from strolls around housing estates, promenades through shopping malls, walking the beat with outreach workers, to pacing out the designs of new urban plazas, the collection aims to demonstrate the centrality of walking to an array of social practices. And, more importantly, it aims to highlight both the gains, and some of the likely pitfalls, of walking as a method.

Walking the City

To paraphrase an urbanist cliché, over 50 per cent of all walks taken by the world's population are urban walks. Probably significantly more. Despite the mid-twentieth century emergence of pro-automobile, anti-pedestrian cities, most of the movement across the world retains a pedestrian element. Moreover, even those cities hitherto enamoured of automated movement are outgrowing the car and re-establishing the millennia-old relationship between urban form and walking. In truly 'smart cities', new technologies of urban governance are still less important than the fact that important institutions and amenities are in easy walking distance of one another. The best 'public spaces' still operate through the pedestrian movement of people through them. In cities in which we feel safe, the fabric of the neighbourhood is still threaded together through the act of walking the beat around the block. And, despite their immersion in digital worlds and 'selfie generated' avatars, urbanites still walk to see each other, and they walk to be seen.

The centrality of walking to city life is reflected in this book, with the majority of chapters in the collection being concerned with distinctly 'urban' walks. Which is to say, each chapter reflects on the mutually sustaining relationship between the individual and the city, as acted out through the act of walking. However, as anyone who lives in a city knows, the relationship between the body and the city is not always an easy one to navigate. At many times walkers' relationships with cities are fraught with obstructions, interference, fear, hurt and sadness. At the same time, privilege is paced out through cities, with some bodies able to go wherever they want, whenever they want. This collection reveals something of the myriad relationships with the city that are paced out by those living within them, building up an account of the variety of walks out of which each day in the city is made.

Learning on the Move

Anyone who has watched a baby take her first steps will know that walking is something we learn, and only after a lot of falling over. The milestone in movement alters our perspective in the world, from crawling low down on hands and knees to standing upright on two feet – bipedal locomotion that with balance and coordination rapidly increases our access to the world and the speed with which we move through it. As we grow and age, we run into more obstacles, and occasionally fall over again, but also continue to learn about the possibilities that are open to us by moving (Sheets-Johnstone 1999). Rhythm, pace and breath unfurl our bodies and the landscapes in which we dwell. The centrality of movement to our knowledge of the world – and the very idea of learning to walk – are also a useful way of thinking about what we might gain from learning on the move with walking methods.

An engagement with pedestrian encounters, and with the pavements and pathways that lead us to places beyond our doorsteps, opens up a broad range of possibilities for re-engaging with the things we seek to understand. Investigative wanders can excavate histories and memories, bringing the past to life. Going out facilitates an ethnographic 'being there', through which we can observe issues unfolding at street-level, if only for a short while. Walking also leads to new places, over bridges that take the researcher's body beyond 'being there' to something more like 'becoming anew', offering novel perspectives and prompting different questions. Instead of thinking about social life from the vantage point of the lecture hall or the classroom, going out for a walk is a way of engaging with the social world and allowing it to ask questions of us. It is an exercise, and a form of training, in sociological attentiveness, as well as a way of letting the sociological imagination roam (Wright Mills 1959). Following different paths, and looking for different clues along the way, the chapters in this collection are testimony to the generosity of the contributors, who offer their own lessons in navigating, and learning from, the city streets.

Reawakening the Body

Discovering the world on foot is also a way in which to reawaken the scholar's body and practice a more sensuous form of scholarship. As Paul Stoller (1997, xi–xii) writes:

> Stiffened from long sleep in the background of scholarly life, the scholar's body yearns to exercise its muscles. Sleepy from long inactivity, it aches to restore its sensibilities. Adrift in a sea of half-lives, it wants to breathe in the pungent odors of social life, to run its palms over the jagged surface of social reality, to hear the wondrous symphonies of social experience, to see the sensuous shapes and colors that fill windows of consciousness. It wants to awaken the imagination and bring scholarship back to 'the things themselves'.

Walking is a brilliant form of exercise for our stiff bodies and a way of reinvigorating our engagement with the social world. It induces a mobile, grounded perspective and foregrounds corporeal, sensual and affective matters. Walking collects together visions, smells, tactilities, sounds and tastes with various degrees of association and intimacy and with "synaesthetic effects" (Tilley 2015, 17–18). Moments of encounter forged between feet and the ground remind us of the emotional and embodied textures of our lives and bring to attention the sensuality of social life. But, as Robin Smith and Kevin Hetherington observe,

"Walking the city streets is not always a pleasurable experience" (2013, 7). The odours that we dress in, consume and leave behind as traces, from sandalwood and coffee to the faint smells of baby sick and shit, the sounds of traffic, accents and announcements, and the ways in which they reverberate differently in space, can be overwhelming, even disgusting at times (see Rhys-Taylor 2013).

The challenge and the opportunity for sensuous scholars is to cultivate and attune their senses, decipher these clues, or perhaps note their absences, as well as show their significance. It is precisely by evoking these ways of knowing that walking, as a method, succeeds where traditional methods with their emphasis on the discursive have left much to be desired. As an investigative method, walking encourages us to think with all our senses, to notice more, and to ask different questions of the world. As such, walking contributes to a burgeoning repertoire of research methods that awaken our "sensual imagination" (Vannini *et al.* 2013), a phrase inspired by C. Wright Mills' call for a sociological imagination.

Walking and Writing

Having attuned ourselves to the embodied nature of social life by walking, the next step is to represent that experience. How we respond to the questions a walk asks of us, and how we go about representing the experience and knowledge gained by walking, are questions that push at the boundaries of scholarly writing and representation. The great philosophers and poets walked in order to be able to write and wrote in order to be able to walk, as though walking and writing were synonymous acts. While, as Tim Ingold and Jo Vergunst (2008, 8) note, the analogy between walking and writing is a beguiling one, we do not want to suggest that the relationship between the two is simple.

The challenge of "fusing the intelligible and the sensible in scholarly representations" (Stoller 1997, xv) is also an invitation to re-imagine the ways in which we write, our forms of argument and modes of representation, and an opportunity to cultivate new skills. Here we join with Les Back and Michael Keith, who argue for a "more artful approach to writing cities that acknowledges that we produce or re-enact the city as we write about it". As they write:

> The description we write of a cityscape will not hold still. The jars of food stacked on the shopkeepers' shelves or crates of fish photographed on the weekend market day will not be there the next time it springs to life for midweek trade. These accounts are epitaphs to a life passed in living rather than eternal truths.
>
> (Back and Keith 2014, 25)

Two such descriptive accounts are included in this collection in the form of short pedestrian essays, in addition to the numerous field notes and thick descriptions that enrich many of the chapters. The essays bookend the collection, offering poetic points of departure and arrival, routes into and beyond the covers of this book. Portraying something of the lyrical qualities of going out for a walk in the city, they are examples of what Les Back (2007, 164) describes as a "literary sociology that aims to document and understand social life without assassinating it". Such literary approaches do not contradict more traditional scholarly accounts, rather they stimulate the sociological imagination and deepen our understanding.

Walking across Expertise

We have already drawn attention to the diverse range of figures and practices that might be encountered in a history of walking. Here, we want to pause and reflect on contemporary engagements with walking across disciplines and expertise. We are interested in what can be learnt from other walking practices – from other walks of life – and how they might inspire the further development of walking methodologies, but we also want to suggest what might be considered distinctive about a sociological walk.

From Sophie Calle to Janet Cardiff, Richard Long to Hamish Fulton, many artists have used walking in their creative practice as method, performance and art form. The briefest introduction to their work reveals an assortment of approaches to the practice of walking. Conceptual artist Sophie Calle's operations take place at street-level, in encounters with strangers and through covert activities of surveillance and stalking. Sound artist Janet Cardiff makes audio walking tours, using narration to guide listeners through the city (see Pinder 2001). Land artist Richard Long's remote walks are brought back to the gallery in the form of sculptures and photography, and walking artist Hamish Fulton's work engages with the experience of walking (see Vannini and Vannini, this volume). These artist's works are, or course, united by their use of walking. But they are also analogous for the extent to which they walk the 'viewer' or listener through 'the social', wading through cultural histories, everyday practices, and both familiar and distant landscapes in the process.

The dialogue between social-scientific methods and art practices can inspire innovation in social science, and it is one of the ways in which the contributors think about walking in this collection. But it is not only philosophers, writers, artists and social scientists that walk with expertise. As Alexandra Horowitz illustrates in her book *On Looking: Eleven Walks with Expert Eyes* (2013), there are a myriad of different expert walkers, with each seeing the world through the lens of their own interests and understanding. The result is often a distinctive attention, focused on a specific corner of the ordinary, a corner otherwise unattended by other walkers. This collection includes walks with many other experts to add to the ambulatory worldview of those offered by Horowitz. Amongst the footsteps gathered here are those of an architect, a hillwalker and an outreach worker. Walking with these experts opens up a space of translation between the expert and the researcher and, to an extent, serves to decentre the authority of the researcher. These 'expert' views, however, are not intended to entirely supplant the insights ascertained by pedestrian social scientists themselves. On the contrary, the sociological attention that is the hallmark of each and every chapter is distinguished by a thoroughly critical engagement with these expert views. While the collection is interdisciplinary – drawing on insights from the worlds of art and geography, as well as the vernacular expertise of city dwellers – each of these angles is refracted through an unabashedly sociological prism. As such, we hope the book makes a strong "case for what is distinctive about the attentiveness we [as sociologists] train on the city" (Back and Keith 2014, 23).

A Stroll Through the Collection

The chapters in this collection are varied, with some offering a more practical, methodologically grounded discussion of the value of walking as a research method and others taking a more abstracted, conceptual approach to the notion of walking. While we have planned a guided route, readers are invited to follow their own desires and make their own paths through the collection, to leap between chapters and retrace their own footprints.

We set out for our first walk on a crisp winter's day in north London with Emma Jackson, who has been walking King's Cross as a sociologist for at least a decade. Her short essay, 'Railway Lands', is an exploration of the dynamic and contested railway lands of Euston, King's Cross and St Pancras, focusing in particular on the reordering of space by two waves of infrastructural and social change, the arrival of the railways in the late nineteenth century and of the Eurostar in 2007. Taking the form of a walk, the essay reflects on sensory traces of these changes in order to explore how the circulation of bodies and capital, and attempts to control unruly public space, have shaped this urban landscape. The walk weaves through the railway stations and the places behind them – including parks, graveyards, canals – using the idea of 'the gothic city' to describe the resurfacing of the uncanny in the encounter between the legible and illegible city.

Next, we head south of the river for a walk through London's postcolonial history of racism and resistance. Les Back's 'Marchers and Steppers: Memory, City Life and Walking' introduces us to Lewisham, the capital of reggae soundsystem culture in Britain. In this impoverished and uncelebrated south-eastern corner of the capital young black people forged a culture of resistance and joy in unlikely places, from church halls to youth clubs to municipal buildings. Visiting the ruins of Jah Shaka's culture shop on New Cross Road, the place where the National Front was confronted and stopped in their tracks in 1977, and the site of the New Cross Fire that killed 13 young black Londoners who had been attending a house party in 1981, the chapter combines autobiography and historical reportage to argue that the echoes of this music – known as steppers – carries a legacy of pain, violence, joy, creativity and affirmation.

In 'Seeing the Need: Urban Outreach as Sensory Walking', Tom Hall and Robin Smith team up to lead us on an urban patrol in Cardiff. Their chapter reports on the work of outreach and street care in the city, showing how a small team of council workers, whose job it is to make repeated tours through the centre of the city, day and night, locate and assist 'vulnerable' adults who may otherwise struggle to access mainstream health and social services. The work of outreach is performed as a repeated patrolling of public, commercial and neglected space in and around the city centre, with eyes and ears open for signs of need and difficulty. The aim is always to discern and uncover, but clients are often hard to find, riddled in among the busy, commonplace cityscape. Outreach, as a mode of urban, pedestrian exploration requires a particular attuning of the senses, in which motion and attention combine to glean clues from the urban environment.

Returning to south London, Charlotte Bates' chapter 'Desire Lines: Walking in Woolwich', walks us through the redevelopment of a small urban square. Pausing at critical points in the history of the square's redevelopment, the chapter discusses the ways in which walking – and desire – inform and reform practices of urban design, mobility and dwelling. Weaving together observations and insights from site walks, interviews, ethnographic observations and documentary analysis, this chapter shows how the practice of walking underlies the ways in which place is desired, imagined, made and lived.

In 'Keep Walking: Notes on How to Research Urban Pasts and Futures', Helena Holgersson returns to three walks in the Swedish city of Gothenburg, and elaborates on what there is to gain from interviewing people on foot. Through encounters in disappearing and emerging neighbourhoods with Jani, Sofia and Karin, and Emir, we are party to conversations that confront the social aspects of city planning, urban inequality and citizenship. Reflecting on the relationship between time and place, memory and emotion, in specific locations and in conversation with very different groups of inhabitants, the chapter shows how the walk-along is also the perfect frame for a story.

Walking interviews have been used with growing frequency to understand the relationships between people, spaces and social worlds, but they typically rely on a single researcher-participant relationship. In Andrew Clarks' 'Walking Together: Understanding Young People's Experiences of Living in Neighbourhoods in Transition', we amble in groups through neighbourhoods and territories, taking in the parks and shelters that offer places to gather. Introducing a mobile focus group method as a way of understanding young people's individual and collective experiences of life in deprived urban neighbourhoods across England, the chapter outlines the challenges and opportunities afforded by the approach and reflects on the implications for knowledge arising from this collective and interactive method.

In 'Westfield Stratford City: A Walk through Millennial Urbanism', Alex Rhys-Taylor calls our noses to attention as he guides us through the mega-mall and upwards on its lifts and escalators. Ostensibly public, largely private, tangled with high-finance, risk and property speculation, digitised, under surveillance, corporately globalised and culturally hybridised, and marked by finite distinctions in culture and socio-economic status, Westfield's success lies in the extent to which the space has come to fully reflect the current social texture of twenty-first century London. As the chapter details, the layout of the mega-mall, and the clustering of specific symbols and sensoria within it, reiterate specific ways of sensing, and making sense of class, citizenship and ethnicity.

Rather than regarding stumbling, tripping and falling as a matter for Goffmanesque social repair or an opportunity for the governance of risk, Mike Michael suggests that the mis-step can be treated as a 'device' that affords a speculative engagement with social processes. 'Walking Falling, Telling: The Anecdote and the Mis-step as a "Research Event"' develops this argument through three autobiographical anecdotes about mis-stepping: falling down the stairs, tripping on a mountain slope and slipping on a pavement. Here, anecdotalising the mis-step in its specificity also suggests particular conceptualisations of 'walking as a method' in terms of its 'emergently causal', 'parasitical' and 'topological' possibilities.

Recounting an 'air walk' held in the south London neighbourhoods of New Cross Gate and Deptford, Jennifer Gabrys' 'Air Walk: Monitoring Pollution and Experimenting with Speculative Forms of Participation' explores how new arrangements and detections of air pollution brought about by the rise of low-cost environmental monitoring technologies might be further developed through practice-based research. The chapter discusses walking as an experiment with forms of participation, and as an entry point for developing distinct approaches to working with monitoring technologies. Moving from descriptive approaches of participation to generative experiments with participation, the walk sets in motion the sites, participant encounters, monitoring kit, infrastructures, urban situations and speculative practices as they come together in this context.

On a listening walk in Edinburgh, Michael Gallagher and Jonathan Prior introduce us to a mode of walking in which listening to the sounds of spaces is the focus. While listening walks have been posited as a means of producing research data about perceived soundscape quality, 'Listening Walks: A Method of Multiplicity', considers the potential of listening walks to act as a research method and pedagogic tool, through which pedestrian sounds, snatches of conversation and the drone of heavy traffic bring to attention the geographies of everyday life. The chapters shows that listening walks provide us with an endlessly repeatable and adaptable method that can address a much broader range of research questions, and be utilised within a variety of teaching settings.

In Scotland's Cairngorms National Park, Phillip Vannini and April Vannini walk together with Chris Townsend, a British walker known worldwide for his multi-day walks. Though their arguments and critiques are distinct, they are similarly inspired by that walk with Chris and similarly motivated by their will to rethink the nature of walk-alongs and to reimagine walking as a 'wilder' way of knowing. In their chapter 'Wild Walking: A Twofold Critique of the Walk-Along Method', Phillip's critique focuses on enlivening the kinesthetic and cinematic potential of the walk-along method, while April's critique concentrates on rethinking the very notion of walking as method.

The collection comes to an end with a luxurious pair of high-heeled shoes. As Caroline Knowles' tells us in her short essay 'Walking W8 in Manolos', the sensory footwork of dwelling demands appropriate shoes. The essay is inspired by an ESRC funded investigation of London's super-wealthy called *The Alpha Territory*. Manolos are W8, the London postcode where one of the highest intensities of high-net-worth people on the planet dwell. In W8 French and American bankers and former debutants rub shoulders with minor royals, celebrities and glitterati. In high-heeled elegance we make our way from the royal borough's central library off Kensington High Street. Meandering some of the back road we pass the new service class pushing prams and cleaning windows and the occasional hedge fund manager steering a uniformed child with a violin. We pass the gaping caverns of basement digs in which nineteenth-century stucco façades acquire swimming pools, games rooms and staff parking, and delicately pick our way down Cornwall Gardens with its manicured window boxes and tastefully identically arranged gardens, until we meet the rush of Gloucester Road and the next postcode breaks the W8 magic. From here, we leave readers to imagine their own future journeys on foot.

References

Anderson, J. (2004) Talking whilst Walking: A Geographical Archaeology of Knowledge. *Area*, 36(3), 254–261.

Back, L. (2007) *The Art of Listening*. Berg, Oxford.

Back, L. and Keith, M. (2014) Reflections: Writing Cities. In Jones, H. and Jackson, E. (eds) *Stories of Cosmopolitan Belonging: Emotion and Location*. Routledge, London.

de Certeau, M. (1984) *The Practice of Everyday Life*. University of California Press, Berkeley CA.

Goffman, E. (1971) *Relations in Public: Microstudies of the Public Order*. Allen Lane, London.

Gros, F. (2014) *A Philosophy of Walking*. Verso, London.

Hall, T. (2017) *Footwork: Urban Outreach and Hidden Lives*. Pluto Press, London.

Horowitz, A. (2013) *On Looking: Eleven Walks with Expert Eyes*. Scribner, New York.

Ingold, T. and Vergunst, J. (eds) (2008) *Ways of Walking: Ethnography and Practice on Foot*. Routledge, London.

Jackson, E. (2015) *Young Homeless People and Urban Space: Fixed in Mobility*. Routledge, London.

Knowles, C. (2014) *Flip-Flop: A Journey through Globalisation's Backroads*. Pluto Press, London.

Kusenbach, M. (2003) Street Phenomenology: The Go-along as Ethnographic Research Tool. *Ethnography*, 4(3): 455–485.

Macfarlane, R. (2012) *The Old Ways: A Journey on Foot*. Hamish Hamilton, London.

Pinder, D. (2001) Ghostly Footsteps: Voices, Memories and Walks in the City. *Ecumene*, 8(1): 1–19.

Rhys-Taylor, A. (2013) Disgust and Distinction: The Case of the Jellied Eel. *The Sociological Review*, 61(2): 227–246.

Sheets-Johnstone, M. (1999) *The Primacy of Movement*. John Benjamins Publishing Company, Philadelphia.

Smith, R. J. and Hetherington, K. (eds) (2013) *Urban Rhythms: Mobilities, Space and Interaction in the Contemporary City*. Wiley Blackwell/The Sociological Review, Chichester.

Solnit, R. (2002) *Wanderlust: A History of Walking*. Verso, London.

Stoller, P. (1997) *Sensuous Scholarship.* University of Pennsylvania Press, Philadelphia.

Tilley, C. (2015) Walking the Past in the Present. In Árnason, A., Ellison, N., Vergunst, J. and Whitehouse, A. (2015) *Landscapes beyond Land: Routes, Aesthetics, Narratives.* Berghahn, Oxford.

Vannini, P., Waskul, D. and Gottschalk, S. (2013) *The Senses in Self, Society, and Culture: A Sociology of the Senses*. Routledge, New York.

Wright Mills, C. (1959) *The Sociological Imagination*. Oxford University Press, Oxford.

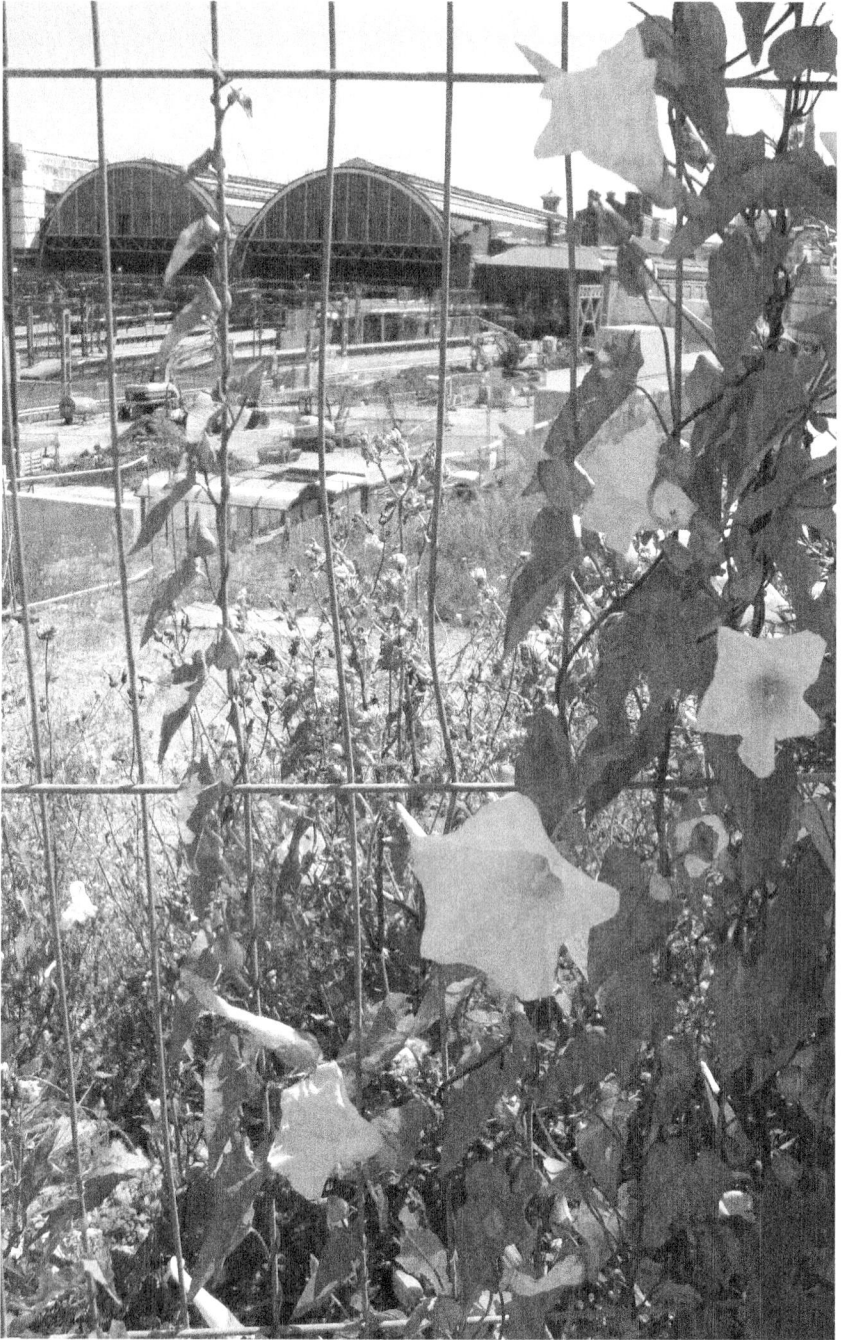

From Camley Street to King's Cross, 2007.
Source: Emma Jackson.

Railway Lands

Emma Jackson

We begin our walk standing outside King's Cross Station. It is a crisp winter's day. Standing at this point we can see, hear and feel that this is a place of motion. There is a steady tide of people entering and leaving the station. Train announcements and occasional sirens punctuate the dominant sound, suitcases being wheeled across stone. The air is heavy with fumes and carries a slight trace of McDonalds fries.

Opportunities arise from this churn of strangers. The drugs and sex markets that have a long association with King's Cross are common features of these places of arrival and departure. We can also start to apprehend attempts at ordering and surveillance at work. Consider the Farmer's Market in front of us. The smells of fine cheeses, the stacks of artisan bread and the striped canopies of the stalls are part of the civilising process of this unruly part of town. Or the 'helpers' around the corner who patrol the now privately owned land of Granary Place. This new streetscape is a testament to the aggressive 'clean up' operation that began in preparation for the arrival of the Eurostar at St Pancras and continues to refigure the landscape.

On our walk, we will move through the railway lands around King's Cross and St Pancras station, from the shiny new concourses through parks, graveyards, canal paths in order to consider the reordering of this space by two waves of infrastructural and social change: the arrival of the railways in the late nineteenth century and of the Eurostar in 2007. We will find traces of 'the gothic city', the resurfacing of the uncanny in this cleansed space.

Before the arrival of the railways, Battle Bridge (the old name for King's Cross) was on the edge of London. In London mythology this name is thought to refer to Queen Boudicca's defeat at the hands of the Romans, although the name is more likely to stem from a battle between the Saxons and the Danes. The name 'King's Cross' refers to a monument erected in 1830 on the site of an old tollhouse that was to mark the site of Boudicca's battle and to honour George IV. Intended to be a police station, the building soon turned into a beer house and became such a nuisance that it was pulled down in 1845, but the name remains (Denyer, 1935). This is a typical King's Cross story.

The advent of the railways[1] greatly shook up temporal and spatial relations in Britain, as Carlyle observed in 1850: 'railways have set the towns of Britain a-dancing. Reading is coming up to London, Basingstoke is going down to Gosport or Southampton.... They are set a-dancing as I said; confusedly waltzing, in a state of progressive dissolution' (Simmons, 1973: 277). This change of pace and throwing together of bodies caused social anxiety and moral panic. In British railway stations various provisions were made to avoid the intermingling of different classes of people, such as waiting rooms stratified by class of ticket. Mixing between the classes was seen as posing a particular peril to the middle-class lady about town, as the railway stations had become a prime location for prostitutes who solicited on the platforms and worked on the trains (Drummond, 2003). Nowadays, other techniques are used to discipline bodies and sort people into spaces around the stations.

Let us cross Euston Road. This is no mean feat. You will be jostled by people with suitcases. The south side of the road has not undergone the same profound change in atmosphere over the last ten years as the area around King's Cross station. The older businesses remain, an Italian restaurant, Reel Time amusement arcade, Ladbrokes. Now we bear left, turning up Birkenhead Street, walking past the terraced houses and the Methodist Church that offers services in Mandarin, Cantonese and English. A homeless hostel sits alongside a hotel called 'Rough Luxe' ('A little bit of rough in a luxurious London', according to its website). At the end of the street Birkenhead Street Estate is walled off by glass and brick, the names of the blocks referencing variations on the now covered river 'Riverside, Riverfleet, Fleetway, Fleetfield'. We turn right across the bottom of Argyle Square, where teenagers play basketball, and cut down Argyle Street, lined with B & Bs and hotels. The Salvation Army is an exception. A sign in their window reads 'This is not a hotel. Ce n'est pas a l'hotel.' You can still pay £15 a night for a shared room on Argyle Street.

Despite the grandeur of the railways, the King's Cross of the nineteenth century was still a mixed area. This is attested to by Charles Booth, measurer and chronicler of London poverty, who could not decide how to classify it according to his colour-coded system:

> The number of streets in the neighbourhood of Argyle Square containing disorderly houses – to supply a provincial demand arriving at King's Cross and St Pancras by the Midland.... Should these streets be marked with a line of black or no?
>
> (Booth, 1898)

The railway lands are confusing places from their inception, places where poverty and wealth rub up against each other.

I've been walking King's Cross as a sociologist for a decade but my acquaintance with it goes back further.

> I recall my brother, over twenty years ago, buying tomorrow's *Guardian* one night at a kiosk where the Farmers Market now stands. His proud explanation that in London you 'can get the news the night before' now seems

quaint and 20th Century. Later, I played gigs at The Water Rats, went clubbing at Bagley's and tried to avoid being solicited on the way to the station's taxi rank.

But the streets on the south of Euston Road are where I began to get acquainted with King's Cross as a researcher,[2] conducting interviews with hostel residents who were being targeted by the Community Safety Partnership as a dangerous 'street active'[3] population who needed to be moved on from public space. While the dust from the regeneration work blew in through the hostel windows, the residents told me that they felt more confined to their small rooms because of the implementation of a range of new sanctions enshrined in the Crime and Disorder Act (1998) and the Anti-Social Behaviour Act (2003) (including: Anti Social Behaviour Orders (ASBOs), Acceptable Behaviour Agreements (ABAs), Dispersal Zones (DZ), Fixed Penalty Notices (FPNs) and Controlled Drinking Zones (CDZ)).

These exclusions were part of the reordering of King's Cross and could be devastating for the individuals who were reliant on the spaces around the stations. While for many the railway station is a place of transit for others it can be, as one hostel interviewee described it, 'a comfort zone'. There are toilets, shelter and opportunities to make money from the people passing through.

> You can spend a whole day long on the station, a whole fucking day long and know that station inside out.
>
> (Ian, hostel resident, interviewed in 2006)

We now walk back towards Euston Road on Argyle Street and take a left. We cross Euston Road for a second time and enter the courtyard of the British Library. The courtyard is walled off from the road, setback, serene. On a sunny day it is a sea of laptops and coffee. The north-west corner provides a view of what the British Library staff call 'the Titanic at Disneyland', the chunky red-brick British Library serving as the cruise liner and the Victorian gothic daftness of St Pancras playing the fairytale castle. We now exit the library courtyard and walk towards St Pancras.

The coming of the Eurostar to St Pancras in 2007 was not about a new connection between London to mainland Europe. The service had been operating out of Waterloo for some years beforehand and the less glamorous Eurotunnel continues to take passengers between Folkestone and Calais. It was about the circulation of capital – a faster connection, a more iconic station and Europe's longest champagne bar. St Pancras was marketed as a place of great luxury, with its 5-star hotel and apartments to match, harking back to its former glories. The first incarnation of St Pancras station housed the Grand Midland Hotel that was at the cutting edge of Victorian technology, fully equipped with gasoliers, electric bells, dust chutes and hydraulic lifts, and the first revolving door in London. However, by 1935 the hotel had fallen behind the times and had to close, becoming offices for the Midland Railway. We can follow the curving driveway up to entrance and take a peek inside but I have never dared to go in. The sign above the new hotel entrance reads 'St Pancras Hotel est. 1873', giving a misleading sense of uninterrupted opulence.

From there we continue east and take the entrance to the upper concourse of the railway station. Standing underneath Paul Day's bronze kitsch colossus of an embracing couple ('The Meeting Place') we can feel the expanse of the station opening around us. The acoustics change. From here we can see the Eurostar trains and Paris beckons.

St. Pancras International opened amid much fanfare in November 2007. I was there the day it opened.

> The sun glints through the spotless glass roof. Lots of happy faced grey haired men in hats crowd around to get a glimpse of the first train leaving for Europe. People appraise the new statues. The orchestra plays something tastefully rousing. A cheer goes up when the first train leaves (I also cheer. I can't help myself. I'm all caught up in the moment). There is excitement in the air. A welcome speech is made by someone important informing us it takes 1 hr 51 minutes to get to Brussels. He then extolls the charms of Brussels but unfortunately the effect is ruined by an interrupting announcement informing us we are all on CCTV.
>
> (Field notes, 14 November 2007)

We take the steps down to the lower floor and slowly move through the station, past the well-to-do shops. There is a piano available for anyone to play on. It always seems to be a passing concert pianist. We exit the station from the King's Cross side and turn left onto Pancras Road continuing past the long queue of black cabs awaiting passengers.

> I walk from the Great Northern Hotel up Battle Bridge Road, looking at the building work still going on at the back of Kings Cross. I read some graffiti on a bricked up window on the Stanley Building 'the music is over but the melody lingers on'. A man in a hard hat shouts at me 'How did you get in here?'. I told him I just walked through. 'Well you can't', he says, 'no pedestrians'. He then shouts at another man in an Eastern European language. I walk back the way I came hearing the thud of a football being passed between the two men behind me.
>
> (Field notes, 14 November 2007)

This site is different now. All of the Stanley Buildings have been demolished bar one that has been turned into offices. These were flats built in 1800 to house railway workers and later provided the home for the protagonists in Mike Leigh's film 'High Hopes'.

Turning right off Pancras Road we enter Camley Street Natural Park's gates, walking up a bark covered path. Camley Street used to be coal yards but now provides a strip of calm alongside the canal where pond life can flourish. It is one of the few places in King's Cross you can sit without having to buy anything. It sits on the site of part of Agar Town, a slum area that was demolished to make way for the railway in 1866. It is estimated that in the original St Pancras development 4,000 houses were demolished in Somers, Camden and Agar Towns displacing perhaps as many as 32,000 people (Swenson, 2006).

> It's cloudy and I'm getting cold. I wander through reeds and around the pond. I can hear someone singing opera in a deep baritone. I follow. I come to a small clearing and a man in a purple shirt is singing. He stops. 'I thought I would take the opportunity,' he says. 'Please, go ahead', I reply, 'I thought it might be a ghost'. 'It is a ghost' he says as I walk off. I look back half hoping that he has disappeared but instead he is taking a picture of St Pancras on his camera phone.
>
> (Field notes, 14 November 2007)

We walk back to the road and swoop under the railway tracks and cut up past the coroner's office to St Pancras Churchyard. It was not only the living who were displaced as part of the coming of the railways. When the Great Midland Railway was being constructed, the burial ground of St. Pancras old church was in the way and so 10,000–15,000 bodies had to be re-interred elsewhere, with Thomas Hardy, then studying architecture in London under chief architect Arthur Bloomfield, overseeing the project. The result was that gravestones were rearranged in odd patterns around the churchyard. In one corner, a procession of headstones look like they are set up for domino rally. Most famously, they cluster in the gnarled roots of an ash tree, known as 'The Hardy Tree'. The churchyard was disturbed by change once more in the latest round of railway construction, Iain Sinclair (2005) writes: 'Tombs are splitting, monuments leaning drunkenly, holes appearing in the earth.' The train brakes screech. A crow caws.

St Pancras churchyard is a psychogeographer's paradise populated by Rimbaud and Verlaine, who lived in a flat in nearby Royal College Street, Percy and Mary Shelley – Percy first saw Mary in Old St Pancras Churchyard while Mary was tending the grave of her mother, Mary Wollstonecraft – ancient Roman remains and highwaymen.[4] I once heard a local poet, Aidan Dun, claim that Jesus was buried beneath St Pancras church. This seems unlikely but you don't have to be a mystical poet to feel the atmosphere in this island of stillness.

We now loop back onto Pancras Road. Dusk approaches but there is still time to catch the last light of the day. Looking down the canal, only one of the Victorian gasholders that once dominated the King's Cross skyline remains, now surrounded by half built apartments and cranes. We walk towards it down the canal. I once came on a bat walk here led by the people from Camley Street. In the dark, we listened to them, learning how to distinguish between daubenton and pipistrelle with the aid of beeping bat detectors, and spooking the odd cyclist and drinker. But in the day time the canal is bustling.

The gasholder stands on our left. It has been planted with grass and turned into a small park. All of the gasholders were dismantled as part of the regeneration of King's Cross. This one was given a lick of paint, moved slightly and put back together. It will soon be joined by another three gasholders that will be reconstructed around the new blocks of flats. A promotional poster on a hoarding depicts life from inside the glass-fronted flats, looking through the old structures towards the canal.

The new park provides a photo opportunity and place where Londoners talk about what used to be. It looks slick but smells of pond water and marijuana. A woman explains to her son about the BT tower, visible across the canal: 'When I was little it was the tallest building in London. And that on the top was a revolving restaurant.' Three lads cut past recalling last night's party: '... and there was Louis, topless! It was jokes ...'.

Moving on, we head down the canal on a temporary walkway that bobs on the water. Cajun fiddle music emanates from a floating bookshop 'Word on the Water'. This new addition faces the newly developed campus for the University of the Arts, now housed in the old Granary Building. Climbing the grey steps to our left, we are now in the heart of the 67-acre King's Cross redevelopment site. An expansive grey-stone square covered in fountains stands between us and the Granary Building, that also houses restaurants, bars and businesses. The names on the buildings recall the past: 'Western Transit Shed', 'Stable Street', the gastro-pub is called the 'Grain Store'. This is privatised space. The Government recently announced its intention to sell the state's 36.5 per cent share in the development. Security guards patrol in fluorescent jackets.

From here we turn down the new pedestrian street of King's Boulevard that runs back to King's Cross Station. It is lined by skeletal trees and adverts for the production of the Railway Children currently taking place alongside us. Other boards tell the story of King's Cross. King's Cross's shady past is part of its marketing – up to a point. The colorful history (minus the drug dealers, sex workers and street drinkers) adds intrigue to this highly regulated space. In this new version of 'old' King's Cross an attempt is made to market a history of the gothic city – Frankenstein and St Pancras Old Church are used as illustrations – while ignoring the processes of cleansing of space and of history that have attempted to expunge those considered undesirable. Alongside, Boudicca is co-opted to sell a new idea of place:

> Trade has been part of the King's Cross experience since Boudicca and her local warriors crossed the River Fleet at Battle Bridge in 61 AD and showed the Roman army the finer points of British bronze and iron. These days, we might invite them round to Vinoteca to settle things over a platter of bresaola and porchetta with Sicilian olives.

But the old King's Cross still lingers. Street drinkers may have decanted their cider into Lucozade bottles but they are still here, although forced into pacing the Euston Road instead of sitting in a station or park. It lingers in the cracked gravestones of Old St Pancras and in the ruins that are shielded from view by hoarding.

We end our walk where we began at King's Cross station. A 'Google Active Art Installation' called Poetrics invites passers-by to say words into a microphone that are then displayed on LED panels. I put my mouth to the red grill and run through some of the words missing from the marketing hoardings.

Notes

1 The Great Northern Railway opened King's Cross as a permanent station in 1852 and the Midland Railway company decided to extend their line from Camden Town to St Pancras in the 1860s. Nearby Euston was built as the first mainline terminal in London 1837.
2 On the project 'Crime Displacement in King's Cross' (www.camden.gov.uk/ccm/cms-service/stream/asset/King's%20Cross%20Report.pdf?asset_id=1373042).
3 Street activity is used to describe street-based drug use, street-based begging, street-based sex working, street-based drinking, street-based rough sleeping.
4 This is terrain covered in depth by Iain Sinclair (1997) and Aidan Dun (1995).

References

Booth, C. (1898) Notebook B354, p. 51, http://booth.lse.ac.uk/notebooks/b354/jpg/51.html.

Denyer, C.H. (ed.) (1935) *St Pancras through the Centuries*. London, Le Play House.

Drummond, D. 'The Impact of the Railway on the Lives of Women in the 19th Century', in R. Roth and M. Polino (2003) (eds), *The City and the Railway in Europe*. Aldershot, Ashgate.

Dun, A.A (1995) *Vale Royal*. Uppingham, Gold Mark.

Simmons, J. (1973) 'The Power of the Railways', in H.J. Dyos and M. Woolf (eds), *The Victorian City: Images and Realities, Vol. 1*. London and New York, Routledge.

Sinclair, I. (1997) *Lights out for the Territory*. London, Penguin.

Sinclair, I. (2005) 'Museums of Melancholy', *London Review of Books*, London, Nicholas Spice, 18 August.

Swenson, S.P. (2006) *Mapping Poverty in Agar Town: Economic Conditions Prior to the Development of St. Pancras Station in 1866*, Working Papers on the Nature of Evidence: How Well Do 'Facts' Travel? No. 09/06. Department of Economic History, London School of Economics.

Black People's Day of Action, New Cross Road, 2 March 1981.
Source: Vron Ware.

1   Marchers and Steppers

Memory, City Life and Walking

Les Back

You only have to walk through the streets of south-east London to feel its para-
doxes. In the thirty years I have been associated with Goldsmiths, University of
London – as both a student and teacher – I am compelled increasingly by the
curriculum to be discovered in the hidden archive of the streets. Strolling out of
the lecture hall or seminar room into this uncelebrated corner of the capital has
always offered a different kind of extra-mural education, if you are willing to get
your shoes dirty.

Accordingly in this chapter I want to argue that walking is not just a technique for uncovering the mysteries of the city but also a form of pedagogy or a
way to learn and think not just individually but also collectively (see also O'Neill
and Perivolaris 2014). This is more than a matter of applying the lens of library
to magnify and interpret city life. Rather, I want to suggest that walking – even
through streets that are well trodden – challenges us to think differently with
almost every next step.

I want to take you on a walk through postcolonial London in the footsteps of
demonstrators and marchers protested competing visions of postcolonial London
life. I also want to take you to where reggae blues dances offered a very different
kind of rhythm – called steppers – and embodied way of being in the city. I have
led groups of students or visiting political activists, writers and even local residents on this historical tour through local streets many times. Richard Hoggart,
author of the classic study *The Uses of Literacy* (1957), was the Warden of the
college when I first came to Goldsmiths as a student in 1981. In the late 1970s
and early 1980s New Cross and Deptford on the south bank of the Thames was
ruined by de-industrialisation, dock closures resulting from containerisation and
urban decline. As sociologist Dick Hobbs (2013: 92) has pointed out, between
1966 and 1976 150,000 jobs were lost as the economic heart was ripped out of
London's dockland communities. Hoggart (1992: 180) wrote in his memoir that
the 'district' – as he used to refer to the college's surrounding areas – is commonly known as "the arsehole of London".

Signs of British empire are everywhere from the ship weather vane on the top
of the local town hall to the ghost of John Evelyn, stockholder in the East India
Company, who in 1671 contributed to the construction of the New Cross Road
(Steele 1993: 33). From the middle of the twentieth century this part of the city

also provided a home for post-war colonial citizen migrants largely from Jamaica and the small Caribbean islands of St Lucia, Barbados and St Kitts. The same year that I moved to New Cross, over a dozen young black Londoners died in a fire at a house party. My point of departure is that within a square mile of the college – literally on its doorstep – unfolded a history of anti-fascist struggle, anti-racism and black liberation, the traces of which still remain albeit uncelebrated and hidden partially in the bustle of everyday life.

Today Goldsmiths and its 'district' is in some ways a very different place. New migrants from West Africa have settled in this part of London, along with others from Latin America, transforming its sounds, tastes and smells. The first signs of gentrification have also started to show – unthinkable thirty years ago – as coffee shops, hipster bars and even organic food delis sprout in the midst of the area's urban ruins (see also Self 2015). Suited and booted property sharks appear in on-line promotional videos extolling "unrivalled investment opportunities" in Deptford as urban grit is transformed into lucrative arty glamour.

Before we go much further I want to make some conceptual points and also offer a few words of caution. For Michel de Certeau the experience of city life at ground level is mysterious, both immediate and often illegible. For that reason he comments that knowledge for the city walker is "as blind as that of lovers in each other's arms" (de Certeau 1988: 93). In order to see beyond the arresting familiarity of the streets we need to transform them into an understood landscape and de Certeau calls this 'space' i.e. where knowledge of a specific place is assembled, historicised and situated. "Every story is a travel story", de Certeau (1988: 115) writes, highlighting this process of making space through telling stories.

On the surface this is very different from the walking-tour guide and yet, as Adam Reed points out in his brilliant study of self-employed tour guides in London, both require what he calls personification (Reed 2002). Urban knowledge is personified and made the individual property of the guide and this, Reed warns, risks closing down understandings of the city. The lengths that the guides go through to get 'into character' is a clue, often dressing in Victorian costumes to speak with greater authority about Dickensian London. Regardless of these limitations, Reed (2002: 138) comments that the guides in his study were able to convey a sense of vitality because they "lived the city that they animated with the category of detail".

So before we begin this journey I want to warn against personification. I am not wearing a costume nor do I claim exclusive access to this story, although I do not deny my own life is woven intimately into it. There is never a single coherent definition of place and no definitive version of its history. Other stories can always be told and different paths taken. This one is analogous to a manuscript available for loan from the infinite library of tales contained in these streets.

In street walking whole systems of meaning and patterns of culture come to life and take shape (Mauss 1979). These Bourdieu (1977: 87) called "practical forms of mastery" that assert a right to be on the street and move through it (see also Robson 2000). As Ingold and Vergunst comment that imperial power too is exercised in a bodily rhythm because "the footwork of colonial occupation is of a peculiar kind, namely the *march*" (Ingold and Vergunst 2008: 13). In the turbulent and violent years of the last quarter of the twentieth century many marches took place along these south-east London streets. Walking here was much more than an everyday stroll; rather political struggles against racism were embodied in ways of moving through the city on foot. Offered here is a spatial story: one that creates an anti-racist space by walking through a profoundly post-colonial place and feeling the traces of its history.

Clifton Rise, 13 August 1977

A short walk from the entrance of Goldsmiths west down Lewisham Way is Clifton Rise. On one corner is the New Cross Inn, a Victorian pub that has stood the test of time and today is a lively music venue. Opposite on the other is the site of the old Kinema, now a nightclub called *The Venue* specialising in tribute bands. Homeless people spend their days at the entrance of the Kinema in the bitter cold collecting contributions from passers-by. Clifton Rise gets its name from the sharp incline that rises out of the flood plain of the Thames at the bottom of the street. There is nothing to commemorate that it was here, on 13 August 1977, that the National Front was stopped in what became known as the Battle of Lewisham.

That summer a moral panic about street crime or 'mugging' was unfolding and reported widely as a racialised form of black crime (see Hall *et al*. 1978). This was as much a result of public concern being orchestrated by the media as it was by the political activities of the extreme Right. The police engaged in a crackdown against young black people, stopping young men in particular and routinely harassing them violently. The atmosphere of the time is captured vividly in Franco Rosso's film *Babylon*.[1] In one scene Blue, the character played by Brinsley Forde, is chased through the back alleys of Deptford by police and beaten viciously. An early sequence of *Babylon* is filmed on Clifton Rise.

Bringing students here invites wonderful collisions with the playful irreverence of south-east Londoners. In 2016 I led a group of earnest oral historians here and a middle-aged locksman approached and asked: "Which way is Israel – take me to the Promised Land!" Such interruptions puncture academic piety and gift helpful reminders to connect and engage with the people whose lives are unfolding here now. Local children often tag along on the walks listening in on the proceedings and sometimes follow the procession riding on their bikes.

In May 1977 the Metropolitan police raided thirty homes in Lewisham and New Cross in a cracking down on alleged street crime. Twenty-one young black people were arrested for alleged involvement in robberies.[2] In response the Lewisham 21 Defense Campaign was set up to support those arrested. In subsequent conflict with the police three more people were arrested. At a community meeting held in June Sybil Phoenix, an important figure in the local black community who set up a community centre in Pagnell Street, condemned the raids, and local black politician Alderman Russell Profitt described the raids as "scandalous and disgusting – a vicious attack on the black community".[3] In July the Lewisham 24 Defense Committee staged a march protesting against the mistreatment by the police. Over 100 National Front activists turned out to attack the march, throwing rotten fruit and caustic soda. The *Kentish Mercury* reported: "Shoppers rushed for cover as racialists stormed down New Cross Road."

At the subsequent court hearings the National Front (NF) Lewisham organiser Richard Edmunds told the local newspapers of their intent to march through Lewisham, bragging it would stage its "biggest-ever rally.... Everybody will know that the Front is marching. Where we had a couple of hundred people in New Cross on Saturday, we will be talking of thousands for our march." The National Front march was billed as a 'march against muggers'. The National Front had made political inroads at the ballot box locally. At a Deptford council by-election in 1976 the combined share of the vote for the National Front and the National Party was 45 per cent. However, in local council elections in May 1977 the vote for the NF waned, with Richard Edmunds receiving 7 per cent of the vote (1,463). The decision to stage a march in Lewisham was – in part – an attempt to reverse the decline in the National Front's electoral fortunes locally. Martin Webster, the national organizer for the NF, made their intention plain to *The South London Press*: "The Reds have had it all their own way.... We believe that the multi-racial society is wrong, is evil and we want to destroy it."[4]

In the week before the march the leader of Lewisham Council supported by three other Labour local councillors handed in a resolution to the Home Secretary for the National Front march to be banned. David McNee, the Commissioner of the Metropolitan Police at the time, issued a public statement opposing the ban. The decision was made for the march to go ahead on 13 August. On the thirtieth anniversary of the march Red Saunders, who had helped found Rock Against Racism in 1976, returned to New Cross and commented:

> Let's not forget the closeness of the Metropolitan Police and the National Front that's a key thing to remember.... Martin Webster used to boast that you'd be stunned how many senior police officers supported the National Front.[5]

Opposition marches and counter-demonstrations took a variety of forms. In the morning a rally took place in Ladywell Field a few miles away and 5,000 people from eighty organisations gathered to hear speeches from local politicians, the Bishop of Southwark, the exiled Bishop of Namibia. What is significant was the diversity of organisations that mobilised against the National Front. Over thirty-five years later disagreement about the organisation and leadership continues, particularly in relation to the role of the Socialist Workers Party (SWP), but all agree that the coming together of the protesters was historic. While much of the political activism had emerged out of the local campaigns against the police harassment, for many activists Lewisham was an unknown place. Jenny Bourne, member of Women Against Racism and Fascism (WARF) remembered:

I have to admit doing something I had never done before or since. I had gone to Lewisham the previous night, just to work out where everything was. Up till then all our protests and marches had been in east and north London, Lewisham felt like an unknown quantity.[6]

Thousand of protesters converged on the top of Clifton Rise where the National Front march had initially planned to assemble. Meanwhile, at the top of the street where the women of WARF assembled, the police tried to clear the crowds with mounted police charging with long batons drawn through the crowd. Jenny Bourne remembered the police "rained down blows on head after head – scattering us, beating us as they went, drawing blood and creating mayhem". The violence of this mayhem was captured on film and often when I take students on this walk I play this footage on my laptop in the exact place where these events unfolded. The film shows one case where a male police officer storms into the crowd and grabs a demonstrator by the throat.

The NF were forced to assemble at the bottom of Clifton Rise in a street running parallel to the New Cross Road called Achilles Street. Jenny Bourne said that in contrast with the anti-racist clashes with the police: "The NF, with hundreds of police shielding them on either side, were escorted down Pagnell Street and through the anti-fascist ranks."[7]

From the top of Clifton Rise we walk east along the stretch of the New Cross Road from which the NF was blocked from walking. Across the street next to the Marquis of Granby pub is where sound system legend Jah Shaka had his culture shop in the 1980s. I would visit Shaka's shop regularly where he sold dread paraphernalia and African artifacts. Although he didn't pay me much mind I learned from him and bought records. The sound system dances where Shaka strung up his sound system provided a refuge and alternative sphere of life for black Londoners in a period of intense violent racism (Bloom 2010: 392–395). The placing of the massive stacks of speakers would re-tune dead spaces like the crypts of churches or youth club gyms with the political and spiritual maxims of reggae's bass culture. Shaka's sound system played conscious reggae and dub and was featured centrally in Franco Rosso's film *Babylon.*

In the sound system world Jah Shaka (Neville Powell) was known as 'Nocky' but he renamed himself and his sound after the warrior Shaka Zulu. Born in Clarendon, Jamaica, he travelled to London with his family in 1956 where he went to Samuel Pepys secondary school in Deptford. William 'Lez' Henry commented that "since the mid-seventies the name Jah Shaka has become synonymous with the Rastafarian roots music, dub wise and Marcus Garvey's black consciousness" (Henry 2002: 155). He cut his teeth with a south-east London sound system called 'Freddie Cloudburst', but by the late 1970s Shaka's sound system was a vital part of black London life. Shaka commented recently:

We had to have something to bring message to the people, to bring message to the people.... Malcolm X, Martin Luther King, Angela Davis and other great people were sending messages for the people to be united around the world ... many people were feeling the pain of suffering ... these messages from these great black leaders ... gave the people hope and hope was very important.[8]

Shaka's sound and dub consciousness was the medium for this message even when it was conveyed wordlessly in rhythm of dub sensibilities.

Today Shaka's shop is home to the *Locks Unique* barbershop and hairdressers. On the sign above the shop is a tree with a human face portrayed in the trunk rooted in the ground but whose dreadlocks reach upward to the sky like branches. I bring students here regularly as a stop on this postcolonial tour. I noticed recently on the lamppost outside *Locks Unique* is a large banner advertising Short Courses at Goldsmiths. The ad promises boldly: "Be part of a powerful legacy of learning." Shaka's shop is the trace of a different legacy of learning that was fostered in the institutions of black London, including supplementary schools and community centres, that was largely ignored and appreciated by the local university. We aim to bridge the gap as we pause to remember and then walk on.

Crossing the New Cross Road and continuing eastwards we pass a small parade of shops by the bus stops. Global connections are threaded through this street (see Hall 2012). At number 355 *Divine Cargo* offers a service shipping parcels and organising international money transfers, next door is *Lady Sandra Hair Style Salon and Cosmetics*. Alternative treatments including herbal medicines and acupuncture are offered at the *Chinese Health Centre* at 359, while a few doors down the old-style laundry service simply named *Launderette* serves all those local people without a washing machine.

I often pause at the end of the parade to show students film footage taken here on the 13 August 1977. A little after 2.00 p.m. that day fighting broke out at the top of Clifton Rise as ten mounted police officers moved in to try and break up the crowds of anti-racist demonstrators; this scene was captured vividly in the photographs of Chris Steele-Perkins, Paul Trevor, Mike Abrahams and Phil McCowan (see Camerawork 1977). The NF marchers, assembled in Achilles Street and lined with police protection, began to march behind a large 'Stop the Muggers' banner. Nick Griffin, a teenager at the time who would go on to be a prominent racial nationalist, remembered:

> I was in the colour party at the front.... The most frightening thing was the noise in fact a lot of people were cowering and its quite pointless because if someone is throwing things at you it's far better to see them coming and it's a better chance of dodging them.... There was genuine local support, enormous local support as far as we were concerned we knew we had several hundred local people on the march with us.... My main memory was that of the noise ... this huge terrifying mob baying for your blood.[9]

As the National Front climbed Pagnell Street they faced the assembly of anti-racists shouting "Scum, scum, scum".[10] The National Front and the police protecting them are pushed back onto the pavement and against the shop front-age. Open fighting breaks out, as the police lines are broken. The film footage corroborates this report from the *Kentish Mercury* published on 18 August:

> One young man, perhaps 16 years old, rushed into the Front ranks and grabbed a flagpole from one of them, broke it in half and held the pieces up while the crowd cheered. Others hurled dustbins and fence stakes into the Front column from close range.

As the National Front activists move off again fearfully the crowd sings "The workers united will never be defeated."

The National Front march proceeded down the New Cross Road through the skirmishes and finally led away to Lewisham train station. As anti-fascists and local black young people held back a running battle broke out with the police. The next day the Battle of Lewisham was covered widely on the front pages of the Sunday newspapers. It is reported that the police had deployed for the first time on the mainland the batons and riot shields used in Northern Ireland.[11] The conflict is reported as a "race hatred battle" between 'extremists'.[12] The *Sunday Telegraph* ran a feature piece by John Smalldon and David Rosenberg entitled 'Why the extremists are on the march' in which they wrote: "Extremists on either side of the fence almost trampled on each other in the stampede to make maximum political capital out of the arrests."[13] Here both Left and Right are conflated with each other and presented as opportunists using the police arrests of black young people and the Lewisham 24 campaign for their own ends.

Jenny Bourne reflected:

> The media had a field-day. Anti-fascism was vilified – with NF supporters and their opponents equated as thugs who wanted no part of democracy. That anti-racism and anti-fascism were essential moral (if not political) positions never got aired in the discussion.[14]

The physical confrontation with the National Front came at considerable cost as the demonstrators left Lewisham that day to tend to their wounds. The political affects were considerable; Martin Webster later commented that the back of the movement was broken that day. However, Jenny Bourne concluded: "We might have won the battle of Lewisham, but we lost the propaganda war."

There is a clue in the way the press coverage at the time referred to 'marchers' and 'counter-marchers'. Perhaps the template for understanding these forms of street politics was set by the Battle of Cable Street where Oswald Moseley's Black Shirt fascists were stopped in the autumn of 1936. The National Front marching through the streets of Lewisham behind their banners was intended to be a pro-vocation – it made racially exclusive nationalism flesh and put in motion their laying a claim to the streets. What unfolded as the 'counter-marchers' confronted them forced them to miss a step and sometimes cower in shop doorways. For the young black people who had been so routinely stopped and searched by the police

– often violently – in the street, in the midst of the demonstration there was a temporary suspension of the power of the law and a fleeting opportunity to strike back.

The struggle over the route of the march, the police protection of the 'right of way' and the attempts to block its passage embodied politically the larger struggle over race and nation. The issue of traversing the streets on foot is then linked to a struggle over who belongs on the streets of south-east London and who is out of place. After 13 August 1977 the National Front as a movement was broken. Nick Griffin, who went on to lead its successor the British National Party, commented:

> It was a crazy strategy to get us into – a piece of bravado by Webster which did the NF an incredible amount of damage. Frightening people off and upsetting and worrying potential voters.... It was a public relations disaster, no doubt about it.[15]

It did not follow, however, that the back of demotic or institutional racism was broken too.

439 New Cross Road, 18 January 1981

The route of the National Front march passed 439 New Cross Road. Just a few years later, in the early hours of 18 January 1981, a devastating fire engulfed partygoers here at a birthday celebration being held for Yvonne Ruddock and Angela Jackson. In the final death toll fourteen young black people between the ages of fourteen to twenty-two had their futures stolen from them that night. Thirteen died in the fire from burns and suffocation while one victim later committed suicide unable to live with the memory of its aftermath.

Dub poet and activist Linton Kwesi Johnson has written that "the most significant date in the history of the black experience in Britain during the second half of the twentieth century is the year 1981" (Johnson 2011: 1). As he notes, it began "inauspiciously" with a tragedy in New Cross. As a teenager I remember passing the ruined house at 439 New Cross Road regularly on my way to college at Goldsmiths. In the doorway was a makeshift memorial, "Thirteen of our children murdered", and beneath these words was a list of their names. The burnt out three-storey house was a reminder of the nature of the offence like an open wound scorched in the body of the city.

Walking the short distance from Pagnell Street we pass the New Cross station and the Amersham Arms and, crossing Mornington Road, SE8, reach the scene of these tragic events. Now there are people living there. Across the letterbox is a message "No Junk Mail". For thirty years there was no marker on the house. On the thirtieth anniversary of the fire a plaque was mounted on the brickwork. It read: "New Cross Fire took place at this site on January 18th, 1981 claiming the lives of fourteen young people."

Eyewitness accounts pointed to arson and the suspicious behavior that night of a man who drove off in a white Austin van. Fire had been a staple weapon of racist violence and there had been other arson attacks on black community centres and youth clubs. Thirty-five years later the origins of the fire remain unknown. There have been two inquests into the New Cross fire, both of which returned open verdicts, and anger remains at the incapacity of the police to determine those responsible. Many believe that the massacre was the result of a racist arson attack. What is undeniable looking back was the shameful indifference to these deaths at the time within the media and the political establishment.

Unlike the Battle of Lewisham that was splashed over the headlines of the Sunday newspapers, in the days that followed there was little coverage of this terrible loss of young life in the newspapers, with the exception of *The Sun* that reported it on the front cover (Holland 1981: 64), and no statement of condolence from then Prime Minister Margaret Thatcher. Joan Anim-Addo pointed out that ten years earlier there had been a racist attack at a party at 47 Sunderland Road, Forest Hill, where three fire bombs were thrown injuring twenty-two people: just eight column inches was devoted to it in the national press (Anim-Addo 1995: 126). The same cold silence of the white establishment conveyed a brutally simple message: the loss of young black lives simply did not matter. Johnny Osbourne sang pointedly in a popular song of the time: "13 Dead (and Nothing Said)".[16]

Out of the ashes of this terrible tragedy came an unprecedented political mobilisation led by the families, the New Cross Massacre Action Committee and the wider black community. It resulted in the historic 'Black People's Day of Action' on Monday 2 March 1981, when 20,000 people from all over the country filed by 439 New Cross Road bound for the Houses of Parliament and Fleet Street. As Paul Gilroy commented, portraits of the young people who lost their lives were carried as a demonstration that their humanity mattered.[17] The image of Owen Wesley Thompson being carried at the top of Clifton Rise photographed by Vron Ware (see p. 20) shows visually the profound insight in Gilroy's remark.

John La Rose, who chaired the New Cross Massacre Campaign, commented in an interview in 1983: "New Cross is an historic event in the history not only of the black community, but in the history of British society" (New Beacon Books 2011: 25). In a way this is my lasting memory. It was that sense of shock that this is where racism can lead – to a massacre, not of what journalists or sociologists grudgingly referred to as 'West Indian youngsters', but to the murder of your neighbours, classmates and friends.

Several years later when I was doing the fieldwork for my PhD I interviewed a local white young woman called Debbie, who said:

> I remember the New Cross Fire because I was quite friendly with the people who lost kids in that fire and I knew quite a few kids.... I felt that quite personally, I was really upset by that. I went on the march and things. I remember it rained. I got soaked to the skin.... That actually did a lot to bring the community around here together ... both black and white people.[18]

Debbie rejected racism and felt that New Cross was a good place to live and bring up her son, who at the time attended Childeric School. She worked as primary child minder, often taking care of black children placed with her by Lewisham Social Services. Her life illustrated how everyday anti-racism co-existed paradoxically in south-east London with the many faces of racism.

Saying nothing in the face of racism was, and is, complicity, whether it is the media at the time ignoring that the violence happened at all, or police harassment and neglect, or laughing at the jokes of racist comedians, or agreeing with casual hatred conveyed over the kitchen table. Being proximate to these events for white residents – like myself – was also a lesson in political humility and learning what it meant to be against racism but respectful of the true costs borne by its victims.

We walk down Mornington Road back onto the floor plain of the Thames through residential streets. At the bottom of the road we meet Douglas Way. I brought music journalist Saxon Baird here in 2014 when he was making a documentary about reggae in the UK.[19] He asked me that day: "Weren't you ever challenged being on the scene and being white?"[20] The people running the sound systems had more important things on their minds than the few white dots on the domino of black London's alternative public spheres (Gilroy 1987).

Of course, there were occasional playful jibes. I remember telling Saxon: "You had to 'check yourself'." It meant understanding the line between respectful affinity and friendship, and violating forms of desire and over-identification. The boundary between the two was constantly being navigated in these worlds. In Franco Rosso's film *Babylon* Ronnie, the white friend in this black sound system posse played by Karl Howman, oversteps this line in the aftermath of the sound system being wrecked and destroyed by white racists. When the group challenges him because "his people did this", Ronnie responds by "talking black" and earns a head-butt and a bloody nose from Beefy who is played by Trevor Laird. I think I learned this lesson too, but bloodlessly. I regard it as a precious gift that was the result of being allowed access to black-hosted spaces at that time. The hypocrisy of south-east London's racial landscape was that by contrast the white racist spaces – particular pubs and nightclubs – were completely off-limits to my black friends. If they ever ventured into them they'd be challenged and met with abuse and often violence.

To the right is the Albany Empire, a community hub and venue that was a vibrant cultural and political centre in the 1980s. The Albany is another institution that grew out of the ashes of fire. Its initial premises were nearby at 47 Creek Road but on 14 July 1978 a fire destroyed the building where Rock Against Racism gigs had been hosted. The following day a note was pushed through the letterbox of the burned out building: it read "Got you". The generation that came of age politically at that moment was aware a fight was going on "for the soul of our country" around race, empire and nation (Widgery 1986: 121).

We turn left down Douglas Way and head back towards New Cross train station, built in 1849. On spring afternoons the sound of blackbirds singing in the trees close by can be heard above the hum of the city. Passing the Waldron

Health Centre we cross Amersham Vale and close to the tracks a soft high-pitch sound signals the next arrival that seems to slow down as the train does. Walking through the Walpole Road underpass a keynote local sound is the rattle of train wheels as they speed along the tracks in percussive four beats.

Crossing Pagnell Street we walk into Fordham Park nearing the end of the journey. The park was named after Charles Frank Fordham, a local politician and the last Mayor of the old Borough of Deptford. In the 1840s the site became John Avann's market garden supplying fruit and vegetables to London's Covent Garden Market. The area was developed for working-class housing in the 1850–1860s. Today the park has been redeveloped with new play areas for children, and along the path is Lewisham's Linear Arboretum. The first tree is the English Oak (*Quercus robur*) and in the path a plaque celebrates its significance. "It is a tree of great cultural and symbolic significance in England", it reads, mentioning it is a popular name for pubs and ships. "Large quantities of oak have come to the Royal Dock in Deptford, one of Henry VIII's main warship building yards." Then there is a quotation from an unspecified ancient source, probably something like E. Keble Chatterton (1911) *The Story of the British Navy*. The quote conveys the hubris of Britain's imperial past: "When large ships for bloody combat we prepare Oak affords plank and arms our men for war, maintains our fires, makes ploughs to till the ground. For use no timber like the oak is found."

The tangled roots of London's imperial past entwine with the postcolonial present. At the edge of the park the Pagnell Street Centre steered by Sybil Phoenix provided an important community resource and set up the Moonshot Youth Club – inspired by the era of space travel – initially based in Telegraph Hill. In her history of black Lewisham Joan Anim-Addo shows in November 1977 – in the aftermath of the National Front march – how local newspapers reported that in local NF meetings threats had been made to burn down Moonshot. At 4 a.m. on 18 December 1977 Pagnell Street was ablaze from an incendiary bomb thrown at the door. The building was gutted. Sybil Phoenix told a local radio journalist: "My name is Phoenix and, so help me God, out of the ashes I will rebuild Moonshot" (quoted in Anim-Addo 1995: 141–142). Over £50,000 was raised and a year later a new foundation stone was laid on the site of the original Pagnell Street Centre; by 1981 the new Moonshot Youth Club was opened.

The youth clubs, the places where sound systems like Jah Shaka's played, and the dances were places of joy and spiritual enrichment but they were targeted by the police and popular racists. In May 1975 a Shaka dance at Moonshot was attacked and several pounds of damage was done to his sound system (Anim-Addo 1995: 194). Shaka did not just play records, rather he used the sound system as an instrument to sculpt sound and create a unique listening experience. The bass sound was so immense that it not only transformed your consciousness but your whole body became an ear: listening through the touch and feel of your skin.

Shaka uses an early Garrard turntable developed in the late 1940s designed to play 78 rpm records because it does not feedback at high volume. The dub plates he plays are very often records made specifically for the sound system and on the microphone Shaka offers lyrical comment and spiritual incantations. Steppers rhythm provides the time signature of a Shaka dance. The details of this are important in order to get close to dub reggae's embodied structure of feeling, a sense of African diaspora aesthetics that is both in a particular space and time yet simultaneously beyond it (Gilroy 1987).

The drive in steppers riddim comes from the drummer who is playing quarter on the bass drum with the right foot known as 'four on the floor', while the left hand plays a rim shot on the third beat of each bar. At the same time the drummer's right hand plays eighth notes on the high hat cymbal with quarter note accents in time with the bass drum. The rhythm that stirs steppers dancing is a variant of Rastafari skank called ital steppers.[21] The springing steps of the rhythm are danced individually in one spot while moving side-to-side with improvised individual moves. On occasion dancers hold a pose like an ancient African idol made flesh for a moment before being released and leaping ecstatically back into life. Carried in the body – in the steps of the steppers – was a different sense of being in place and time, where the dance was an embodied psychic realm and an alternative public space (Gilory 1987; Henry 2006).

One of the trademarks of Shaka's performance was his 'echo chamber' comprising of an HH analogue tape loop delay. The signal from the sound would repeat and reverberate within the space, suggesting a historical resonance beyond it. Another aspect of Shaka's performance was his use of a siren that would often be played hauntingly through the echo chamber. Shaka commented recently that he used the siren to alert the dancers to threatening forces that are gathering. He told an audience in Tokyo in 2014 "It's like you are throwing a spear", pausing to simulate the sound of a spear being thrown. "It's a warning it causes the people to think."[22] Perhaps it's a sign of a different time but today Shaka's siren is available from Apple in the form of the Dub Siren DX as a phone app. [23]

Walking down the path there is a foxglove outside Moonshot Youth Club. The premises have been renovated with a new glass entrance area and it is home to the Double Jab boxing club. I remember coming to a Shaka dance here in the mid-1980s and there were so many people queuing up to go into the dance that the queue went around the building twice. It was a sign of how vital the music was, it kept the people strong but it kept them sane in hostile times too.

Between 1973 and 1976 the poet Linton Kwesi Johnson studied sociology at Goldsmiths. In 1997 he reflected:

> I was trying to formulate a kind of sociology of reggae.... I coined the phrase 'dub lyricism' and spoke about reggae DJ's as poets, because I saw them in a similar light to the griots, being people doing oral poetry, spontaneous oral poetry.

> (Harris and White 1999: 60)

I bring students to this spot often and quote from an essay by Linton called 'Jamaican Reggae Music' published in the journal *Race and Class* that I think was his undergraduate dissertation. I know this passage by heart and it shaped my own understanding of why reggae mattered:

> It is a music that beats heavily against the walls of Babylon, that the walls come a-tumbling down; a music that chucks an heavy historical load that is pain that is hunger that is bitter that is blood, that is dread.
>
> (Johnson 1976: 397)

Looking across at the football pitch and the expanse of patchy badly bruised grass I imagine another point of assembly. It was here in Fordham Park that demonstrators gathered on 2 March 1981 for the Black People's Day of Action. It was a historic coming together of 20,000 black people and their associates in the aftermath of the tragedy of the New Cross Fire. As it weaved its way through south London children and young people scaled the fences of their schools to join it. Many of the demonstrators who were on the march that day would go on to become the most articulate voices to emerge from postcolonial London.

The Black People's Day of Action was historic because it marked a political and cultural turning point. John La Rose commented:

> The New Cross Massacre campaign gave an enormous self-confidence to the black population in Britain – that has expressed itself politically, cultur-ally, since 2nd March, 1981. At Brixton, the youths who were fighting against the police in open insurrection, were saying, "They burnt us out in New Cross we are burning them out now".
>
> (New Beacon 2011: 25)

The fire this time, to paraphrase James Baldwin, was also channeled culturally through music, art and literature (see Back 1988).

Last Steps, Sitting Down and Taking It In

Walking down the path of the linear arboretum some more words are set into the concrete of the renovated park. This time from musician Alex James who studied French at Goldsmiths but earned acclaim as the bass player in the rock band *Blur*. The quotation is from his memoir *Bit of a Blur* (James 2007: 34 35) and celebrates the social life of Fordham Park, endless summer games of cricket and the *Dew Drop Inn* that was located on the northern edge at the bottom of Clifton Rise. James recalls 'The Dewie' fondly as the "best pub in New Cross" and the quotation in concrete is located close to where the pub used to trade, although the building has now been converted into flats. James (2007: 35) wrote: "In London, pubs are wonderful places ... they are the synapses of the city, full of connections and paths that lead in all directions."

I am sure Alex James's late 1980s' characterisation of the Dew Drop as a convivial haunt of urban diversity is accurate. Just ten years earlier *The Dew Drop Inn* was a notorious racist space and a stronghold of local National Front support. I remember the association during the 1980s when I was a youth worker at Moonshot. Reggae DJ and sociologist Lez Henry has described being attacked by white patrons of *The Dew Drop Inn* in the 1970s after a Jah Shaka sound system dance in the nearby Moonshot Youth Club.[24] Perhaps the celebration of Alex James at Fordham Park, a Goldsmiths student and white musician, is an odd choice given this history. Part of the paradox of postcolonial London is that *both things are equally true* of this iconic local place that provided a haunt – at different times – for National Front supporting local racists and budding art school rock stars.

Further along the path snakes around an artificial mound. Here there is a stone memorial to the fourteen young black people who died in the New Cross Fire. Their names are etched into the stone. When I bring students here I often play Linton Kwesi Johnson's tune 'New Crass Massahkah'. The lyric celebrates the harmless pleasures of the blues dance which is then attacked violently and engulfed with flames.[25] John La Rose commented in 1983 that the perspective of the young is "to mash up Babylon, to create a new society, where social relations are not so barbaric as they are, that is something which is not humane, and make it more human" (New Beacon 2011: 31). Or, as Jah Shaka puts it, "the truth carries no colour".[26]

This side of Fordham Park borders on Childeric Road where Debbie – the anti-racist white child minder mentioned earlier – brought her son to school. London's racist past is uncannily present even as the children laugh in the play area close by. This street was also the scene of some of the most infamous police raids during the late 1970s where we began. Journalist Paul Foot documented one such raid in June 1977:

> 5.30 Monday Morning. Six policemen break down the door of 21 Childeric Road in Deptford, South East London, with an axe. Another six smash down the back door. They pour inside, overturning furniture, ripping open drawers, and turning people out of their beds. Christopher Foster, aged 16, is frog-marched into the road in his underclothes. Insults and questions are shouted at him. He and four other young people in the house are rushed to Penge police station. These include Cathy Cullis, a young white girl. She is stripped to her underwear in a cell. Two policemen come and joke about the 'disease' she has caught living with black people.
>
> (Quoted in Renton 2006: 53–54)

Looking across to Childeric Road from the memorial, number 21 is just a few houses to the left.

There is a bench in front of the memorial, it is the end of my walk and I often sit here to take in what has been learned. The value of walking and teaching is to invite students to feel the social landscape and its haunted past, to open themselves to its unfolding life and link this to its facsimile in writing that is documented in the books read in the library. The walk is subtly different every time and something unexpected unfolds with each group. There are things that I only see or notice when I am alone too. Looking at the memorial from the bench I notice that in the background is *The Dew Drop Inn* that seems to be a white shadow cast over it. This illustrates London's metropolitan paradox where brutal forms of racism co-exist and are contiguous with spaces of resistance, expressive cultural forms and everyday multiculture.

To close, I want to draw out some conclusions about the value of trying to learn the city by walking it. The ambulant insight produced along the way enables us to get a feel for the marchers as we follow in their footsteps and the spectral shouts of the demonstrators and develop a sense of what was claimed or contested within these embodiments of urban life. It also invites an understanding of the co-presence of racism and multiculture and the nearness of love and hate or discord and harmony.

This is not to suggest that understanding is simply a matter of proximity or getting close. As de Certeau commented 'being there' can be spellbinding, as blinding as a lover's embrace. Instead I want to argue for the value not just of proximity but the value of returning. This is perhaps why anthropologists commonly revisit the sites of their ethnographic fieldwork repeatedly during the course of a scholarly lifetime (Caplan 1997).

Cities reveal their secrets – both past and present – in small installments. Tracking back on foot offers an invitation to conduct an anthropology of the near but it also involves making links between that sensuous lived encounter and the dusty official record archived in the library. All of this is necessary for the kind of urban pedagogy I am proposing, a form of slow release understanding achieved through *staying there*, taking another attentive stroll and thinking again on your feet.

Notes

1 Directed by Franco Rosso *Bablyon*, 1980 made by Diversity Music Limited in association with the National Film Finance Corporation, screenplay by Martin Stellman and Franco Rosso.
2 This account is drawn from the Lewisham '77 website that was developed and compiled on the thirtieth anniversary from activists' accounts and local and national newspaper coverage; see 'Racism and Resistance in South East London: A Chronology', http://lewisham77.blogspot.co.uk/2007_07_01_archive.html, Thursday, 26 July 2007, downloaded 2 April 2016.
3 'Racism and Resistance in South East London: A Chronology'.
4 *South London Press*, 5 August 1977, p. 4
5 Red Saunders, 'Lewisham '77', a walk in August 2007, www.youtube.com/watch?v=Vl9x-oK_qZs, downloaded 4 April 2017.
6 Jenny Bourne, 'Lewisham '77: Success or Failure?', Institute of Race Relations website, www.irr.org.uk/news/lewisham-77-success-or-failure, downloaded 2 April 2016.
7 Bourne, 'Lewisham '77: Success or Failure?'.
8 Jah Shaka, 'Red Bull Music Academy Lecture', Tokyo, 7 November 2014, www.youtube.com/watch?v=3QNWpnwWgc4, downloaded 6 April 2016.
9 Interview with the author, 2 April 1998.
10 This footage is available on YouTube, www.youtube.com/watch?v=hK0aURnC314&nohtml5=False, downloaded 20 June 2016.

11 *Sunday Telegraph*, 14 August 1977, p. 1.
12 *Observer*, 14 August 1977, p. 2; *The Sunday Times*, 14 August 1977, p. 1.
13 John Smalldon and David Rosenberg, 'Why the Extremists Are on the March', *The Sunday Times*, 14 August 1977, p. 15.
14 Bourne, 'Lewisham '77: Success or Failure?'.
15 Interview with author, 2 April 1998.
16 Johnny Osbourne, '13 Dead (and Nothing Said)', www.youtube.com/watch?v=gin Km0F7Qsw, downloaded 20 June 2016.
17 From an interview with Paul Gilroy in *The Time Machine*, BBC Radio 4, broadcast Saturday 31 October 2015, www.bbc.co.uk/programmes/b06l2vw7, downloaded 14 April 2016.
18 Interview with author and fieldnotes, 23 January 1987.
19 Saxon Baird, 'Dread Inna Inglan: How the U.K. Took to Reggae', Afropop Worldwide, https://soundcloud.com/afropop-worldwide/dread-inna-inglan-how-the-uk-took-to-reggae, downloaded 12 April 2016.
20 The full recording of the thirty-five minute walk with Saxon Baird is available at https://soundcloud.com/saxonius/lewisham-and-soundsystem, downloaded 20 June 2016..
21 Thanks to to William 'Lez' Henry for sharing this insight.
22 Jah Shaka, *Red Bull Music Academy Lecture*, Tokyo, 7 November 2014, www. youtube.com/watch?v=3QNWpnwWgc4, downloaded 6 April 2016.
23 This app is now available on iTunes, https://itunes.apple.com/us/app/dub-siren/id317311446?mt=8.
24 See 'Interview: Dr. William "Lez" Henry on Racism in the UK, Rastafari and the Transcendent Nature of Sound Systems', Afropop Worlwide, www.afropop. org/16795/interview-dr-william-lez-henry-on-racism-in-the-uk-rastafari-and-the-trans cendent-nature-of-sound-systems, downloaded 20 June 2016.
25 Linton Kwesi, 'John New Cross Massahkah', www.youtube.com/watch?v=FUMYA qAlAXA, downloaded 12 April 2016.
26 Jah Shaka, *Red Bull Music Academy Lecture*.

References

Anim-Addo, J. (1995) *The Longest Journey: A History of Black Lewisham*. London: Deptford Forum Publishing.
Back, L. (1988) '"Coughing up Fire": Sound Systems in South-East London', *New Formations*, 5 (Summer): 141–152.
Bloom, C. (2010) *Violent London: 2000 Years of Riots, Rebels and Revolts*. Houndmills, Basingstoke: Palgrave Macmillan.
Bourdieu, P. (1977) *Outline of a Theory of Practice*. Cambridge: Cambridge University Press.
Camerawork (1977) 'Lewisham: What Are You Taking Pictures for?' *Camerawork*, Number 8.
Caplan, P. (1997) *African Voices, African Lives: Personal Narratives from a Swahili Village*. London: Routledge.
de Certeau, M. (1988) *The Practice of Everyday Life*. Berkeley, Los Angeles and London: University of California Press.
Gilroy, P. (1987) *There Ain't No Black in the Union Jack: The Cultural Politics of Race and Nation*. London: Hutchinson.
Hall, S. (2012) *City, Street and Citizen: The Measure of the Ordinary*. London: Routledge.

Hall, S., Critcher, C., Jefferson, T., Clarke, J. and Roberts, B. (1978) *Policing the Crisis: Mugging, the State and Law and Order*. Houndmills, Basingstoke: Macmillan Press.

Harris, R. and White, S. (eds) (1999) *Changing Britannia: Life Experience with Britain*. London: New Beacon Books.

Henry, W. (2002) 'Jah Shaka', in A. Donnell (ed.), *Companion to Contemporary Black British Culture*. London and New York: Routledge, p. 155.

Henry, W. (2006) *What the DJ Said: A Critique from the Street*. London: Nu-Beyond.

Hobbs, D. (2013) *Lush Life: Constructing Organised Crime in the UK*. Oxford: Oxford University Press.

Hoggart, R. (1957) *The Uses of Literacy: Aspects of Working-Class Life with Special Reference to Publications and Entertainments*. Harmondsworth: Penguin.

Hoggart, R. (1992) *An Imagined Life: Life and Times 1959–91*. London: Chatto and Windus.

Holland, P. (1981) 'The New Cross Fire and the Popular Press', *Multiracial Education*, 9(3): 61–80.

Ingold, T. and Vergunst, J. L. (eds) (2008) *Ways of Walking: Ethnography and Practice on Foot*. Aldershot: Ashgate.

James, A. (2007) *A Bit of A Blur: The Autobiography*. London: Hachette Digital.

Johnson, L. K. (1976) 'Jamaican Rebel Music', *Race and Class*, XVII(4): 397–412.

Johnson, L. K. (2011) 'We Have Not Forgotten', in New Beacon Books (eds), *The New Cross Massacre Story: Interviews with John La Rose*. London: New Beacon Books, pp. 1–4.

Keble Chatterton, E. (1911) *The Story of the British Navy from the Earliest Times to the Present Day*. London: Mills and Boon.

Mauss, M. (1979) *Sociology and Psychology*. London: Routledge and Kegan Paul.

New Beacon (2011) *The New Cross Massacre Story: Interviews with John La Rose*. London: New Beacon Books.

O'Neill, M. and Perivolaris, J. (2014) 'A Sense of Belonging: Walking with Thaer through Migration, Memories and Space', *Crossings: Journal of Migration and Culture*, 5 (2/3): 327–338.

Reed, A. (2002) 'City of Details: Interpreting the Personality of London', *Journal of the Royal Anthropological Institute*, 8: 127–141.

Renton, D. (2006) *When We Touched the Sky: The Anti-Nazi League 1977–1981*. Cheltenham: New Clarendon Press.

Robson, G. (2000) *'No One Likes Us, We Don't Care': The Myth and Reality of Millwall Fandom*. Oxford: Berg.

Self, W. (2015) 'Afterword', in M. Beaumont, *Night Walking: A Nocturnal History of London*. London and New York: Verso, pp. 411–413.

Steele, J. (1993) *Turning the Tide: The History of Everyday Deptford*. London: Deptford Publishing Forum.

Widgery, D. (1986) *Beating Time: Riot 'n' Race 'n' Rock 'n' Roll*. London: Chatto and Windus.

Seeing the Need: Objects That Might Match the Tenor and Drift of Outreach Inquiry.
Source: Tom Hall.

2 Seeing the Need

Urban Outreach as Sensory Walking

Tom Hall and Robin James Smith

What does looking for something look like? Perhaps looking *at* something, holding something as the object of an unwavering attention, requires an immobility; and perhaps we too readily take this as a model for what it is to see more generally. Certainly, this is a conceptualisation of what it is to attend to something that has held good for much of social scientific inquiry over the past 100 years or so. An object, the ontology of which is assumed fixed, a priori, is isolated and abstracted from context, held in (ideally) unwavering focus whilst various inquiries are made. This is what we commonly construe as intelligence. Whether we are talking here about inquiries into social organisation or social phenomena or persons, for some time the social scientific preference has been for this static, rather than mobile or relational, mode of inquiry (Büscher *et al.*, 2010). In practice, of course, the notion that observer and observed are best aligned in immobility if things are to be properly examined is a straw target and easily recognised as such. *All* perception involves movement and interaction; in the absence of movement (of any kind) perception itself is stalled (see Noë, 2004). In addition, movement relates to a particular formation of reality and knowledge. As Henri Bergson (2007: 22) has it,

> [i]ntelligence starts ordinarily from the immobile and reconstructs movement as best it can with immobilities in juxtaposition. Intuition starts from movement, posits it, or rather perceives it as reality itself, and sees in immobility only an abstract moment, a snapshot taken by our mind, of a mobility.

And, of course, the chapters gathered in this collection variously examine and illustrate the relationship between motion, the senses and knowing. Retaining the inextricable relation of mobility and perception, we draw out a distinction between how this is differently configured in the act of looking *at* something as opposed looking *for* something. Regardless of the degree of movement involved in the actual business of seeing, to look *at* something is always to have it located already, as co-present, to hand, or available for viewing through some mediated means. Looking *for* something, on the other hand, is more obviously, always and unavoidably, to move; to be engaged in a search for an object or person is to be directed by the idea of something sought but not as yet to hand.

In the context of this collection, and of our research more generally, we are interested in the confluence of movement and perception in relation to knowledge of place and the city. We do not, however, intend to look at this relation held still, isolated and analysed through formal sociological method but instead to 'go out' (Molotch, 1994) and look *for* it in action in the work of our key informants. At this point it will help to introduce these individuals, if briefly: we are concerned with a team of council workers based in Cardiff whose job it is to make repeated tours through the centre of the city, day and night, looking to establish contact with, and minister to, 'vulnerable' adults who may otherwise struggle, on their own, to access mainstream health and social services. Rough sleepers make up a significant proportion of this population, but take their place alongside assorted others, all of whom the council outreach workers aim to enrol and assist as clients. In due course we will consider the working practice of this outreach team in some detail; it provides our case study. But first we want to consider movement, and particularly walking, as a method employed to various ends not least by social researchers – but also, and crucially, by almost everybody else.

Moving and Method

Like other researchers with an interest in knowledge, perception and place (including all of those collected in this volume), we take walking to be an essential method through which to access and analyse these intertwined phenomena. Increasing numbers of social scientists have appropriated walking as a professional method in recent years to better access or 'reveal' whatever it is that a given informant or setting is presumed to hold for their inquiries. Such work has taken on a variety of forms of 'go-along' (Kusenbach, 2003) and other such guided walks, variously contrived for the purposes of professional inquiry in and through which the act of walking together is said to 'produce an affinity between personal narratives and the movement through place' (Moles, 2008). And such work has undoubtedly added much to the ways in which such researchers get at and gain understanding of the everyday experiences of their informants. Yet, two points remain. The first is that, despite the seemingly overwhelming theoretical complexity of everyday life for the analyst, members experience only practical difficulties in methodically organising movement, perception and knowledge. The second is that, quite outside of any professional research design, walking is an already established practice, accomplished by members in step with other tasks such as talking or guiding or asking for directions, and a whole range of stuff getting done involving knowledge and perception (e.g. Ryave and Schenkein, 1974; Psathas, 1992; Mondada, 2009; Laurier *et al.*, 2016). Indeed, people routinely engage in their own pedestrian projects, both ordinarily and on occasion as part of some professional remit. The point being, whatever it is that walking might be argued to bring to social scientific inquiry, whatever it might 'open up', people are in any case already doing it: strolling around the city centre to see what is going on, perhaps for fun, perhaps as participants in a guided tour, perhaps as a dog walker or street cleaner; walking with a colleague outside of the workplace to talk privately and freely about a sensitive matter; showing a visitor around your home town, taking in the sights. Despite the availability of other means of achieving something like the same purpose – one could use maps, or talk on the phone, or browse a set of postcards, or recruit some more enhanced technological mediation – there would appear to be something in the immediacy and intimacy of walking that finds it consistently enrolled by people in their lives and work.[1]

Importantly then, and in keeping with the above, the walking that we want to consider and reflect on in this chapter is not recommended or applied as *our own* method.[2] Our informants – Cardiff's city centre outreach workers – have already settled on walking as *their* method. We will explain and show why so below, but suffice to say here that there are other options available to them – they could ride bikes, or spend far more time than they do using their works minivan – but their routine *modus operandi* is to go out and walk the streets of the city centre, on the look-out *for* something. In the remainder of this chapter, we aim to outline something of the use of walking as a means by which to reach out to the rough sleeping homeless: vulnerable adults available to view – in public distress or difficulty – but not always to hand and needing first of all to be found. We proceed by thinking about mobility and perception in relation to differently formatted search practices.

Patrol and Perception

Persons with a professional remit for the tracing and location of objects or persons, lost or unknown, may at any one time, be engaged in one or another of a number of search formats. Police officers, for example, may be dispatched to search for a suspect at his or her place of work, or last known address. They may be provided with a description or picture – a mugshot or artist's impression – of a suspect whose location is unknown, so that they may, rather more loosely, keep an eye out for them. Setting out from the police station and into the city to look for one person, whereabouts unknown, would be a chancy undertaking and very likely a waste of time; but being alive to the possibility of their discovery whilst moving through the city on other business is efficient. (On other occasions, police officers will simply be out patrolling, not looking out for anyone in particular, just keeping an eye on things generally and letting members of the public see them doing so.) Outreach workers are not police officers, but we make mention of the police here to permit reference to Egon Bittner's (1967) classic article on policing and peacekeeping on skid row. The article is directed to a great many of the practical methods US police officers employ in their work with the homeless outside of situations requiring actual law enforcement – where action might be taken in consequence of a crime (already) committed. These practical and peacekeeping skills are various but a common initial difficulty faced by the police in a great many cases has to do with the fact that the very people they aim to encounter and somehow manage – for whatever purpose – are *homeless*. The word glosses over an array of miseries and sufferings but is also a membership category tied to predicates including the lack of a series of stable and tied locations such as might be tied to other categories of person such as 'employee' or 'home owner'. Members of skid row are unreliably located and lead lives that lack a readily available structure and predictability. On occasion, this presents police officers with an immediate problem:

> That a man has no 'address' in the future that could be in some way inferred from where he is and what he does makes him a person of *radically reduced visibility*. If he disappears from sight and one wishes to locate him, it is virtually impossible to systematize the search. All one can know with relative certainty is that he will be somewhere on some skid-row and the only thing one can do is to trace the factual contiguities of his whereabouts.
>
> (Bittner, 1967: 706)

The US vernacular aside, this is a challenge that any outreach worker dealing with the rough sleeping homeless in a UK city centre would unhesitatingly recognise. Working with the homeless starts out, every day and repeatedly, as a job of work that looks like *searching*. Having held off thus far from describing the practice of outreach in any detail, we will now make good and provide a detailed account of just what this business of tracing the factual contiguities of another's whereabouts looks like in the middle of Cardiff.

> Half past six on a sunny afternoon, now turning to evening, in the centre of Cardiff. Jeff, an outreach worker, is stood in the foyer of Marland House waiting for his colleague Dennis and in the meantime talking to a security guard about the (derelict) Central Hotel, around the corner, which has been secured behind plywood hoarding over the last couple of days in preparation for demolition. Jeff wonders if anyone might still be 'in' there. This will be worth making sure of, before the bulldozers get to work.
>
> Dennis arrives, carrying a box of one-cup sachets of powdered hot chocolate. Together, Dennis and Jeff leave the building turning left towards the train station and then left again on to Great Western Lane where Dennis' car is parked. Dennis opens the boot, puts the box inside and shuts it again. Leaning against the passenger side door, smoking a cigarette, Jeff briefs Dennis on the day's news, which includes the (provisional) good news that Barry O. has been moved into a flat on Salisbury Road and the sad news that Ryan G. is dead; an unsuspicious death, his health just gave out says Jeff. Other clients will want to know, if they don't already.
>
> Leaving the car where it is and returning to Central Square, Jeff and Dennis spend ten minutes with a group of street drinkers sat on benches opposite the train station, shouting and hooting at passers-by (at least one of the drinkers was a good friend of Ryan G. and none of them seem to have heard the news; but Jeff and Dennis make no mention, given how drunk everyone is – saving this task for a quieter time, perhaps later tonight, or tomorrow morning). Next, they turn their backs on the train station and walk

over to the bus terminus where they spend ten minutes slowly walking up and down each of the stands, stopping at one point to speak to a man sat on his own on a bench – he doesn't answer back (this is Bernard W; he doesn't often answer back, or say anything at all). Jeff spots Suzie B. at a payphone by the public toilets, trying to make a call but dropping money on the floor. She is heavily made up, and not wearing much. She staggers over to Dennis and asks to borrow his phone. Dennis gives her 30p instead, to try again at the phone box.

Jeff and Dennis walk off together towards St. Mary Street, but Suzie follows. She wants to talk and needs to sit down. She has some things she wants to tell Jeff, with whom she has always got on well. Back on Great Western Lane the three of them share a low wall, as seating, and Sarah rehearses the events of the last few days, an account which includes details of an assault, arrest, collapse and her being 'back on the gear'. This last item is not news at all, in the sense that it was already apparent. Suzie asks for some condoms, and Jeff gives her a handful. Suddenly purposeful, she heads off towards Wood Street, weaving along the pavement.

The two outreach workers stand up and start walking, turning right and then left to cross St. Mary Street onto Mill Lane, then left onto The Hayes and along Working Street, and then right onto Queen Street. At various points they come across people they know, and entangle themselves in conversation for a minute or two: Brian N., who used to be a client but has been housed and off the drink for over a year; Sarah A. who wants £1 to buy a tray of chips (with whom Dennis has a stern word about seeing the doctor, as agreed); and then Ian D., sat on a bench opposite the Oxford Arcade. Ian detains Jeff and Dennis a little longer than either of them would have wished, but won't take the cue that they are ready to move along. (Talking with Ian requires a degree of patience as there is an odd and slightly obsessive, sometimes paranoid, pattern to his conversation.)

All the way along The Hayes and Working Street and now Queen Street the pace has been slow. Jeff zigzags from one side of the (pedestrianised) street to the other, as if window shopping. Dennis pauses here and there, then catches up. The two of them confer at various points. There is a seemingly offhand character to their movement, a 'moseying' quality; they appear unfocused – not really going anywhere, not in any sort of a hurry, and (again, seemingly) repeatedly distracted by this or that. Jeff makes a call on his mobile to check on the availability of bed-spaces at a local hostel.

Passing a short blind alley running alongside JD Sports, Dennis pauses again. A pile of something – blankets? – has caught his eye. He turns off Queen Street and down the alley to take a closer look, turning the pile over with the toe of his boot. Nothing of any further interest, it seems; but as Dennis is poking about two boys emerge from the dog-leg end of the alley, looking guilty and protesting they were doing no more than collecting discarded JD Sports carrier bags. Dennis doesn't ask any further questions – he knows at least one of the boys – Roy G. – (and his mother). Roy has been

sleeping rough in the Wood Street car park the last few nights, in the stairwell behind the fire door, by the ramp at the back. Jeff recognises the other
boy from somewhere, but can't think of his name. The two boys are gone,
quickly. Jeff and Dennis turn back onto Queen Street, walking steadily up
towards the Capitol Centre where they turn left onto Park Lane. Here the
pace slows even more, as the two of them rummage around, peering into the
backyards and rear parking spaces of the buildings either side. A pile of
rubbish, a discarded shoe, sheets of cardboard, bottles. They double back
and turn left and then right, then double back again to turn left and right
again – Windsor Place and Windsor Lane; and then back onto Queen Street
with the Capitol Centre now behind them.

A left turn onto Charles Street where, up ahead, a crowd is assembled
awaiting the arrival of the evening 'soup run' (hot drinks and sandwiches
distributed by volunteers from local church congregations). No sign, as yet,
of the teenage crowd that has taken to hanging out here in the evenings,
causing difficulties on occasion. Keith L. is here, talking, talking, talking.
Also deaf Colin. Someone new, with two dogs on ropes, and a rucksack on
his back – Dennis goes across to have a word. Jeff works the crowd a little,
asking questions, gathering up the news and gossip. Quite a few people are
asking about Ryan. There are some donated clothes available this evening,
and a scrum quickly develops as people crowd around, holding up tracksuit
trousers and sweatshirts for closer inspection then setting them aside or
stuffing them into carrier bags. There must be more than thirty people jost-
ling around a single trestle table. 'Spot the homeless person', says Jeff,
shaking his head.

By half past eight the two outreach workers are retracing their steps, back
along The Hayes and then Caroline Street, crossing St. Mary Street and then
Great Western Lane. This short distance, easily covered in under ten
minutes at a brisk pace, takes them half an hour. Back at the car Jeff recalls
the other boy's name, from by JD Sports: he is Darren W., and is (supposed
to be) resident at a local authority children's home. Jeff places a call, and is
told that Darren has not been 'home' for three days now and has been
reported missing. Jeff and Dennis' sighting will now be passed along to the
police.

Back on Great Western Lane Dennis opens the boot of his car and checks
the contents: hot chocolate sachets, also crisps and a large box of condoms.
He opens the driver's-side door and gets in; Jeff walks around the car and
gets in the passenger seat. They drive off together, under the railway bridge
and onto Callaghan Square and Herbert Street, looking out for Suzie who
will have started work now – others too.

What we have here is an instance not of police patrol but outreach patrol in
the city centre of Cardiff. Jeff and Dennis are street-based care workers
employed by the local authority to attend to the rough sleeping homeless (and
yes, as such their duties do include a degree of peacekeeping and what could be

called soft policing). Their principal task, and the way in which they themselves would describe the work they do, is to be available – there, out on the streets – regularly and routinely enough as to make reliable and repeated contact with vulnerable adults whose lives have somehow come unstuck in the middle of the city; persons who are considered 'hard-to-reach' by institutions that would offer them the various services that would cater to their multiple, intersecting and complex needs. However, in the context of our discussion here, these individuals are to be considered hard-to-reach in a more literal sense – geographically; they are hard-to-reach because precariously located, because in constant mobility, because sometimes squirrelled away out of sight and hoping to escape attention and hence not always so easy to find.

The work of outreach as assistance is beyond our remit in this chapter. Outreach workers seek out clients in order to then intervene in their lives in some way, offering remedial measures, support and advocacy. This is hard work; some clients are hard to win over, and can seem variously stuck in their present circumstances. But we provide no account, here, of the interpersonal and therapeutic work of 'unsticking'. Outreach workers are there to help, certainly; but we are not setting out to ask 'How do they do that?' Instead our question is: 'If outreach workers are there to help, how do they get *there*?' Getting there is a job of work in itself, and has to get done (repeatedly) before an outreach worker can even begin to try to help anyone.[3]

Ways of Walking

What can we say about whatever it is that outreach workers are up to in the passage above? Whatever else they are doing they are surely walking. Stepping out of their office at Marland House and onto the street, about to begin an evening's outreach patrol, outreach workers may pause to light a cigarette or button a coat (and in doing so may also have a quick look around, taking in their immediate surrounds and the things and people in it that matter or might do so), but then they are off, moving through the city. It would make no sense to do anything else. 'Doing outreach' means taking a look around, on foot; it comes before and is complementary to any of the work that might get done with a client once found, or back at the office following that encounter – data entry, waiting lists, phone calls made to local hostels, GPs' clinics, treatment programmes and court officers.

So outreach workers walk, and must do so in order to see what is going on. Most of the places in which they spend most of their time are close enough to hand to make this practicable, and in another sense it is only ever walking that is going to get you where you really need to be, as an outreach worker; you couldn't drive a car to or through all the places that an outreach worker might want to go, nor could you poke around and circle in the ways that outreach practice seems to require. There are of course a number of ways of walking. Outreach workers out and about in the middle of Cardiff are not the only ones doing it; almost everybody walks in the course of any given day. But people walk in different ways: they stroll, stride, prowl; they trip along, or trudge (see Tilley, 2008: 267). What we are concerned with here, however, are ways of walking associated with varieties of purpose. How a person walks depends to a considerable degree on what they are up to, perhaps where they are going but more importantly what they are doing. And in this outreach workers are somewhat distinctive in their movements, set apart from many of the other pedestrians with whom they share pavement space. They are most obviously distinct from the 'commuter', a category of pedestrian on his or her way from one location to another and aiming to get there directly in order to get on with whatever it is they can only accomplish once they arrive. Commuters are people with places to be. Outreach workers have places to be, too, and things to do; but the locations and activities that matter to outreach can only be arrived at by a close attention paid in the meantime to where an outreach worker is already and through which he or she is moving. Outreach workers on patrol are *searching*, are looking for something or someone: a client, or if nothing so definite then at least some sign or indication that one might be to hand. As such, their walking practices are apt to be more environmentally engaged than those of someone in a hurry to reach a point of arrival. Outreach workers dawdle; there is no rush nor can there be, because where they want to be is where they are already, out and about, looking around. They also seem, at times, uncertain, moving in ways that give them the appearance of someone not altogether sure of their location; they meander and branch off then double back; they complicate what might have seemed a simple enough task; they appear easily distracted. All of which gives outreach patrols a distinctive look and choreography, available to view at different scales: traced out as a line of movement on a map an outreach patrol takes the form of a visual log of what looks like rummaging around (see Hall and Smith, 2014).

To rummage is to search, and to search is always to search for something. But there are different ways in which one might set out to search, depending on whether the something one is trying to find is something known to be lost in the first place, is something for which one is looking. Sometimes we search for things without knowing with absolute certainty what it is that we are after, even at the same time as we can be sure that we will recognise them for what they are if and when we come across them. This distinction – between an object or person sought and a more general casting about in pursuit of *the sort of thing of person one might be after* – is one we will now elaborate.

Searching and Streetcombing

We are concerned with searching, as an activity realised in movement and particularly, in our case, in the practice of walking. Of course, searches can be enhanced by technological means and mediated in a number of ways – consider the mountain rescue team aboard a helicopter employing a thermal imaging camera; but walking is our concern. To search is to move, in order to see (what can be found); and this is significant for the understanding of the relationship of the task at hand to perception (Schutz, 1962). All searches, in one way or another, are bound up with perception of an environment but, importantly, the way in which that environment is perceived, and thus accomplished, is shaped in and through the practice of searching; the phenomenal field 'changes its arrangement through the course of the search' (Laurier, 2005: 3). Which is also to say that searches do not simply take place within an area or territory but are a constitutive element of the setting itself. Someone engaged in a search is not 'perceiving the environment' in some general sense but is seeing in and through the practical purposes they are about – looking to find that which they are after. And we can note here that perception stands, or can do, for a fuller array of sensory engagements than that of sight alone; and we can note, further, that walking as a relatively unmediated mobility practice more fully allows for the deployment of such an array than do other ways of moving around (a mountain rescue crew aboard a helicopter cannot touch or too easily smell the environment they nonetheless see below them; outreach workers, on foot, can and do).

To search for something is to see an environment according to what one is looking for, what is absent; and sometimes very specifically so. Perhaps, in searching for an object known to be missing we hold an idea or image of that object in our head, in advance of the movements we might then undertake to locate it. This would be to act as the police officer (see above), issued with a suspect's description; we organise our perception of the environment according to that specified object we already know to be missing, perhaps looking to 'match' some aspect of what is available to view with the image we hold of what it is we are after and have mislaid. The practice is in no way the preserve of uniformed officials. Everyone knows what it is like to have lost and then to look for something – car keys, a pair of glasses. Where are they? We begin with likely last places, followed by immediate surrounds and then out further to trace pathways between more distant sites. (Given time and no results, the search may then turn to increasingly unlikely and exotic locations for the given object to have been placed – the bread-bin, the fridge. Sometimes, it turns out, the object has been in plain sight for the whole time, right under one's nose but somehow invisible to the search.)

One of the difficulties with finding one's glasses or car keys is that these objects are small and portable enough to have been relocated – perhaps innocently, perhaps mischievously – by a third party. Even so, the objects themselves are inert, and one can hope they are still wherever it was you lost or left them. Other problems – nice for the analyst and much less nice for the searcher – are introduced if the lost or sought object can itself move during the process of the search. Objects in the environment that move (themselves) are that much harder to find. They won't keep still, or can't be relied on to do so, are not reliably *anywhere*, and may even act in ways intended to frustrate being found – ducking out of sight, slipping round a corner, squirrelling themselves away. We are back with the street homeless and the work of outreach, also Bittner and persons of *radically reduced visibility*. Jeff and Dennis and their colleagues are often enough engaged in just this sort of challenging search, looking out for a known individual, a client of the team, out there somewhere in the city this evening, no one knows quite where – almost certainly not exactly where last seen – but who must be found. The urgency of the situation will vary. Perhaps they have a letter to deliver, a tribunal decision in relation to benefit entitlement. Perhaps there is news regarding a long-awaited room at a local hostel. Perhaps things are very much more urgent than that, an emergency even; a client has been reported seriously injured and collapsed outside the shopping centre, only on arrival at the scene he is gone – where? Searching for a client under any such circumstance, more or less mundane or serious, is business as usual for an outreach worker, a repeated task. Not a week goes by that they aren't called out to conduct a search of this sort. If the situation is genuinely urgent the search will have that character too, an impatient and hurried quality – but any such hurry held in tension with the imperative not to rush and risk missing things. More haste less speed. Searching is distinctive in this, as a mobility practice; if you know the location of the thing you are looking for you can run there directly or jump in a taxi, but if you are searching for it you would be better to move carefully, however urgent your business. And searching under these circumstances – looking for a homeless client somewhere in the city, quite possibly on the move themselves, quite possibly keeping a low profile – cannot be systematised, as Bittner has it. You cannot hold the territory still, prohibit interruption, banish other parties, subdivide the ground and methodically attend to every square metre in sequence. Instead, as described already, Jeff and Dennis cast about. But who are they looking for?

Spot the homeless person, says Jeff – a joke; the point being that a great many more people gather to take advantage of the food distribution on Charles Street in the early evening than are actually sleeping rough or likely to be doing so that night. But spotting the homeless person is also a job of work for any outreach worker; and the task is not always particular, directed to this or that person, known to be homeless and sought as an *individual*. Notwithstanding the occasions on which outreach workers set out on foot to search for a particular 'missing' client, the greater part of their walking practice – outreach patrol – is not geared to any such specific objective. The aim, instead, is to have a more general look about and scout the territory, not searching for any one person any more than for any one indication that such a person might be to hand. Outreach workers don't leave their office in the early evening to look for a certain blanket (blue, stained, ragged) in a particular doorway (red, recessed, littered) any more than they might look for a specific (brand of) discarded syringe or any other single indicator that might be taken to signify in the context of their employment. They look for blankets, for doorways, for syringes and any number of other *unspecified* signs that they might be onto something. They don't look for Darren W. or JD Sports carrier bags so much as for persons and objects that might somehow – in their appearance and in combination and in context – match the more general tenor and drift of inquiry that provides the baseline rationale for outreach work. All of which is to say that they don't know what they are after exactly or what they might find, not because they lack purpose but because their searching is non-specific and liable to be that much more productive as such. This distinction, between, on the one hand, searches directed to the location of a particular object and, on the other, to wider indefinite inquiries, can be found in Jakob von Uexküll's classic study of the perceptual worlds of animals and humans (2010; first published 1934). Looking for some particular thing or person we move ourselves so as to secure a match for a search image held in the head; casting about more generally, we operate with no such determinate image but instead with what von Uexküll's refers to as a search 'tone'. Operating according to tone '[w]e do not look around for one particular chair, but for any kind of seating' (Uexküll, 2010: 117). These observations hold good for outreach workers, who are not looking for somewhere to sit down but for an opportunity to assist. Walking the city streets of Cardiff in the early evening, Jeff and Dennis are not determined in their movements by a single search image they hope to match to things observed – this person, that object – instead they are looking around for the sorts of need out of which an outreach worker might make something. We can call this practice, in this instance, *streetcombing*. In ideal type, this is a sort of search and walking set apart from inquiries directed to the seeking out and finding of anything in particular; streetcombing looks different being done; it looks inexact and unhurried, abstracted, even at the same time as it is keenly interested.[4]

We should note, of course, that ideal types are just that. In practice things are muddier, certainly so with outreach patrol, which folds into itself at the same time *both* specific inquiries and a more open, inquisitive dispensation; the two cross tracks. Called out in relation to some or other incident and looking for one client in particular, outreach workers are nonetheless – to varying degrees, depending on the urgency of the primary task – open to other discoveries. Similarly, out on patrol and casting about for anything that might snag their attention they may very well also have it in mind to keep an eye out for this or that client in particular, not seen for the last three days and consequently a source of mild but growing concern.[5]

Conclusion: Seeing the Need

As we've indicated above, outreach workers are engaged in an exploratory movement, a purposeful wandering (Yarwood, 2010), alive to the possibility of discovery of vulnerability, damage and need. Outreach workers do not and cannot systematise their patrols, 'walking the grid' as others do – for example, crime scene officers (Ludwig *et al.*, 2012), archaeologists (Goodwin, 1994) and surveyors. Sometimes the team might be on the look-out for a particular person, but more often than not they are engaged in an act of diagnosis both of the city's appearedly vulnerable adults and the spaces that may provide for need and vulnerability: public spaces, not as squares and streets and plazas but as a space of retreat, shelter and seclusion (see Lagae *et al.*, 2006: 34).[6] Beginning to see *to* need is reliant upon being able to see need and vulnerability and damage for what it is, in the many forms that it might take. This cannot be done at a distance, or in a hurry, or systematically. And it is also about the observer or searcher being open and available to contact too, for all the risks and trouble that that might entail. As we've suggested, this involves a good deal of patience and care and time spent not looking *at* something, or even systematically *for* something precisely defined, but rather an open attentiveness.

We anticipate that readers of this collection will have recognised something of a relationship between outreach work and ethnography. Outreach workers, in part, operate in a manner akin to what we (ethnographers, generally) like to call an ethnographic sensibility (Atkinson, 2014). They are ostensibly outsiders, operating on turf that is not their own in becoming experts in the lives of others. Indeed, the team themselves will talk (in introducing a novice to the work, for example) about 'entering the world' of rough sleepers, and of being 'privileged' to be able to spend time talking with and listening to their clients. They are good at it and take pride in the various sneaky means[7] of gaining access to this world and maintaining and managing field relationships. Outreach workers, in and through their fieldwork, develop empathy and insight through bodies that are 'tuned up' to the same crap that their informants are taking (Goffman, 1989: 125). They learn to take the perspective of a rough sleeper and see the city accordingly: Would I sleep there or not? Too busy? Too isolated? Too open? Will I be seen? Does the rain get in under that stairwell? No? Good. Seems dry; and an air vent too. Perfect.

Outreach workers do what they do partly because they believe in it and want to make a difference, but partly for reasons external to the immediate encounter. They have ulterior motives, sometimes, not always fully disclosed to those they spend time with. Information gained is documented and recorded in various ways, and extracted from the site for another audience. And sometimes outreach workers bring unwanted attention to the lives and presence of their clients that might have otherwise remained under the radar. In this way, both outreach work and ethnography can be described as Janus-faced (Rowe, 1999) and the work of 'finks' (Goffman, 1989).

We have, then, come to share a sensibility and method with the team, walking along beside them, learning to see with 'outreach eyes' – a turn of phrase Jeff is fond of using; gaining a 'vulgar competency' (Garfinkel, 2002) in the team's practical methods. And we think that there might be much to learn from this case in terms of how it is that social research might better search out, see, and see to social problems. In addition to demonstrating something about searching and seeing and walking in the urban context, we suggest that our case might also be read as a lesson in humility for social science methodology, perhaps adding weight to the call for 'slow methods' (see, for example, Grandia, 2015). Rather than developing ways of isolating social phenomena in order to hold them still, as objects of attention, we might better think about developing practical skills through which to recover something of the 'open, exploratory, spirit' (Faris, 1967: 130) first practised by the Chicago ethnographers but subsequently pressured by the rise of structuralism and statistics, specialisation, and the contemporary demands and priorities of funding regimes and narrowing definitions of 'impact'. We might do more to recognise that engaging with the world 'is not an automatic faculty but a skill that needs to be trained' (Back, 2007: 7). As noted by Shilling (2012: 4), there is much worth in returning here to C. Wright Mills' reminder that it is the 'imagination … that sets off the social scientist from the mere technician' (2000 [1959]: 211), an imagination that goes beyond arid technical programmes of training in methods, but that requires its own apprenticeship in learning and understanding. It is in this sense that we make a case here, in closing, for a practical sociological imagination, exercised as a tenor and drift of inquiry directed towards everyday mobile situated encounters. As we have aimed to make visible in the description of outreach work, moving slowly and carefully, and going out without a fixed image of what it is you might be looking for, can be the best way not to miss what is really there.

Notes

1 Moreover, the result would not be the same. Knowledge of place produced from maps or mediations is not only of a different order to that gained from walking, but produces a different place (Hall and Smith, 2014).

2 Our methodological recommendation, if we were to make one, would be to take heed of 'Sacks' Gloss' (see Garfinkel, 2002) and try to find some 'work gang' who are already engaged in handling whatever the phenomena happens to be that the project is interested in.

3 The possibility that these two tasks – looking for someone and looking after them – might not be so wholly distinct, the one separate from and preceding the other, is explored by Hall (2016).

4 As Anne Brewster has it, 'to beachcomb is to become entangled with things incidentally, to become curious, to recollect' (2009: 126). So too with streetcombing. Note also that searches of this sort do not come to a conclusion in anything like the way that specified searches do. When you find your car keys you are done searching. But an indefinite search can continue … indefinitely; that is, until time is in some way 'up' or it is felt that the area or territory under inspection is exhausted of possibility (for today). This gives indefinite searches a cumulative nature: the beachcomber discovers a relation between their finds and the tides and adjusts his or her practice accordingly; the browser in the bookshop discovers a new favourite author but remains open to new discoveries – perhaps prompted by the varied endorsements on the back of the book they now hold; the woodland forager may discover a good patch for mushrooms and make it their business to revisit. And so on. So too with outreach in the city.

5 This crossing of tracks is more widely characteristic of searching as an undertaking or accomplishment. Searching for a lost cat, for example (see Laurier *et al.*, 2002), may be initiated as a very specific activity at first – going looking, enrolling other people, placing posters on lampposts – but this cannot be kept up indefinitely. If initial searches prove unsuccessful one's inquiries transform into a more diffuse and partial attentiveness to the possibility of seeing the cat in the course of doing other things.

6 A brief supporting treatment of this description of 'diagnosis' work is provided by Degen *et al.* (2010).

7 These words are taken from Goffman (1989). We suspect that today's research ethics committees would look dimly upon them, despite their continued closeness to the reality of many field relations.

References

Atkinson, P. (2014) *For Ethnography*. London: Sage.

Back, L. (2007) *The Art of Listening*. London: Bloomsbury.

Bergson, H. (2007). *The Creative Mind*. New York: Dover Publications.

Bittner, E. (1967) The police on skid-row: a study of peace keeping. *American Sociological Review*, 32 (5): 699–715.

Brewster, A. (2009) Beachcombing: a fossicker's guide to whiteness and indigenous sovereignty. In H. Smith and R. T. Dean (eds), *Practice-Led Research, Research-Led Practice in the Creative Arts*, pp. 126–149. Edinburgh: Edinburgh University Press.

Büscher, M., Urry, J. and Witchger, K. (eds) (2010) *Mobile Methods*. London: Routledge.

Degen, M., Rose, G. and Basdas, B. (2010) Bodies and everyday practices in designed urban environments. *Science Studies: An Interdisciplinary Journal for Science and Technology Studies*, 23(2): 60–76.

Faris, R. L. (1967) *Chicago Sociology 1920–1932*. London: University of Chicago Press.

Garfinkel, H. (2002) *Ethnomethodology's Program: Working out Durkheim's Aphorism*. London: Rowman & Littlefield.

Goffman, E. (1990) *The Presentation of Self in Everyday Life*. London: Penguin.

Goffman, E. (1989) On fieldwork (transcribed and edited by Lyn Lofland). *Journal of Contemporary Ethnography*, 18(2): 123–132.

Goodwin, C. (1994) Professional vision. *American Anthropologist*, 96(3): 606–633.

Grandia, L. (2015) Slow ethnography: a hut with a view. *Critique of Anthropology*, 35(3): 301–317.

Hall, T. (2016) *Footwork*. London: Pluto Press.

Hall T. and Smith, R. J. (2014) Knowing the city: maps, mobility and urban outreach work. *Qualitative Research*, 14(3): 294–310.

Kusenbach, M. (2003) Street phenomenology: the go-along as ethnographic research tool. *Ethnography*, 4(3): 455–458.

Lagae, J., Çelik, Z. and Cuyvers, W. (2006) Reading public space in the 'Non-Western' city: a dialogue between Zeynep Çelik and Wim Cuyvers. *OASE (DELFT)*, 69: 32–42.

Laurier, E. (2005) Searching for a parking space. *Intellectica*, 41–42: 101–115.

Laurier, E., Brown, B. and McGregor, M. (2016) Mediated pedestrian mobility: walking and the map app. *Mobilities*, 11(1): 117–134.

Laurier, E., Whyte, A. and Buckner, K. (2002) Neighbouring as an occasioned activity: 'finding a lost cat'. *Space and Culture*, 5(4): 346–367.

Ludwig, A., Fraser, J. and Williams, R. (2012) Crime scene examiners and volume crime investigations: an empirical study of perception and practice. *Forensic Science Policy and Management: An International Journal*, 3(2): 53–61.

Moles, K. (2008) A walk in thirdspace: place, methods and walking. *Sociological Research Online*, 13(4).

Molotch, H. (1994) Going out. *Sociological Forum*, 9(2): 221–239.

Mondada, L. (2009) Emergent focused interactions in public places: a systematic analysis of the multimodal achievement of a common interactional space. *Journal of Pragmatics*, 41(10): 1977–1997.

Psathas, G. (1992) The study of extended sequences: the case of the garden lesson. In G. Watson and R. M. Seiler (eds), *Text in Context: Contributions to Ethnomethodology*, pp. 99–122. London: Sage.

Rowe, M. (1999) *Crossing the Border: Encounters between Homeless People and Outreach Workers*. Berkeley, CA: University of California Press.

Ryave, A. L. and Schenkein, J. N. (1974) Notes on the art of walking. In R. Turner (ed.), *Ethnomethodology*, pp. 265–274. Harmondsworth: Penguin.

Schutz, A. (1962) Common-sense and scientific interpretations of human action. In *Collected Papers*, Vol. 1. The Hague: Martinus Nijhoff.

Shilling, C. (2012) Series editor's introduction. *The Sociological Review*, 60(S1): 1–5.

Tilley, C. (2008) *Body and Image: Explorations in Landscape Phenomenology 2*. Walnut Creek, CA: Left Coast Press.

Uexküll, J. von (2010) *A Foray into the Worlds of Animals and Humans: With a Theory of Meaning*. Minneapolis, MN: University of Minnesota Press.

Wright Mills, C. (2000 [1959]) *The Sociological Imagination*. New York: Oxford University Press.

Yarwood, R. (2010) Risk, rescue and emergency services: the changing spatialities of Mountain Rescue Teams in England and Wales. *Geoforum*, 41: 257–270.

Walking, Sitting, and Skateboarding in General Gordon Square.
Source: Charlotte Bates.

3 Desire Lines

Walking in Woolwich

Charlotte Bates

As anthropologist Tim Ingold (2007, 1) notes, it takes only a moment's reflection to recognise that lines are everywhere. This is because,

> As walking, talking and gesticulating creatures, human beings generate lines wherever they go. It is not just that line-making is as ubiquitous as the use of the voice, hands and feet – respectively in speaking, gesturing and moving around – but rather that it subsumes all these aspects of everyday human activity, and, in so doing, brings them together into a single field of inquiry.

In this chapter, I want to trace the generation of lines in the urban landscape by following one particular typology of line, the desire line.

In every town and city today, unofficial paths created by walkers cut across the land. An aerial view of almost any urban park is likely to reveal a criss-cross of tarmac paths, pressed grass, and worn earth tracks, generated by people straying from designated pathways and treading other routes from place to place. Urban planners and landscape architects call these improvised routes 'desire lines' or 'desire paths'. They are what Ingold (2007, 43) describes as 'traces' – enduring marks left on solid surfaces by continuous movement. These informal paths can form with as few as fifteen traversals of an unpaved route (Kohlstedt 2016). More often than not, desire lines appear beaten into grass, trampled-down and worn bare by frequent footfall and the human desire to find shorter or more easily navigated routes. One of the most famous lines of desire is artist Richard Long's 'A line made by walking' (1967). As a student, Long paced up and down in a field in Wiltshire until the flattened grass caught the sunlight and became visible as a line. A black and white photograph records a fixed line of movement, art made by walking in landscape.

Desire lines are often understood as highlighting the failure of urban planners and landscape architects to anticipate and provide official pathways in just the right places. As Fran Tonkiss (2013, 7) writes,

> a great deal of urban form is made not on the basis of conscious design objectives, but out of our intentions to do *other* things: to make a living, find

a space to sleep, get from A to B and on to Z according to routes and along desire paths unanticipated by the transport planners.

Sometimes these unanticipated routes are made official with tarmac, at other times their use is curtailed with the addition of signage and physical barriers. These ways tell of the tension between the regulated and signposted circulation of pedestrians in the city and the traces of more personal forms of movement left by urban dwellers – pedestrian 'tactics' that disrupt and resist the 'strategies' of urban planners and the 'rational plan' of the city (de Certeau 1984).

In this chapter, I explore what can be learnt from desire lines. The chapter takes as an example the redevelopment of a small urban square in south London, designed by landscape architects Gustafson Porter and completed in 2011. Pausing at critical points in the history of the square's redevelopment, I discuss the ways in which walking – and desire – inform and reform practices of urban design, mobility, and dwelling. While urban planning is traditionally conceived as a 'connective activity' (Madanipour 2010, 352), General Gordon Square is much more than a network of connected points. As Ingold, drawing on Lefebvre, writes, place can better be understood as a knot of entangled lifelines, a 'mesh-work' of reticular patterns left by people whose movements 'weave an environment that is more "archi-textural" than architectural' (Lefebvre in Ingold 2007, 80). Ingold's diagram, which depicts a squiggle of winding routes and a geometric set of straight lines, illustrates how 'the meshwork of entangled lines' and 'the network of connected points' (Ingold 2007, 82) have significant and contrasting implications for our understanding of urban form and urban living (see also Moles and Saunders 2016). Following the meshwork of desire lines that have been generated over years of design, planning, and everyday use, I show how the practice of walking underlies the ways in which place is desired, imagined, made, and lived.

Throughout, the chapter juxtaposes and blends insights from two different perspectives, sociology and landscape architecture. Whereas landscape architecture is preoccupied with the physical qualities of public space and often ignores its nonphysical qualities (Miller 2007, xi), sociology tends to overlook the materiality of public space, focusing instead on its social and political relations (Neal *et al.* 2015, 465). So while, as Tonkiss (2013, 28) writes, 'Thinking about cities in terms of physical form, as those concerned with their design are obliged to do, jars somewhat with a recent critical concern in other disciplines to understand the urban in terms of networks, connections and mobilities', it also offers an opportunity to reimagine, and rematerialise, our understanding of place and mobility. Accepting that a focus on questions of size and shape – the width, surface texture, and gradient of a path, for example – might seem 'a rather plodding, even out-dated, way of representing the city' (Tonkiss 2013, 28), the chapter takes the dimensions of urban form as a point from which to investigate how the materiality of place structures everyday urban experience, illuminating how the urban landscape supports or restrains particular movements, activities, and feelings. Drawing on what can be learnt from General Gordon Square,

I suggest that the materiality of place is not merely a context for social life, but is co-constitutive of urban living.

Recognising that social life has a physical texture, and that the materiality of the urban environment mediates our relationships, with ourselves and each other (see also Bates *et al.* 2017), seems obvious when walking the city streets. Where and how people move is a continuous negotiation between the body and the environment. Experiences of moving, and being moved, are defined not only by our own physical and psychological capabilities and skills, but also, and more importantly, by the qualities of the urban environment, which shape our movements. As philosopher Maxine Sheets-Johnstone (2010, 171) writes,

> Spatial qualities – a rounded, curved space, as in wending one's way on a downhill slope in skiing, or an angular, jagged space, as in dodging this way and that in a game of tag – are qualities that movement itself creates.

In other words, spatial qualities make a particular movement the movement that it is. Weaving together observations and insights from site walks and interviews with the project architect, interviews with the access consultant and access panel group, interviews with local residents, ethnographic observations of social life in the square, and documentary analysis gathered over two years, the chapter considers how urban walking shapes and is shaped by where and how we live.

'I Used to Avoid Walking Across It, Especially at Night Because I Didn't Want a Rat Running Over My Foot'

Woolwich was once the heart of the British Empire's military-industrial complex. Post mid-century many local industries closed down; the Royal Arsenal, which closed in 1967, had employed 100,000 people at its peak. From the mid-twentieth century through to the new millennium, the area became a run-down and deprived part of the capital. The British National Party was active locally in the 1990s and the area witnessed a series of racist attacks, including the murders of Rolan Adams on 15 February 1991, Rohit Duggal on 15 July 1992, and Stephen Lawrence on 22 April 1993. In more recent years Woolwich's reputation has been compounded by the riots of 2011 and the murder of soldier Lee Rigby on 22 May 2013.

Corporate and council investment is now beginning to transform Woolwich, and new and planned housing and transport developments are making it a relatively affordable and desirable place to live. In 2012 Woolwich Central, a development of 960 homes and a Tesco superstore was completed, and in 2018 a Crossrail station will open, creating new and faster transport links to the city, Heathrow airport, and other parts of the world. At the nearby Woolwich Arsenal development, luxury waterfront apartments have replaced old council estates and derelict land, and signs of gentrification are visible with new coffee shops, cafes, and restaurants opening in the area. A report from the Royal Borough of Greenwich indicates that the Woolwich Riverside ward has experienced a population increase of 50 per cent between 2001 and 2011. New communities have also rapidly emerged, as immigrants from Nigeria, Ghana, Nepal, and Eastern Europe have settled in the area. These physical, social, and cultural changes are remaking Woolwich, and while its other histories have not yet been completely erased by regeneration (see Holgersson, this volume) they are beginning to fade from the collective memory. The transformation of General Gordon Square, named in memorial of British Army officer Major General Charles George Gordon (1833–1885) who was born in Woolwich, is one small part of this regeneration masterplan. The design concept, to create a unified space that would transmute a derelict place into a vibrant hub of multicultural life, was realised by Gustafson Porter in 2011. In some respects, the regeneration of Woolwich is a 'good news' story in which the contradictory and tension-laden nature of urban development is glazed over (Imrie and Lees 2014, xii). As Kristine Miller (2007, xiv) observes, the results of development do not necessarily benefit the people who live there; we live in a society in which a few landowners profit from increases in land value while existing residents face rising rents or are priced out. Yet, I want to argue, General Gordon Square plays a vital role in sustaining people and the place in which they live (see also Bynon and Rishbeth 2015).

I had never set foot in Woolwich prior to the summer of 2014, but this is how one local resident described the old General Gordon Square to me in an interview:

> As I remember the square, it had a pond in the middle with some kind of not very nice looking water, I remember seeing large rats running around so I used to avoid walking across it, especially at night because I didn't want a rat running over my foot, and there were a lot of street drinkers.

Numerous online blog posts reinforce this description with accounts of cat-sized rodents prowling the square and of the fountain being used by street drinkers as a public convenience. While General Gordon Square had previously been a pedestrian no-go area, the roads surrounding the square were heavily congested with traffic. Bus routes surrounded the square and people stood in crowds on the narrow pavements with nowhere to comfortably wait, sit or rest. There was something fundamentally wrong with the way the town centre was working. As architect Jan Gehl writes (2011, 75), life between buildings is a process. Places where nobody wants to be drastically reduce opportunities for activities to stimulate and support one another, from children playing, to people sitting on benches, or people simply walking by. Living public spaces disintegrate when nothing happens in them, and instead of supporting social life they become a contributing factor to vandalism and crime in the streets (see also Jacobs 2011 [1961]).

Walking through the new square with the architect on a warm and sunny August afternoon, I felt the free mingling of strangers and sensed a culture of conviviality, civic regard, and cohabitation. No longer a space to be avoided or of anti-social loitering, General Gordon Square had become a hive of relaxed and lively social activity. Mothers were feeding babies, there were children playing in the new water feature known locally as 'Woolwich Beach', young people were skateboarding, and people passed through, sat alone or chatted in groups while generally enjoying the ambience. This place was doing the summertime thing. How had the transformation occurred? As we walked and talked together, the architect explained the design process that has altered the way the space works and is used today.

Pedestrian Flows

In order to understand the dynamics of General Gordon Square and its neighbourhood, Gustafson Porter turned to Space Syntax, an international firm providing spatial analysis of the functional performance of buildings and urban places. Pedestrian surveys and spatial modelling were used to examine the relationship between the built fabric of the city and urban activity patterns. Studies of pedestrian behaviour included gate counts of different user groups over different times of the day, and following and mapping the activities of people within the square. In addition, spatial accessibility analysis was used to demonstrate how different spatial layout options would affect a range of social and economic issues, from retail performance to pedestrian wayfinding and safety.

These studies showed, as local residents had also recounted, that people were avoiding setting foot in General Gordon Square, choosing instead to move around it. The report described the centre of the square as spatially segregated and visually enclosed by overgrown vegetation, creating fear of crime. Pedestrian flows through the square were recorded as very low, with few people taking the shortest path through the middle of the square and a sharp decline in pedestrians entering the square after 6 p.m. The pavements around General Gordon Square were found to be overcrowded, generating pedestrian congestion and impeding natural flows through the area. Overall, Woolwich town centre was not found to be a popular place, as the report stated: 'There is not much recorded evidence to show that people enjoy the environment.'

To mitigate these problems, the firm recommended increasing visibility into and through the space, reducing level changes, visual clutter, and dense foliage, aligning pedestrian crossings to desire lines, and opening up diagonal routes through the centre of the square. By unifying the space, the report suggested, it would be possible to create a sense of identity for the area as a whole, and if this could be achieved the design would be able to create a 'sequence of spaces catering to the different needs of users by providing places for moving, browsing and shopping, as well as places to rest and contemplate the surroundings'.

This analysis of the existing built environment and vision of the future square shows how planning and design decisions can impact on the ways that people move and interact in public space. Following people, and tracking their desire lines, illuminated where the optimal paths should be. Just as the reconstruction of paths in New York City's Central Park was based on paving desire lines that had been created by park visitors over many years (Barlow Rogers 1987),

General Gordon Square's future pathways emerged from the existing routes and flows that were tracked throughout the day. Taking into account existing and future draws and destinations and working with the topography of the land, curved diagonal routes through the square were eventually designed to accommodate movement between the public transport stations and the main shopping street, making not just quicker routes but nicer routes to get from one point of the town centre to another.

These observational tracking exercises – literally following people – show how different pathway configurations can bring people together spatially or keep them apart, highlighting a relation between the patterns of urban form and the patterns of activity in the city, and providing quantitative evidence of street life. They also hold something in common with what Margarethe Kusenbach (2003, 463) refers to as 'natural' go-alongs, in which researchers follow informants into their familiar environments and track outings as closely as possible, with respect to the particular day, the time of day, and the routes of the regular trip. But as David Seamon (1994, 44) notes, 'The need is to integrate this emphasis on movement and spatial connectedness with other conceptions of urban and community design.' What is missing from spatial analysis, and what the go-along – by accompanying, instead of following – is able to access, is the 'stream of perceptions, emotions and interpretations that informants usually keep to themselves' (Kusenbach 2003, 464). While the personal and social dimensions of walking are often overlooked by urban planning and transport studies, in which walking is presented as a self-evident phenomenon (Middleton 2016, 9), there is much more that can be learnt from an engagement with pedestrian encounters.

Disability Routes

Gustafson Porter also commissioned an access management consultant to support and advise on access within the new square. As Alexandra Horowitz (2013, 228) observes, the street changes for anyone who is temporarily or permanently injured. While most people choose their route by sight to destination, surface condition, street furniture, clutter, lack of signs or tactile pathways can impede disabled people. From a disability perspective, the old square and its surrounding roads were distinctly unfriendly. Factors contributing to its avoidance by disabled people included the heavy traffic surrounding the square, the lack of straight crossing points, the steep gradient across the site, and the poor visibility due to planting and lighting conditions.

These points were investigated in a series of access consultation workshops and site walks with the access panel, design team, and client representatives. In March 2009, the group met to walk the site together. Before going out, the architects made a presentation, which included a clay plaster model of the design. This became a useful communication tool, as Peter, who is blind, ran his hands across the clay, feeling the levels as the architect described them – a photo caption in the access report describes how the architect 'walked' Peter through the site model by 'touch'. The group then made a walk around the square together, with the architect explaining the plans in situ and making notes while David, who has paraplegia and uses a wheelchair, Peter, a blind man who has a guide dog, and Joanne, a deaf woman, made their own observations from their different experiential perspectives. They reported the uneven surfaces, which impeded ambulant disabled people and mobility aid users, the curved routes within the square, which were disorienting for vision impaired people, the pathways that were too narrow at seating points so that people using the benches felt exposed, and the low level wooden rails, which blocked access to grassed areas and were also a trip hazard that 'give a painful bruising to the shin if you walked into it'. As Joanne later explained in an interview with me, it was important to actually go out and look at the site, because

> not being an architect, just looking at plans is difficult. Being in the space helps to visualise what it will be. It makes you think about the impact of what they are proposing ... and gives a better feeling of how the plans will work.

As well as investigating the site through the 'audit bodies' (Friedner and Osborne 2013) of the access panel, a range of wearable simulation devices were provided on the walk. Glasses that simulate visual conditions such as glaucoma and tunnel vision, weights that affect the gait and cadence of movement, and headsets that reduce hearing were passed around, allowing the design team and client representative to experience the site in differently embodied ways. One man was recounted as having been transformed from a strong and confident individual to somebody who did not want to move, because he was not sure where his next step would be.

Authentic or simulated, the site walk highlighted the practical knowledge that 'filters' our perception of the environment (Kusenbach 2003, 467), establishing the physical and emotional challenges presented by the existing site. As forms of embodied participation, access audits and simulation exercises are considered to be both valuable and controversial. Sadly, access audits are often perceived as obligatory tick box exercises, and disabled peoples' bodies are habitually 'devalued, oppressed, and ignored by planners, architects, society, and the state' (Friedner and Osborne 2013, 44). Wearable simulations, which mimic the physical experience of being elderly or impaired with specially designed goggles, gloves and even whole-body suits, are sometimes deemed offensive amongst the disabled community, although their use does appear to assist designers in developing a more diverse understanding of the body into their practices (see Kullman, 2016). But, as Michele Friedner and Jamie Osborne (2013, 53) write, when done well, participating in access audits can transform stigmatised bodily difference 'into a valued vantage point to both share and discuss with others', making personal and bodily experiences sources of authoritative knowledge and generating important insights that can (re)shape a design.

Discussions between the access panel, design team, and client representatives highlighted the need to reduce changes in level and gradients across the site, minimise pedestrian travel distances, enhance seating, consider surface treatments for ease of mobility, visual definition and wayfinding, and take into account the layout, height, and selection of planting. Working together and thinking in different ways, the lens of accessibility provided another route into understanding the square and its dynamics, illuminating what is at stake in making inclusive public spaces.

'It is Only by Moving Through Space That You Can Appreciate How It Has Been Thought Through'

There is something about walking together that brings to life our relationships with place. As I walked and talked with the architect on that summer afternoon, I sensed his attachment to the project and began to understand something of the labour that had gone into making this place. The months of planning, weeks spent modelling, testing, and adjusting measurements and plans, the meetings and conversations in which decisions were negotiated and made, the construction, and more adjustments to the design. I also felt I had gained some respect by asking to meet in this way. We shared a sense that moving through the space was the best way to understand how every detail, large and small, had been thought through.

As Sarah Neal notes, walking interviews can emphasise participants' personal relationships with a space (Neal *et al*. 2015, 466). They also draw out the distinctive ways in which different people experience, and possess knowledge of, cities. In her book, *On Looking: Eleven Walks with Expert Eyes* (2013), Alexandra Horowitz shows that people have their own expert ways of seeing the otherwise unattended and ordinary elements of the city. The book includes a walk around the block with eleven different experts, including a typographer, a sound engineer, and a blind woman, in addition to Horowitz's toddler and her dog. Kusenbach's example, from a walk-along in Gilmore Junction, neatly illustrates the same point:

> Why does Ross 'always' take notice of a background environmental feature such as street lights, even during the day? Before retiring, Ross used to work in the City's Department of Street Lighting for many years. Because of his professional experience, Ross routinely notices and evaluates street lighting conditions as a prominent feature of the urban landscape.
>
> (Kusenbach 2003, 467)

Walking through General Gordon Square with the architect highlighted the professional expertise that is forged from training and experience – a certain knowledge of and feeling for the urban landscape, a way of reading plans and interpreting spaces, and a particular familiarity with the site.

Walking together was also a way of accessing what Maxine Sheets-Johnstone calls 'thinking in movement', a corporeal-kinetic knowledge of space that we learn from infancy, but commonly take for granted as adults. She writes:

> As adults, we nevertheless have the possibility of experiencing fundamental aspects of space, that is, fundamental aspects of what we already know as 'space' simply by paying attention to our experience of movement. However untrained we might be in such an endeavor, by paying close attention, we have the possibility of experiencing a diversity of spatial qualities ... for example, a resistant space as we walk into a strong wind or shove a heavy box across a floor; an angular space when we feel ourselves cutting sharp corners; a yielding space in the course of running across an open meadow; a circular space in molding our arms to pick up a large bowl. Whatever the spatial quality, we experience it kinesthetically.
>
> (Sheets-Johnstone 2010, 173)

Building perceptions and conceptions of the space in the process of moving ourselves (Sheets-Johnstone 2010, 174), we noted the smooth surfaces underfoot, the wide pathways that allow bodies to move freely, and the long stone benches that kick back at just the right ergonomic angle, with arm rests that provide support to stand up. We observed the different ways in which children and adults move within the square too – the children running through the water and leaping over the terrace ledges, exploring the space with more energy and freedom than the adults, who roam within the designated paths at a more leisurely pace. The site also acted as a prompt for questions and memories to emerge and unfold as we made our way together. At the end of the walk, we continued talking over coffee in a café situated on the corner of the square, formerly the on-site planning office during the months of construction.

It is perhaps unsurprising that the practice of walking informs the discipline of landscape architecture. This does not mean that it should be taken for granted. The ability to think through human movement is fundamental to good design and the success of a project, as the architect explained in an interview,

> Fundamentally walking will shape a design because desire lines, topography, materiality, signifiers in the landscape to draw you through, support in a landscape to allow you to be there, all those things are essentially for the person in the space and therefore you need to understand fundamentally why or how a person's going to walk through it.

Understanding the whys and hows in turn involves thinking through the multiple different ways in which people walk. While some people are in a rush and just want to get from A to B as quickly as possible, others may not have a reason to get from A to B but want somewhere to spend time and linger, and some people have great difficulty walking. People walk on foot, with walking aids, dogs, shopping trolleys, and pushchairs, and some people wheel in manual or electric wheelchairs and mobility scooters. These diverse pedestrian mobilities offer untold insights into human movement.

As has already been highlighted, there were once many obstacles to walking in Woolwich. The roads with high kerbs, the guard rails, the badly located and controlled crossing points, the steep gradients which had resulted from years of sporadic development, the gradual accumulation of street furniture and clutter. Looking back from the top corner of the new square, we paused to take in the space as it works today. A road on one side of the square has completely disappeared and another is closed to traffic during the day, so that the square is now eased from traffic and linked with the shopping street by a shared surface, prioritising pedestrian use. There is clear visibility through the square, making the space feel safer and connecting it with the surrounding area, while dense planting near the bus stops creates a barrier to the busy road route and reduces the sound of traffic. Long benches provide a choice of places to sit, pause, and rest, alone or in groups, and lavender and sarcococca scent the air. Recalling the moment the site was opened, the architect described how people flooded into the space, remarking, 'it was literally like water, you just suddenly are channeling water where it wants to go'.

Everyday Life in the Square

Having traced the history of the square's redevelopment, I want to turn now to the everyday life of the square as experienced by Ann, a white woman in her fifties who has lived in Woolwich for the last fifteen years. Ann has rheumatoid arthritis, a condition that affects the joints in her hands and feet, causing pain and swelling, and restricting her strength and mobility. She was diagnosed with the condition six years ago, and it has changed her perspective on the urban environment, as she told me in an interview:

> I tend to be much more conscious now of disability needs, I'm always looking around and observing and thinking about that kind of thing. It changes your mindset when you actually have a disability yourself, you don't notice those things before – I'm much more aware now.

Sitting in the square together, she points to a block of grey flats within sight. It is not far away, no more than a five minute walk, but the journey to meet me took her three times that long.

Ann likes to walk and does so almost everyday, it helps to keep the joints moving and walking is recommended for people with arthritis. But her walks now are done slowly, with small paces and in stops and starts, as she pauses to sit between each little bit of the journey; walking for Ann takes time, perseverance, and patience. Although she favours walking along the river, which appeals more to her tastes and personal biography, shaped by a childhood spent in a coastal town, she often passes through the square on her way to and from the shops, pausing to rest and stretch her feet. As she remarked, 'it's quite nice to walk in a space without traffic, especially when you're slow crossing the roads'. The smooth surfaces and wide walkways also make the square a nice place to walk through, and are a welcome relief from the busy market nearby where she sometimes shops for fresh fruit and vegetables. When we met, she was still feeling the effect of her hands being knocked by shopping bags as she passed through the market crowds on her way to the square. Such injuries are an everyday hazard of walking in crowded places, and she would not dream of visiting a busy place like Oxford Street anymore.

Ann also avoids the town centre after 7 p.m., and is not the first person to have remarked that Woolwich can still be a hostile and aggressive place at night. Sitting together in the square, we engage for a while in the classic outdoor activity of 'people watching'. Ann remarks,

> I observe lots of different groups sitting here…. I love to see people enjoying themselves and having their community in a nice public space…. It probably shows a lack of community centres and I think that the square has become a kind of community centre, which is nice.

The Nepalese women are sitting together, sharing a cigarette, and people are perched on the terrace ledges watching the Rio 2016 Olympics on the big screen TV (which, coincidentally, was originally installed in the square for the London 2012 Olympics). The idea that the square is a big community centre is appealing, and suggests that the regeneration of General Gordon Square has played an important role in making Woolwich a more inclusive, safe, and multicultural neighbourhood. Yet, while she enjoys seeing the many different faces in the square, Woolwich's history and reputation have not yet been completely remade. Ann's experiences of walking with her Muslim son and daughter-in-law, who wear Islamic dress, illuminates this point:

> It's quite sad when your son is told to go back to his own effing country, and I can't do anything except maybe swear back, but I feel vulnerable as a disabled person when that happens so I tend not to go out with them now.

Despite the visible changes in Woolwich and the popularity of the new square, incidents like this one continue to inflect the lives of those who live there. The example illustrates some of the social factors that influence where and when we walk, and with whom.

Walking Lessons

In a study of urban design in two English towns, Monica Degen and Gillian Rose (2012, 3277) recount how walking in Milton Keynes is experienced as an isolating and lonely experience of moving through the town on 'autopilot', while walking in Bedford is a slower-paced and less programmed 'amble' or 'stroll'. In this chapter, I have shown how the relationship between

the design of the urban environment and the way people walk is a multi-
layered and ongoing process, in which lines, bodies, and landscapes are intertwined. Prior to 2011, General Gordon Square was a place that people rarely
set foot in. Today, people walk, run, jump, skate, glide, and wheel in and
through it, gathering in groups to share a convivial moment or watch the big
screen TV. The square illustrates the impact that design can have on the ways
in which we move through and dwell in space, and provides examples of how
the materiality of the landscape can encourage people to come together (see
also Bynon and Rishbeth 2015). It also shows how the everyday journeys and
encounters that are made in public space can (re)generate a neighbourhood,
resonating with Sophie Watson's (2006) description of urban public space as
a site of potentiality, difference, and enchanted encounters. As archeologist
Christopher Tilley (2015, 25) writes, 'The biography of a person, or a group,
can be found in the sum of the paths that are walked.... Changes in the character of these paths are part and parcel of the transformation of social
relations.'

The square also illustrates how mobility and dwelling are co-dependent. As
Caroline Knowles (2010, 374) writes, 'Travel is part of dwelling, not its counterpoint.' Walking in urban space is not a simple process of moving from A to B,
but depends on a whole host of factors that may be encountered on the way,
from the surface of the pavement to the behaviour of other people. And popular
spaces for walking also need to be places for staying, or dwelling in, as Gehl
(2011, 129) notes,

> It is not enough merely to create spaces that enable people to come and go.
> Favorable conditions for moving about in and lingering in the spaces must
> also exist, as well as those for participating in a wide range of social and
> recreational activities.

But, while urban planning and transport literatures position walking as a practice
that unproblematically encourages 'social mixing', 'community cohesion', and
'social interaction' (Middleton 2016, 1), I do not want to suggest that the relationship between walking and urban regeneration is unproblematic. As Gehl
(2011, 17) writes,

> Life between buildings offers an opportunity to be with others in a relaxed
> and undemanding way. One can take occasional walks, perhaps make a
> detour along a main street on the way home or pause at an inviting bench
> near a front door to be among people for a short while.

Yet, at the same time, it must be recognised that such opportunities can also be
challenges, and risks.

This is not a cosy picture of urban regeneration, for despite the tangible
changes to the square and its newfound conviviality, it remains a contested
space. Who can walk there and in what circumstances – with whom, wearing

what, or when – are questions that still need to be asked. Just as walking can maintain social relations (Middleton 2016), it can also break them, as Ann's example of walking with her family showed. The question of who is included or excluded from this public space also needs to be asked. The square is a success story for many groups of people, from the Nepalese women who regularly meet there, to the children who have a new place to play, and the disabled people whose access to the town centre has been vastly improved. Yet as Miller (2007, x) observes, 'public life is not spontaneous. It is bound by regulation and codes of conduct. These codes and regulations not only control what can happen on the streets and sidewalks, plazas and parks, but also who can be present there.' Who constitutes the public of General Gordon Square is similarly carefully controlled. Recall how the square was once avoided, in part because of the street drinkers who occupied it. Following a series of anti-social public drinking bans, street drinkers have now moved out of the square, enabling Woolwich's other communities to reclaim the space, but displacing some of the problems previously experienced in the town centre to surrounding areas. Interestingly, given the topic of this chapter, the logic of such bans relies in part on increasing the distance between the factors that encourage street drinking – the proximity of alcohol outlets, benefit offices, and 'anti-social behaviour hospitable architecture' – and thereby making them further to walk between.

Aside from the systematic exclusion of groups and individuals, General Gordon Square may also be considered a victim of its own success – too busy and popular to provide the quiet retreat from the city that many people seek out in urban squares and parks. It has long been recognised that cities 'jar the nerves' (Fitzgerald *et al.* 2016, 222). As Georg Simmel argued in his classic essay 'The metropolis and mental life', urban living is distinguished by an intensification of '*nervous stimulation*' (1964 [1903], 410, italics in original). What is experienced as urban 'buzz' by some people can feel uncomfortable to others, and while the square may be an acquired taste, this again raises questions about our ability to provide inclusive public spaces for people with different needs and desires to dwell in together. Several of the people whom I interviewed expressed a preference for walking in quieter places, such as the river or the common.

Ingold (2011, 148) writes:

> Proceeding along a path, every inhabitant lays a trail. Where inhabitants meet, trails are entwined, as the life of each becomes bound up with the other. Every entwining is a knot, and the more that lifelines are entwined, the greater the density of the knot.

If walking weaves places together, and places are like knots, then General Gordon Square might be drawn as a dense squiggle in the urban landscape, a knot made by the power of movement as possible and present lines that meet, intertwine, and pass by.

Acknowledgements

This case study was part of a European Research Council (ERC) Advanced Investigators grant entitled 'Universalism, universal design and equitable access to the designed environment' (project number 323777). Special thanks to Gustafson Porter for supporting the study, and to all of the interview participants for sharing their time, thoughts, and experiences.

References

Barlow Rogers, E. (1987) *Rebuilding Central Park: A Management and Restoration Plan.* MIT Press, Cambridge MA.

Bates, C., Imrie, R., and Kullman, K. (2017) Configuring the caring city: ownership, healing, openness. In Bates, C., Imrie, R., and Kullman, K., *Care and Design: Bodies, Buildings, Cities.* Wiley-Blackwell, Chichester.

Bynon, R. and Rishbeth, C. (2015) Benches for everyone: solitude in public, sociability for free. [Online] available at: http://youngfoundation.org/wp-content/uploads/2015/11/The-Bench-Project_single-pages.pdf.

de Certeau, M. (1984) *The Practice of Everyday Life.* University of California Press, Berkeley CA.

Degen, M. and Rose, G. (2012) The sensory experiencing of urban design: the role of walking and perceptual memory. *Urban Studies*, 49 (15): 3271–3287.

Fitzgerald, D., Rose, N., and Singh, I. (2016) Living well in the Neuropolis. *The Sociological Review*, 64 (1): 221–237.

Friedner, M. and Osborne, J. (2013) Audit bodies: embodied participation, disability universalism, and accessibility in India. *Antipode*, 45 (1): 43–60.

Gehl, J. (2011) *Life between Buildings: Using Public Space.* Island Press, London.

Horowitz, A. (2013) *On Looking: Eleven Walks with Expert Eyes.* Scribner, New York.

Imrie, R. and Lees, L. (2014) *Sustainable London? The Future of a Global City.* Policy Press, Bristol.

Ingold, T. (2007) *Lines: A Brief History.* Routledge, London.

Ingold, T. (2011) *Being Alive: Essays on Movement, Knowledge and Description.* Routledge, London.

Jacobs, J. (2011 [1961]) *The Death and Life of Great American Cities.* Modern Library, New York.

Knowles, C. (2010) 'Mobile sociology'. *British Journal of Sociology*, 61 (1): 373–379.

Kohlstedt, K. (2016) Least resistance: how desire paths can lead to better design. [Online] available at: http://99percentinvisible.org/article/least-resistance-desire-paths-can-lead-better-design.

Kullman, K. (2016) Prototyping bodies: a post-phenomenology of wearable simulations. *Design Studies*, 47: 73–90.

Kusenbach, M. (2003) Street phenomenology: the go-along as ethnographic research tool. *Ethnography*, 4 (3): 455–485.

Madanipour, A. (2010) Connectivity and contingency in planning. *Planning Theory*, 9 (4): 351–368.

Middleton, J. (2016) The socialities of everyday urban walking and the 'right to the city'. *Urban Studies*, 1–20, doi:10.1177/0042098016649325.

Miller, K. (2007) *Designs on the Public: The Private Lives of New York's Public Spaces.* University of Minnesota Press, Minneapolis MN.

Moles, K. and Saunders, A. (2016) Ragged places and smooth surfaces: audio walks as practices of making and doing the city. *Journal of Urban Cultural Studies*, 2 (1): 151–164.

Neal, S., Bennett, K., Jones, H., Cochrane, A., and Mohan, G. (2015) Multiculture and public parks: researching super-diversity and attachment in public green space. *Population, Space and Place*, 21: 463–475.

Seamon, D. (1994) The life of the place. *Nordisk Arkitekturforskning* [*Nordic Journal of Architectural Research*], 7 (1): 35–48.

Sheets-Johnstone, M. (2010) Thinking in movement: further analyses and validations. In Stewart, J., Gapenne, O., and Di Paolo, E., *Enaction: Toward a New Paradigm for Cognitive Science*. MIT Press, Cambridge MA.

Simmel, G. (1964 [1903]) The metropolis and mental life. In Simmel, G., *The Sociology of Georg Simmel*. Free Press, New York.

Tilley, C. (2015) Walking the past in the present. In Árnason, A., Ellison, N., Vergunst, J., and Whitehouse, A., *Landscapes beyond Land: Routes, Aesthetics, Narratives*. Berghahn, Oxford.

Tonkiss, F. (2013) *Cities by Design: The Social Life of Urban Form*. Polity, Cambridge.

Watson, S. (2006) *City Publics: The (Dis)enchantments of Urban Encounters*. Routledge, London.

Walking Through the Re-Used Industrial Area Where the Old Paint Factory Used to be Located.

Source: Helena Holgersson.

4 Keep Walking

Notes on How to Research Urban Pasts and Futures

Helena Holgersson

What did the daily passing of the empty lot where the paint factory once stood mean to Jani, who used to work there as a young man after he came to Sweden from Finland in the 1960s? Why were Sofia and Karin, who were involved in the marketing of the new up-scale residential area about to be built there instead, investigating stories of the 'good old days' in the area? And what did the shopping centre that Emir brought me to, only weeks after he had gotten his residence permit, have to do with his future?[1] I have been using walk-alongs (Kusenbach 2003) as part of my methodology for ten years now, and by now I have walked Gothenburg with a number of people who live their lives here under very different circumstances. In this chapter I will return to three walks and elaborate on what there is to gain from interviewing people on foot. I suggest that one issue that seems impossible to ignore as you accompany people on their everyday routes in the city is time, and I will look closer at how and why my co-walkers talk about the past and the future during our walks. I will also argue that this is something that researchers who are interested in inclusive urban politics ought to pay attention to. My research revolves around the social aspects of urban planning, and more specifically the conflicts of interest that are always part of this process and how they are negotiated in the everyday life of the people affected. In my PhD project I used ethnographic methods to investigate the spatial aspects of non-citizenship (Holgersson 2011, 2014c) and in the following project I further elaborated on walking methodologies, as we researched the gentrification of an old industrial area close to the harbour (Holgersson 2014a, 2014b; Thörn and Holgersson 2016). Both studies focused on urban inequality and had an ambition to listen to the voices of those who live their life in the city, but whose bodies are absent from the shiny pictures of future vision documents (cf. Back 2007).

In my discussion on how the past and the future appear in my co-walkers' narratives I take as my starting point sociologist Pepper Glass's recent appeal to walking ethnographers to start treating the past as *performed* rather than *born* (Glass 2016). This means not just inserting a background section in the beginning of our publications, unreflectingly treating the past as historical facts that shape the present. Instead, he argues, we need to treat the past as an analytic theme and empirically study how it emerges in our ethnographic data.

The present shapes the past as much as the other way around, he argues, and urges us to look more closely not just at *how* people talk about the past as they pass through different urban environments, but *why* they do so. Glass's discussion resembles writings on collective memory that underline that the past is not just objective facts but a tool of the present (cf. Nora 1989; Trouillot 1995; Puwar 2011). What ethnographic studies contribute are illustrations of what this might mean in everyday life.

Glass's findings add to our knowledge of how people use the past as they negotiate their place in the socially stratified city, questions that – when I think about it – have been at the core of everything I have written about in the past ten years. So have negotiations about the future though, which is why my answer to his call became to analyse my co-walkers' performances of the future too, from the same perspective. Studying places that do not yet exist, Michael Borer (2010) suggests that we complement the concept of *collective memory* with the concept of *collective imagination*, which he then goes on to describe as part fantasy, part investment. What I find most interesting here is who gets to invest in their own future and that of Gothenburg. There are of course no facts about the future, but in contemporary cities there are constant efforts to formulate single, indisputable, visions that make every other way forward seem unrealistic, and position critics as reactionary or nostalgic. This theme has been extensively analysed in writing on post-political policies and urban planning (Swyngedouw *et al.* 2002; Mouffe 2005; Mukhtar-Landgren 2008; Holgersson 2014b).

Walking Through the Past and the Future

The Walk-Along as an Ethnographic Tool

Ethnographers use walking as a research tool in many different ways. Many focus on their own walking. In Tim Ingold and Jo Lee Vergunst's *Ways of Walking* (2008) the invited authors tell us about their walks in industrial ruins in the UK, along a beach in Canada, on slippery pavements in Aberdeen, up a hillside in Himalaya, at a carnival in a small Spanish village and so on. Naturally, the book does not offer any definitive argument, but what the writers all seem to be arguing is that walking helps them portray events and environments in an embodied and multi-sensed way. Then there are others, like myself, who instead ask people who they otherwise would have interviewed in the traditional way to take a walk with them instead, interviewing them on foot. Methodologically I initially drew from ethnographer Margarethe Kusenbach's (2003) work on go-alongs.

It was actually when I searched for recent articles citing Kusenbach that I stumbled over Glass' work. Like me, he felt the need to develop the traditional research interview in order to create a more place-sensitive methodological toolbox. But while he (and his research assistants) drove through the city with his informants, in what Kusenbach calls *ride-alongs*, I asked mine to take me out walking, which she refers to as *walk-alongs* (ibid.: 464). A walk-along basically entails interviewing someone whilst moving through environments familiar to her/him. But the reason why the article 'Street phenomenology: The go-along as ethnographic research tool' has become so widely cited (cf. Lee and Ingold 2006; Büscher and Urry 2009; Carpiano 2009; Anderson 2015) – and the concept of walk-along so popular – is that Kusenbach's formulation of a specific walking method enabled researchers to expand on how it combines interview and participant observation. Kusenbach (2003: 463) differentiates between *natural* and *contrived* go-alongs, and I worked with the latter. In my study on the urban geography of non-citizenship I asked irregular migrants to take me to places that meant something to them, and we ended up in parks, shopping centres, allotment areas and so on. And in the gentrification study I asked all interviewees to meet me in the partly demolished industrial area that we were to talk about.

Kusenbach seems to have been mostly walking with 'ordinary' people, researching everyday life in 'ordinary' neighbourhoods. Working within the fields of irregular migration and gentrification, my perspective is quite different, which is why my selection of interviewees has been more strategic. My advice to researchers interested in democratic aspects of urban planning is to focus on walking with 'vulnerable' and, not least, 'powerful' people (Holgersson 2014c). On the one hand I have been walking with people who are excluded from future visions (irregular migrants, people at risk of displacement), and on the other hand with the people in charge of the redevelopment of the city (developers, employees of construction companies, marketers and civil servants). This enabled me to elaborate on how the past and the future are being narrated in Gothenburg at the moment, and on which groups of residents are included and excluded in contemporary historical accounts and future visions respectively, and, most importantly, on the consequences of this inclusion/exclusion.

In her article Kusenbach (2003: 466ff.) puts forward five analytic themes that go-alongs helps us explore further:

1 *perception* (how different people perceive the same environment);
2 *spatial practices* (the meaning that people put into the same activities);
3 *biographies* (how people connect their life stories to specific places);
4 *social architecture* (how people relate to others inhabiting the same space as them);
5 *social realms* (how place shapes social interaction).

Although my research focuses much more on power relations than hers, I found this list useful as an analytic point of departure. But I also added one more point:

6 *the role of the researcher* (walking as a common activity and more of a conversation than an interrogation).

With both groups of co-walkers in the old industrial site, my role as a researcher was affected by us walking. In the case of 'vulnerable' people my impression is that they were empowered by getting to show me around 'their area' rather than coming to the university to meet me. Moreover, they asked me many more questions than I usually get during traditional interviews, which reassured me that they knew what kind of study they were taking part in, and what the outcome of it would be. On the other hand, the 'powerful' people lost some of their authority outside of their offices. It also felt important to bring them to the place that all their models and maps depict. I am not arguing that walking puts the researcher and researched on an equal footing, but that this relationship is unsettled and, at best, partly evens out, depending on who your co-walker is.

Performing the Past and the Future

In his study in Ogden, Utah, Glass's initial research questions focused on how various groups of residents related to different areas in this segregated city. But as he started analysing his ride-alongs, using grounded theory methods, he found that the theme of 'memories' kept growing, and realised that he needed to pay their accounts of the past some serious sociological attention (Glass 2016: 94). In the gentrification study, my experience was very similar to this, and time became a recurring theme in my publications (cf. Holgersson 2014a, 2014b). However, since there were always other main questions, I felt motivated to bring those different threads together in dialogue with Glass and Borer. There was clearly more to be written on this. In his article Glass starts off by advocating us to understand the past as performed:

> Ethnographers and other researchers of the present tend to treat the past as born, understanding it as an essentialized, objective foundation, comprised of historical facts that were recorded as having happened. In contrast, interviewees in my study performed the past, largely made up of autobiographical experiences, as tools of present interaction. The past here is not of 'before' and influencing the 'now'; it is a product of the present that shaped the past. It emerges not from tangible documentation by professionals, but from people constructing it through memory and imagination.
>
> (Glass 2016: 107)

Glass of course is referring to Pierre Nora's (1989) work on the relation between memory and history, where he describes memory as how people continuously remember – as individuals and collectives – and history as how society organises the past. Even though Nora describes memory as a process, and history as trying to destroy it (ibid.: 9), I follow Glass in preferring to talk about performing the past (and the future) rather than seeing it as collective memory (and collective imagination); while memories (and dreams) are things, performance is an activity (Glass 2016: 98).

In my previous work on urban inequality I often included a section on the history of Gothenburg, and of the area in question, in the introduction. Not to do so in such articles seems difficult, but we need to be aware of how time-bound such background sections are, and this is something that we need to keep reminding ourselves and our readers of. The past and the future are both products of the present, constantly being renegotiated (Borer 2010; Glass 2016). It is not hard to find examples of dated historical narratives or future visions – in the movies as well as in urban planning. As part of his ambition to research how his interviewees perform the past, Glass looks more closely at how they invoked the past for specific purposes in conversations – sometimes as a *strategy* to say something about the present, sometimes as *reverie* in order to reimagine old times (Glass 2016: 93). Proceeding from my own walk-alongs, however, I want to add that the future can be analysed in similar ways. My own co-walkers certainly used it both to criticise the present and to joyfully remember 'good old days'. I will offer illustrations of this in the next section, where I return to three walk-alongs that I made.

In his study of time, place and urban redevelopment, Borer focuses on the neighbourhood of City View in Greenville, South Carolina, and more specifically on involving local residents in renovating an old firehouse. On their ideas of the future he writes:

> While collective memory is part history and part commemoration […], collective imagination is part fantasy and part investment. Any type of investment in one's community – whether it is through time and participation, funding and financial support, or constructing meaning and sentimental value – is necessarily future oriented.
>
> (Borer 2010: 108)

There seem to be no plans for general redevelopment of the area, and the interviewees take their future here for granted and perceive the invitation to participate in the planning process as an opportunity. In my research project on the gentrification of the old industrial area the situation was very different. Few of the people renting premises in the run-down buildings would be residents of New Kvillebäcken, which made the future plans mostly appear as more of a pending threat than an opportunity.

It is in itself sociologically interesting to examine how and why people talk about the past and the future, but working in the field of critical urban studies I soon move on to thinking about what the political implications of the findings might be. My co-walkers' accounts were clearly part of larger narratives. I always have C. Wright Mills' (1959/2000) classical discussion on the relation between history and biography with me, and after having acknowledged how we should avoid using static historical facts in our analyses, I still want to analyse my co-walkers' stories against the backdrop of the parallel processes of Gothenburg's transition from industrial city to post-industrial city (e.g. Thörn 2011), the dismantling of the social democratic welfare state (e.g. Larsson *et al.* 2012) and the change from labour immigration to refugee immigration (e.g. Schierup *et al.* 2006). Or maybe rather in relation to how these developments are narrated and understood in relation to each other. Throughout the two fieldworks mentioned above I became increasingly interested in how people make sense of the images of Gothenburg's past and future that are produced as part of the enormous project to redevelop the old harbour and industrial areas of the city. That we as researchers also perform the past and the future does not mean we should stop writing – nor walking – but this needs to be repeatedly acknowledged.

Returning to Three Walks

Walk One: Biography, History and Place

The first walk-along that I chose to reanalyse is one that I made in 2011 with Jani, a 65-year-old man who came to Sweden from Finland with his family when he was 15 years old, as part of the big labour migration programme of the 1950s and 1960s (e.g. Schierup *et al.* 2006). Among the walk-alongs I made this is probably the one where the conversation most explicitly revolved around the past and the future, and I have since returned to the transcript with more explicit questions on this topic. The walk Jani and I made was as part of the research project on the gentrification of a reused old industrial area, and at the time of our meeting the old tin buildings were in the process of being knocked down in order to make room for an up-scale residential area – New Kvillebäcken. Jani was the chair of a Finnish association with premises right across the street from where the new area would soon be materialising, in the block that most probably would be next in the bigger redevelopment project of which New Kvillebäcken was part (Thörn and Holgersson 2016). In the venue, where there once was a textile factory, then a mosque, Finnish seniors make radio broadcasts, engage in karaoke and tango nights, hold zumba workout sessions, language classes and soup lunches. Interestingly enough though, one of the first jobs that Jani had found in Sweden 50 years ago, he told me as we passed an empty lot at the edge of the area, was in a paint factory that used to be there, pasting labels on cans. The now demolished building seems to be what Glass refers to as *a ghost* in his everyday life, reminding him of seemingly good old days. Glass (2016: 13) finds that while people who use the past as a strategy often do so to critique the present, people who perform the past as reverie are trying instead to make the present enjoyable.

Jani might have told me about his first job in a traditional interview as well, but it was as we moved through the area that he shared this. In my experience researchers interested in the connection between biography, history and place have a lot to gain from interviewing people on foot (cf. Kusenbach 2003). As the walk continued we kept talking about his time at the paint factory, and about post-war Sweden where the industrial city was imagined as the end of history. It was not a coincidence that he and his family settled on Hisingen, north of the river that separates Gothenburg. This was one of the areas where the industrial expansion took place, and where public housing areas were built to supply the industrial workers with good housing. Here is an extract from the interview:

'Did a lot of Finns work there?' I ask Jani.

'Not … in that factory, I was the only one.'

'So it was because you lived here …?'

'Yes, they needed people. In those days you could just go there and ask […]. It was not like today!'

I laugh.

'It's very different now.'

This illustrates how the past can be used to describe the present. That Jani had just knocked on the door of the paint factory asking for a job in the 1960s would most likely not have been considered interesting information had it not been so unlike the way the labour market functions today, as thousands of young people once again come to Sweden. The Afghan, Iraqi and Somali teenagers of today primarily come here to seek asylum, but they will eventually need to become 'employable' in a very different labour market than the one Jani entered 50 years ago (Sernhede 2014).

My motive for choosing to start off with Jani's walk-along was that he so clearly performed the past as both a strategy and as reverie in the way Glass discusses. But how he performed the future is just as interesting. As we walked through the partly demolished industrial area it was constantly present, often in the form of rumours of future plans. The Finnish labour migrants are almost archetypical Hisingen residents of the 1960s, but he doubted if there would be room for their association in, or around, New Kvillebäcken in a decade or so. In many cases I had more information about the redevelopment project than he had. When the project had been officially launched by the chair of the municipal board, in an empty lot, a few months before our walk, he and the other current inhabitants of the area had not been invited. Instead he had been watching the spectacle from the window of the Finnish association. Many of the people I met in the area shared Jani's worry about the upcoming redevelopment, and how it would affect the surrounding areas (see Despotovic and Thörn 2015). Just before our walk, huge containers bearing New Kvillebäcken posters had been stacked, two-high, at every corner of the site, and to Jani they represented the impending takeover. Jani did not know if one could register for an apartment yet, and he did not understand which small businesses and organisations would have the means to pay rents for premises in the newly built area. Not Finnish seniors for sure.

Since the rest of the industrial area was also planned to be redeveloped, Jani eventually risked physical displacement. But more importantly, he was already being *discursively displaced*. In a visionary film of New Kvillebäcken, pictures were used to visualise the future of the area, but the old inhabitants were absent from these images.[2] In other words, they were still physically present, but already written out of the area's future (Holgersson 2014a). When the marketing director of the municipal developer in charge of the project was asked in a radio interview who he thought would live in the future area, he answered 'more modern people' (P4 Göteborg 2012). Where the 'outmoded' people are planned to go remains uncertain. In her study of the gentrification of the old working area of Partick in Glasgow, Kirsteen Paton (2010: 137) discusses how gentrification – and the middle class – is being perceived as 'the antidote' for old industrial cities struggling to reinvent themselves. In an age of post-political urban planning, when redevelopment projects are often presented as inevitable and the only way forward, it becomes crucial to pay attention to the voices of those excluded from the future visions – and to walk the city with them. Nora (1989: 9) argues that the official writing of history aims at destroying collective memories. When it comes to the future this would correspond to official future plans presented as the only way forward, supressing ideas of alternative roads ahead. The people who rented premises in the run-down industrial buildings also had thoughts on how the area could be developed, of course without them having to leave.

Walk Two: Marketing the Future, Ignoring the Past

The second walk-along that I am going to dwell on here was made in 2011 as part of the same research project as the walk with Jani. Sofia and Karin were two women in their mid-twenties who were involved in the marketing of New Kvillebäcken, one for a communication bureau and one for the municipal developer. I selected this walk because it is interesting in relation to my walk with Jani, and because of the way the two women perform the future, sometimes using (selected parts of) the past. At the time of our meeting it was the job of these two women to create marketable images of the not-yet-built residential area, which included campaigns such as the ads on the containers that Jani pointed out and running a blog that was supposed to attract the attention of potential future residents. The big posters read: 'With a bit of imagination you could … smell the aroma of fresh coffee coming from the kitchen in your new three-room flat', '… see people having a crayfish party on their balcony', '… hear children laughing in the shady courtyards between the houses' and '… watch the setting sun as it sinks behind the rooftops', which gives us some clues to the kind of future area that the developer was imagining. Here are Sofia, Karin and I talking about the blog, and how to write post after post about a neighbourhood that does not yet exist:

> 'You're supposed to get a feeling of "What might life in Kvillebäcken be like?"', says Karin.
> 'Yes', Sofia agrees.
> 'What will it be like then?' I ask.
> 'A mixed city!' Sofia answers, and laughs a bit.
> Karin also laughs, and then continues 'No, but it's up to the people that move in, who form …'
> 'It definitely is', Sofia assures me.
> And then Karin says 'But then of course, we put a lot of emphasis on questions of sustainability … and a sustainable and environmentally friendly life …'
> '… with a relaxed city lifestyle and … yes …', Sofia fills in.

I interpret the laughs as expressions of ambivalence towards the possibility of creating the atmosphere of an area from above in this way, before anyone has even moved in. Then I think their focus on sustainability is worth attention. As architectural researcher Carin Bradley (2009) has shown, in a Swedish context 'an environmentally friendly life' is connected to a white middle-class consumerist lifestyle (cf. Quastel 2009; Checker 2011), and this fits well with the overall themes of the blog. In one post there is a list of things to do to save the world; one point is to recycle one's Nespresso capsules. Words such as 'mixed city', 'sustainability' and 'a relaxed city lifestyle' are important nodes in discourses on an urban future that is often presented, and thought of, as inevitable today. And it is with this specific image that Jani has trouble identifying himself. This use of the future is very strategic as it – often implicitly – paints a picture of an unsustainable past in order to legitimise major redevelopment. What I also find interesting here is how contemporary both the past and the future are. Parts of the vision of New Kvillebäcken that were formulated as the project started were already hopelessly dated long before people could move into the new houses. It was the future anno 2008 and wifi was still novel technology.

What struck me, as Karin, Sofia and I walked past the demolition sites and the remaining old industrial buildings, was how unfamiliar my co-walkers were with the past and the present area – and its inhabitants. None of them had ever lived on this side of the river, and before this project they had not had much reason to come here either, they told me. Their focus was on the maps and models of the future area and its potential residents. As we entered the area one of the women 'checked in' on Facebook. I did not react to this as it happened, but reading through the transcript of the walk I realise that she 'checked into' New Kvillebäcken. Where Jani pointed at a demolished factory, they saw buildings that were not yet erected. However, having left their office and come to the area, it was impossible for them not to give the people about to be displaced a thought. Given that other employees at the municipal developer were in charge of negotiating the buyout, they knew very little about these residents. They therefore started asking *me* about them, whether we had interviewed them as well, and if so, what they thought about it all. That is not likely to have happened had we not been in the area, talking whilst walking.

Glass points out how people with a personal history in an area see 'ghosts' – such as closed cafés, restaurants, shops and schools, demolished houses – in their everyday life, while people who move into an area make a future there by investigating the past (Glass 2016: 103). This is probably why 'storytelling' has become very fashionable in the marketing of redeveloped areas (Jensen 2007). This involves revealing selected parts of the past to create a feeling of authenticity – another, even more strategic, way to perform the past. Future-oriented nostalgia is another way to describe it (Davis 1979). In the New Kvillebäcken case, potential buyers and tenants could watch the visionary film, where a fictive future resident describes how the soul of old Kvillebäcken will still be present as a 'charming ingredient' in the new area (Älvstranden 2008). Since all the old buildings will be demolished it is quite hard to understand what that actually means, and Sofia and Karin did not have a good answer to this. It seemed to me as if they wanted to latch on to the storytelling trend – they had ideas of asking people to send them memories from the area and of making a historical walk there – but this was not easily done in the case of Kvillebäcken. Moreover, this kind of commercial storytelling is always about smoothly bringing out a marketable past, but in Kvillebäcken the selection would probably have been too obvious. In the ten years prior to the redevelopment the old industrial area had been dramatically stigmatised as a dangerous and crime-torn area (Thörn and Holgersson 2016), seemingly too recently to become a set of charming yet thrilling stories. A woman from one of the construction companies involved in the projects did see the future potential in this though, she told me during our walk. Skipping the past 30 years or so was another idea, proposed by a man from yet another construction company. This would enable the marketing group to tell the story about the prosperous and hopeful post-war times that are so often romanticised in Sweden at present. But which old inhabitants do you interview about the good old days after everyone has been displaced? Their memories might not fit in with the historical walk that Karin and Sofia had in mind.

Walk Three: Lost in Time, Stuck in Space

The last walk-along that I have returned to was one of the first ones I made. I was researching the geography of non-citizenship and realised that I needed to supplement the traditional interviews that I had already conducted with more place-sensitive methods. Margarethe Kusenbach's work caught my attention and I asked my interviewees to take me to a place in Gothenburg that meant something to them. This set of walks was made as a test, and instead of recording the conversation I made detailed notes. In 2006 I met up with Emir, a young man in his early twenties, who had lived irregularly in Gothenburg for a few years with his parents and younger sister. The family had fled from Bosnia. Compared to the two walks above, time was not such an explicit topic in our conversation, which is why I saved it until last. Still, going through it again I realise that although the people I met were stuck in time (cf. Brekke 2004), irregularity is all about the past and the future. As part of their appeal, Emir's family needed to once more 'tell their story' in order to prove their need for protection. A more strategic way to perform the past is hard to imagine. As for their future, their everyday life was lived one day at the time – psychologically as well as financially – but they were constantly reminded that unlike the people around them they could not make future plans.

The past was not a main theme during this set of walks. Although my interviewees had already created some memories in Gothenburg, most of their past had taken place elsewhere. However, in his article Glass (2016: 103) notices that while passing different locations his interviewees did not just remember past events tied to those particular places. Much like mine, they were also reminded of times spent in somehow similar settings, and the people that they associated with those places. To my co-walkers the motive for bringing up memories from the country that they had left resembles what Glass describes as reverie, although for them, reminding themselves of 'good old days' was a much more bittersweet activity than for Glass's informants. What I want to underline here is the potential to get people to share stories of their past during a walking interview, regardless of whether the person's history is located somewhere else. It seems to be both about the form of the conversation and about the passing through a diverse physical landscape where all sorts of sensory experiences can lead one's thoughts back in time (Rhys-Taylor 2007).

As I kept reanalysing this walk I found that there is something really interesting to learn about how people perform the future here too. One of the biggest benefits to interviewing Emir on foot instead of sitting down was an in situ insight for me of what it might mean to live, and keep on living, in a place where you cannot plan your future. This was nothing we explicitly talked about, but something that struck me during our walk. As Kusenbach (2003) describes, walk-along is as much a participant observation as an interview. Roots are often used as a metaphor in discussions on individual pasts, but during my walks with irregular migrants in Gothenburg I realised that our futures need them too; an imagined future needs to be placed to make sense. A couple of weeks before I was to meet up with Emir for our walk I had received a joyful text message from him simply saying 'Hi! We've got our residence permit!' In this research I asked people living, or having recently lived, under the threat of deportation to take me to a place in the city that meant something to them. Around 2005 this group was often referred to as 'hidden refugees' in Sweden, and described as living 'outside society' and 'underground'. However, as I started my fieldwork I realised that most of the men and women I met moved through Gothenburg as part of their everyday routine, to get to and from work, but also to visit friends and relatives or just to get out of their crowded apartments. This was when I added walk-alongs (and mental maps) to my research design (Holgersson 2011; 2014c).

Theoretically, my motive for interviewing on foot was that walk-alongs, combining interview and observation, would help me bring out the spatial aspect of what anthropologist Nicholas de Genova (2002) characterises as *deportability*, a condition where you are at constant, but not immediate risk of, being arrested and deported. In this particular case I expected the guy to take me for a walk in the area in the north-eastern suburb where he had been staying up until now. As an irregular migrant he had been collecting empty tins along the tram lines, and thus moving through large parts of Gothenburg in his everyday life. He preferred not to leave the apartment though, he told me, and the central node of his map was 'home'. But now he wanted to meet up at Drottningtorget, a square right next to the Central Station, and go somewhere for a coffee. When I arrived he was already there, waiting at the newsstand. I spotted him from a long distance. Chatting, we started walking towards what he described as his favourite café, which turned out to be located well into the shopping centre Femman. He preferred the seats in the display window, he told me, 'so that you can watch people passing by'. He was looking forward, not back, and the café seemed to symbolise his new position. During our walk I realised that in order to perform the future you need a place in the world. And that he now, once again, had one.

Conclusion

Walking is a very enjoyable activity, especially walking with others. It is not hard to romanticise. On my way back to the office after having interviewed someone on foot I often felt that my job is amazing. I do not remember not getting along with anybody I walked with. At the same time though, as a social scientific method walk-alongs have great potential in helping us bring out the conflicts of interest that are built into urban planning. I realised this back during my first set of walk-alongs with irregular migrants almost ten years ago, and then again during the more recent Kvillebäcken walks. But stumbling over Glass's (2016) work on the connection between walking and performing the past while working on an abstract for my chapter in this book I saw an opportunity to return to some of my walk-along notes and transcripts, focusing solely on this – but also examining how they performed the future. To summarise, I argue that both these processes play important parts when people negotiate their position and place in the city – and in society.

Drawing on C. Wright Mills (1959/2000) I then started thinking of how the ways in which people's private troubles correspond to current public issues affect how they perform the past and the future. Jani's and Emir's stories need to be interpreted against the backdrop of a Swedish present in which different actors are struggling over how to describe the connections between deindustrialisation, the transformation of the welfare state, economic crises, globalisation, increasing refugee migration, and the growth of racist parties and movements throughout Europe. And this is also the present in which Karin and Sofia are trying to produce images of a bright future, hoping to attract the attention of the 'modern people' who have been identified as the target group for the marketing of New Kvillebäcken. No wonder that the concept of future-oriented nostalgia (Davis 1979) seems so fitting to describe current urban branding campaigns. A more strategic – and selective – use of the past than commercial storytelling is hard to find.

In the introduction I explained how my interest in the discussion on how people perform the past and the present lies with the political implications. Summing up, trying to tie the three walks together, I want to linger on the issue of what it means to be – or not be – able to participate in the planning of the city's future. Emir's problem was not the lack of an invitation to citizen dialogues over the forthcoming redevelopment of the central riverbanks of Gothenburg, but being unable to look forward at all. Future plans need to be placed somewhere, and waiting for asylum makes that impossible. To urban ethnographers, the reason why irregular migrants are such an interesting group to walk the city with is the fact that they live their life in the city without ever being considered in the planning process. What does it mean for a city that thousands of its residents are stuck in the present, not being able to link their individual dreams to any collective imagining, not investing anything? As Les Back points out in *The Art of Listening* (2007), we need to listen more carefully to these stories, devoting them some serious sociological attention.

Jani's story is more clearly linked to Borer's (2010: 96) discussion of how people's sense of belonging is affected by redevelopment processes. He has not been invited to participate in any dialogue over the future of the area where the Finnish association, in which he invests most of his spare time, and rents premises, is based. And he does not recognise himself in the marketing of New Kvillebäcken. The redevelopment of the old industrial area was initiated by the municipal development company Älvstranden, which makes it relevant to ask how the city deals with all the people who are being discursively displaced as plans for the continued expansion of the central city are presented, for instance in the form of the blog Sofia and Karin are running. It is crucial to make visible present inhabitants' dreams of the future. And to pay attention to their roots. Where are these future visions placed? For individuals to be able to dream of and invest in a future in Gothenburg they need to know that there is room for them in the future city as well. This is not just true of irregular migrants (cf. Mukhtar-Landgren 2008)

Above, I have offered a number of arguments why urban ethnographers who are interested in the political implications of how people perform the past and the future need to consider including walk-alongs in their methodologies, but I left one for last. A walk-along is the perfect frame for a story. As I already touched upon, together with artists, photographers, novelists and journalists, sociologists are – or at least ought to be – storytellers (cf. Becker 2007), and writing about walks you made gives you a better chance, I argue, to bring both your interviewees and your arguments alive. Combining participatory observation and interview enables you to discuss not only what was said, but also what happened along the way – and what the way looked, sounded and smelled like. Walks also have a beginning and an end. I left Jani at the venue of the Finnish association, where he had invited me in for coffee and a cinnamon bun. My walk with Sofia and Karin was made on a rainy spring day, over lunch, and as soon as we reached the corner of the area where we started they headed back to their offices. And after Emir and I had left the café in the shopping centre, he took the tram back to the suburb where he was still staying. Me, I went straight back to the university to make field notes and upload the recordings.

Notes

1 The personal names are fictitious. The places carry their own names.
2 The film 'Kvillebäcken – Continental and Gothenburgian' was previously posted on YouTube: www.youtube.com/watch?v=MPf-TaD5GFA (last accessed 14 November 2013), but has since been taken down and is no longer accessible to the public.

References

Anderson, Jon (2015) *Understanding Cultural Geography: Spaces and Traces*. London: Routledge.
Back, Les (2007) *The Art of Listening*. Oxford: Berg.
Becker, Howard (2007) *Telling about Society*. Chicago: University of Chicago Press.

Borer, Michael (2010) 'From collective memory to collective imagination: time, place, and urban redevelopment', *Symbolic Interaction*, 33(1): 96–114.

Bradley, Karin (2009) *Just Environments: Politicizing Sustainable Urban Development*. Stockholm: Royal Institute of Technology, School of Architecture and the Built Environment.

Brekke, Jan-Paul (2004) *While We Are Waiting*. Research report, Institutt for samfunnsforskning, Oslo.

Büscher, Monika and Urry, John (2009) 'Mobile methods and the empirical', *European Journal of Social Theory*, 12(1): 99–116.

Carpiano, Richard (2009) 'Come take a walk with me: the "go-along" interview as a novel method for studying the implications of place for health and well-being', *Health and Place*, 15(1): 263–272.

Checker, Melissa (2011) 'Wiped out by the "greenwave": environmental gentrification and the paradoxical politics of urban sustainability', *City and Society*, 23(2): 210–229.

Davis, Fred (1979) *Yearning for Yesterday: A Sociology of Nostalgia*. New York: Free Press.

de Genova, N. (2002) 'Migrant "illegality" and deportability in everyday life', *Annual Review of Anthropology*, 31: 419–437.

Despotovic, Katarina and Thörn, Catharina (2015) *Den urbana fronten. En dokumentation av makten över staden*. Stockholm: Arkitektur Förlag.

Glass, Pepper (2016) 'Using history to explain the present: the past as born and performed', *Ethnography*, 17(1): 92–110.

Holgersson, Helena (2011) *Icke-medborgarskapets urbana geografi*. Gothenburg: Glänta produktion.

Holgersson, Helena (2014a) 'The urban geography of Swedish non-citizenship'. In Francisco Martinez and Klemen Slabina (eds), *Playgrounds and Battlefields: Critical Perspectives of Social Engagement*. Tallin: Tallin University Press.

Holgersson, Helena (2014b) 'Post-political narratives and emotions: dealing with discursive displacement in everyday life'. In Emma Jackson and Hannah Jones (eds), *Stories of Cosmopolitan Belonging: Emotion and Location*. Milton Park: Routledge Earthscan.

Holgersson, Helena (2014c) 'Challenging the hegemonic gaze on foot: walk-alongs as a useful method in gentrification research'. In Timothy Shortell and Evrick Brown (eds), *Walking in the European City*. Farnham: Ashgate.

Ingold, Tim and Vergunst, Jo Lee (2008) *Ways of Walking: Ethnographic Practice on Foot*. London: Ashgate.

Jensen, Ole (2007) 'Culture stories: understanding urban branding', *Planning Theory*, 6(3): 211–236.

Kusenbach, Margarethe (2003) 'Street phenomenology: the go-along as an ethnographic research tool', *Ethnography*, 4(3): 455–485.

Larsson, Bengt, Letell, Martin and Thörn, Håkan (2012) *Transformations of the Swedish Welfare State: From Social Engineering to Governance?* New York: Palgrave Macmillan.

Lee, Jo and Ingold, Tim (2006) 'Fieldwork on foot: perceiving, routing, socializing'. In Simon Coleman and Peter Collins (eds), *Locating the Field: Space, Place and Context in Anthropology*. Oxford: Berg.

Mouffe, Chantal (2005) *On the Political*. Milton Park: Routledge.

Mukhtar-Landgren, Dalia (2008) 'City marketing in a dual city'. In Katherine Tyler and Bo Peterson (eds), *Majority Cultures and the Politics of Ethnic Difference*. New York: Palgrave Macmillan.

Nora, Pierre (1989) 'Between memory and history: les lieux de mémoire', *Representations*, 26: 7–24.

P4 Göteborg (2012) 'Afternoon session', *Sveriges Radio*, 27 December.

Paton, Kirsteen (2010) 'Making working-class neighbourhoods posh? Exploring the effects of gentrification strategies on working-class communities'. In Yvette Taylor (ed.), *Classed Intersections: Spaces, Selves, Knowledges*. Farnham: Ashgate.

Puwar, Nirmal (2011) 'Noise of the past: spatial interruptions of war, nation and memory', *Senses and Society*, 6(3): 325–345.

Quastel, Noah (2009) 'Political ecologies of gentrification', *Urban Geography*, 30(7): 694–725.

Rhys-Taylor (2007) 'The irrepressibility of Mangifera', *Eurozine*, 23 April. Online: www.eurozine.com/articles/2007-04-23-rhystaylor-en.html.

Schierup, Carl-Ulrik, Hansen, Peo and Castles, Stephen (2006) *Migration, Citizenship and the European Welfare State: A European Dilemma*. Oxford: Oxford University Press.

Sernhede, Ove (2014) 'Youth rebellion and social mobilization in Sweden', *Soundings*, 56: 81–91.

Swyngedouw, Eric, Moulaert, Frank and Rodriguez, Arantxa (2002) 'Neoliberal urbanization in Europe: large-scale urban development projects and the new urban policy', *Antipode*, 34(3): 542–577.

Thörn, Catharina (2011) 'Soft strategies of exclusion: strategies of ambience and control of public space in Gothenburg', *Urban Geography*, 32(7): 989–1008.

Thörn, Catharina and Holgersson, Helena (2016) 'Revisiting the urban frontier through the case of New Kvillebäcken, Gothenburg', *City*, forthcoming.

Trouillot, Michel-Rolph (1995) *Silencing the Past: Power and the Production of History*. Boston: Beacon Press.

Wright Mills, C. (1959/2000) *The Sociological Imagination*. Oxford: Oxford University Press.

Shelter in a Park.

Source: Mobile Focus Group Participant.

5   Walking Together

Understanding Young People's Experiences of Living in Neighbourhoods in Transition

Andrew Clark

The 'mobilities turn' in the social sciences has sparked interest in methodo-logical attempts to understand how movement can make social and material realities (Büscher and Urry, 2009). This includes the possibilities for using walking interview methods to understand how neighbourhoods and com-munities of place are interpreted or experienced on the ground (Carpiano, 2009; Fincham *et al.*, 2010; Hall *et al.*, 2006; Moles, 2008). Although diverse in approach, walking interviews attempt to recreate the interview method while on the move, be it by foot or vehicle. They have been considered a useful way of understanding the social and physical aspects of locally situated daily experience. In doing so, it is claimed that they can better access the 'small details' of neighbourhood life and enable alternative, perhaps more grounded, perspectives to emerge that better resonate with participants' own interpretations of their lives (Fink, 2012; Hogan, 2009). It has also been sug-gested that walking interviews can illuminate how individuals situate them-selves in a localised socio-spatial landscape as well as reveal the ordinary, frequently hidden dimensions of life that may remain unremarked upon in static, room-based interactions (Evans and Jones, 2011, Kusenbach, 2003). So, walking alongside an individual can provide metaphorical insight into what it is like to temporarily 'live the life' of another (Anderson and Jones, 2009: 399) by providing privileged access to the geographically situated lived real-ities that constitute everyday experiences (Pink, 2008a).

While there is a growing literature about conducting one-to-one interviews on the move, there has been little, if any, consideration or discussion of the possibil-ities of adopting the approach to group settings (Carpiano, 2009). These possibil-ities underpin discussion in this chapter. I outline how a mobile focus-group method was developed and implemented to assess young people's experiences of living in deprived urban neighbourhoods undergoing regeneration. I consider the challenges and opportunities afforded by the approach, including how the tech-nique produced individual and group insights into the material, social, biographical and embodied production of neighbourhoods and reflect on the implications for knowledge arising from the explicitly collectivist and inter-activist nature of the method. Paying attention to walking provides insight not only into how individuals experience the world, but also come to make it (de Certeau, 1984). This chapter aims to go beyond discussion of the approach as another research 'tool' to consider how encouraging groups of individuals to move through and interact with the environment produces particular versions of neighbourhood experience. Reflexive accounts of how tacit or everyday knowledge is produced in research thus need to be attuned to the ways in methods actively create versions of the social world through their situated and embodied practice (Law and Urry, 2004).

Research Context

The mobile focus group method described here was developed as part of an England-wide mixed-method evaluation of an initiative to promote inclusive activities, primarily targeted at young people living in urban localities under-going economic, social and physical regeneration and redevelopment.[1] Under-standing young people's place in the production of neighbourhood life has long been of interest. Research has explored issues of territoriality, safety and risk, social interaction and identity formation at various scales. Frequently, research has identified how young people may become stigmatised in neigh-bourhood places (e.g. Brown, 2013; Deuchar, 2009; Pickering *et al.*, 2012). Work has highlighted how an adult majority may label a younger minority as antisocial for misappropriating the street or public spaces as sites for social gathering, leading to calls for initiatives and schemes that can mark young people out as problematic, or requiring some form of intervention in the guise of neighbourhood regeneration or urban redevelopment (Neary *et al.*, 2013). Indications are that in such contexts young people are marginalised from urban regeneration and restructuring politics, processes and outputs (Skelton and Gough, 2013). For instance, Watt's (2013) work on the regeneration of parts of East London for the 2012 Olympic Games revealed how for many young people, the Olympics, and their associated regeneration neighbourhood-based legacies, were 'not for them'.

Yet rather than the passive or receptive agents of the neighbourhoods they inhabit, young people draw on social and spatial resources to get on with their ordinary, everyday lives, even amidst significant neighbourhood change (Neary, 2015). That young people are active participants in the production of neighbour-hood life is becoming recognised in both research and practice around neigh-bourhood development and regeneration (Goodwin and Young, 2013). Greater involvement of young people in processes of involuntary household relocation can enable empowerment (Lawson and Kearns, 2016), and listening to young people has been considered beneficial not only as a means of democratic involvement, but also for understanding more about community development including neighbourhood regeneration processes (Greene *et al.*, 2016). Thus young people occupy a somewhat paradoxical position in urban restructuring and redevelopment processes, particularly as they operate at the neighbourhood scale. In part, they are caught up in discourses of disorder and deviance, presented as a risk requiring intervention to ensure appropriate behaviour in public. At the same time, their role as neighbourhood actors and active place-makers means that their inclusion in redevelopment programmes is vital in order to shape and achieve the aspirations afforded by particular schemes and projects.

It is this context that the initiative that was the subject of the wider evaluation was developed. The initiative promoted a number of out-of-school schemes and activities for young people (typically aged 12–18) living in deprived urban areas. While the wider evaluation assessed various measures and outcomes, the mobile focus groups intended to elicit participants' views about the initiative, how it was experienced in varying local contexts, and its position in the everyday experiences of life for young people in changing neighbourhoods.

The mobile focus group approach was developed as a means of prioritising young people's voices and was based on established rationale for undertaking both mobile interviews outlined above, and conventional focus groups. The latter included the potential to obtain a variety of opinions within a relatively short space of time and provide insight into how groups of individuals come to make collective sense of phenomena (Caretta and Vacchelli, 2015; Kitzinger, 1994). More pragmatically, the evaluation funding organisation was also keen that the team obtained as much insight from as many different young people in the most effective way. It is also relevant to acknowledge that those whose views we wanted to gather are frequently 'over-researched' and can be wary of outside researchers and more formal data-collection techniques that may bear similarity to those used by individuals in positions of authority (Bagnoli and Clark, 2010; Barker and Weller, 2003; Clark, 2008). In developing a technique that could be differentiated from more established, possibly more formal, approaches we aspired to encourage participants to engage more authentically in the evaluation process, or failing that, at least consider their involvement to be less onerous than other techniques.

The mobile focus groups were completed in a range of English towns and cities. These included large urban metropolises, industrial towns and coastal resorts. The specific neighbourhoods that were the focus of the visits were heterogeneous, ranging from high-density Victorian terraced housing to post-war edge-of-city public housing estates, and mixed low and high-rise apartment blocks. Some had transitioned to housing association management while others were a mix of privately owned and privately rented properties. Most were undergoing physical regeneration (or were due to do so), variously comprising retrofitting existing properties, large-scale demolition and the construction of new-build properties. Common to all the neighbourhoods were high indicators of multi-deprivation and economic instability.

Eight focus groups with fifty-five participants were undertaken. All members of the groups were recruited from already existing youth clubs and organisations being funded by the wider initiative. The smallest group comprised three members and the largest twelve. With the exception of the smallest groups, two researchers attended all the walks. The walks were conducted at the same times the groups met, typically on weekday evenings. On arrival, the researchers were introduced to the groups and requested a 'small group of volunteers to show the researchers around the neighbourhood and talk about what it was like to live there'. The request was always well received. The walks were audio and visually recorded and a collection of disposable cameras were shared among members of the group with the suggestion that individuals also photograph aspects of their neighbourhood.

Each walk began by asking participants to 'show the researchers around the neighbourhood' (see Clark and Emmel, 2010). Rather than ask participants to lead me on a predetermined route, participants were encouraged to decide between themselves where to go, with the only provisos being that the group stayed together and within walking distance of the youth centre where we initially met. As we ventured forth, the groups were asked about the spaces being walked through, along with life in the neighbourhood more generally. Discussions covered what they liked and disliked about where they live; where they do and do not go; everyday routines and activities that were locally situated; how the neighbourhoods had changed over time; and how they perceived and experienced local facilities and infrastructures. The walks lasted between sixty and seventy-five minutes and usually took in the paraphernalia of neighbourhood life: shops, youth or community centres, schools, playgrounds, food takeaway establishments, and houses where participants, their friends or family currently or had previously lived.

A Brief Summary of Findings: Roots, Belonging and Boredom

Neighbourhoods are simultaneously material or physical phenomena, locations for social exchange and interaction, as well as being uniquely personal, subjective experiences. They are locations intimately tied to identity, memory, biography and social relationships, which mean that individuals' neighbourhood experiences vary from the mundane, seemingly ordinary, to at times the exceptional and unique (Rogaly and Taylor, 2009). All these features emerged on the group walks. Where we walked, and just as importantly, where we did not walk, revealed how different individuals and group construct different microgeographies of the neighbourhood. Resonating with Lewis' (1985) autobiographical description of London as a checkerboard of safe and dangerous places, the walks revealed the relatively familiar places of comfort and security, as well as those to be avoided; not all the time, but certainly at particular times of the day or night, or depending on the presence or absence of other people. Participants spoke about how they engaged in the social life of the neighbourhoods, offered partial histories of what had changed and remained the same, and provided insight into the intricate geographies of belonging and not belonging that were tied to time as well as space. They also narrated locally well-known stories about historical events, gossip and hearsay about different parts of the neighbourhood or groups within it. So, the mobile focus groups begin to unearth something of how young people's territoriality comes into being not just in geographical contexts, but also through historical, diurnal and seasonal rhythms.

PARTICIPANT 1: I wouldn't feel safe walking on the [park] at night or the alley way between [supermarket] and the reservoir. People used to go up on the hill and smoke and drink. A homeless person lived there at one point.

PARTICIPANT 2: … If you go through [the park] and there are people here, then you don't stay. It depends on who is here. There's less hassle in the summer because people will just chill out…. People hang out here straight after school until midnight. This is where we used to … skate. It's a criminal offence now. People drink alcohol and smoke drugs here so not many people come here now…. A lot of the skaters have moved to the recreation ground where they have a skateboard ramp.

(Walk in Northamptonshire)

Showing me where they lived permitted participants to reveal the intricate micro temporal and spatial bases of their neighbourhood practices. They took me to specific streets and parks they considered more or less safe to be in, and explained, in detail knowable only to those intimate with the locations we were passing though, when, where and how they assessed the relative safety of those places. The walks revealed the importance of boundary-makers such as fences, walls or particular streets that signified differences in where participants felt they could and could not go, or that enabled a sense of security, and contributed to their sense of ease in the area. These were nuanced articulations that often needed to be understood in their situational contexts and which may have evaded adequate description through room-based focus groups. For instance, a walk in London took me across a main road that dissected the neighbourhood group members were drawn from. For one young person this meant venturing into a place she had never visited despite living in close proximity:

RESEARCHER: Did you say this bit scares you?

PARTICIPANT 1: Yeah 'cos I'm not used to this side, I'm only used to that side. All my life I've never gone over this side. Not even to the shop …

PARTICIPANT 2: It's like rivals groups, there's two sides.

PARTICIPANT 1: … where this lot [male participants] live is on that side. That's why we don't get along. We live on different sides…. We still have a bit of hatred.

(Walk in London)

In encouraging participants to move within and between places of comfort and discomfort, the walks were thus both familiar and disruptive to routines and habitual movements. As the comment above suggests, participants constructed a sense of belonging through the intricacies of location but such belonging was frequently ambiguous. On the one hand, they demonstrated a 'sense of pride' in what they revealed, highlighting particular phenomena that they liked, were proud of, or considered worth showing to a stranger. Some walks took on some of the qualities of a visitors' tour (though without the hyperbole or romanticism), with participants keen to indicate how they felt they belonged to where they lived and how they participate in localised spaces. Yet participants also spoke of the difficulties of life for themselves, their parents and their neighbours living in an environment in need of economic as well as physical improvement. They talked candidly about their embarrassment of being from an area considered somehow less good than other places in their towns and cities, and expressed anxiety at being in some way stigmatised on account of where they lived. This externally imposed stigma became evident in their questioning their own sense of local belonging:

PARTICIPANT: It's much better than what its reputation is. It's got a very bad reputation. Certain individuals give it a bad name and the whole place gets labelled.

(Walk in London)

PARTICPANT: I heard people at school say, [the estate] is like, for little scruffs, but I just says, 'yeah, shut up' [laughs].

(Walk in South Yorkshire)

In doing so, paradoxical perspectives emerge of young people wanting to be simultaneously proud of where they live, suggesting for example that these places are 'not as bad' as others may make out, while pointing out environmental, economic and social challenges that required attention.

In spite of much commentary about the decline of local geographies in the construction of social networks it is clear that young people still continue to rely on spatial propinquity to form and maintain relations with others. This includes neighbourhood infrastructures that have become taken for granted in their routines and activities. Shops, parks, schools and friends and relatives' houses were all presented to me on the walks. Outside of home and school, the neighbourhood continues to be an important place where young people choose to spend time away from parents and adult surveillance, and engage in the seemingly mundane but socially relevant acts of 'hanging around' and 'being bored'.

PARTICIPANT 1: This is a rough estate. There's a lot of violence. And there was something like an attempted murder few years ago, and if you go straight down there, there was a murder there last year I think. An old man got murdered.
PARTICIPANT 2: It's not dangerous. It's just the people that are on it.
RESEARCHER: What's good about it?
PARTICIPANT 3: It's got parks and it's close to [food takeaway] where you can get burgers.

PARTICIPANT 2: I don't see anything bad, apart from the fighting. But it gets boring sometimes.

(Walk in Lancashire)

PARTICIPANT: Everyone used to go outside the shops, having a beer [laughs]. But you don't really see them anymore. People used to just hang outside the shop and ask me to get them cigs and stuff.... I get cans [of beer from the shop] and sit with my mates. We go on the streets. That's what everyone does.

(Walk in Greater Manchester)

'Hanging around', or to be more precise given that such activity relies on maintaining momentum, 'ambling around', is a key part of young people's lives. Where they gather with friends to 'do nothing' indicates an intricate 'geography of boredom' that is essential to young people's daily experiences that inform where, when, with whom and how they belong in place. The mobile focus groups thus offer a way of understanding how identities and belonging are locally situated and the importance of 'being there' to appreciate what this means in practice.

Places are made through the gathering together of bodies, things, time and space rather than static sites (Tuan, 1977). The mobile focus groups, like other mobile methods, offer insight into the dynamic and fluid ways in which neighbourhoods are constructed by the movement of bodies through space (Lee and Ingold, 2006; Pink, 2008a). However, the walks offer more than an empirically observable exploration in the form of a whistle-stop tour of key sites, or an overly romanticised trail through neighbourhood life (Kusenbach, 2012). Rather, they reveal the interpretive, multi-sensory dimensions of neighbourhood life and, crucially, how neighbourhoods are the product of such experiences (Degan and Rose, 2012). Experiencing the dampness and cold of an autumnal evening congregating on a playground, the uneasiness of gathering winter darkness waiting outside a takeaway for it to open, and the moving at pace through parkland to keep up with friends on bicycles all reveal the sensorial nature of neighbourhood life. Likewise, wandering around an edge-of-town housing estate on a wet afternoon in late summer can better reveal the sense of boredom and frustration about the lack of things to do and places to go than any number of words (however well articulated) in a room-based focus group. This is not just because life 'feels' different when on the move (Moles, 2008), but because young people experience neighbourhood life peripatetically. That it is through movement that they produce neighbourhood places means it is necessary to pay attention to both the *walking* and the *talking* as simultaneously product (or data) and practice.

The Methodological Potential of Talking and Walking Together

It is challenging and frustrating to attempt to adequately capture in written form the complex, nuanced, multi-sensual dimensions and embodied practices that make up people's experiences of place (Tuan, 1977). Paying attention to the process of moving, as well as the spaces we are moving through and between, is central to realising both the substantive and the methodological potential of mobile focus groups. To be explicit, the mobile focus group method thus conjures up neighbourhoods that are not just based on representation, or even empathetic understanding, but are also real, experiential entities located in the moment of interaction between researcher and participants, and which are productive of place itself.

The interactional, inductive and situated practices of mobile focus groups bring many of the benefits of other walking methods. This includes enabling knowledge to emerge in situ with the environment structuring as well as informing the unfolding narrative (Anderson and Jones, 2009; Fink, 2012). So, rather than being the detached, objective focus of discussion, the environment directs and affects dialogue by prompting and interjecting in 'three-way-conversations, with interviewee, interviewer and locality engaged in an exchange of ideas' (Hall *et al.*, 2006: 3). The emergent knowledge is thus grounded in lived experience. Just as important as those experiences revealed on the walks are those that are not. For instance, young people living in the two coastal towns offered no discussion of the trappings of the local tourist economy such as amusement parks or beaches. Those living in larger cities rarely ventured into city centres or beyond the confines of the geographies afforded to their daily activities-spaces of school, home, friends' houses, a local shop and the places in-between.

As an interaction, the technique also provides telling insight into how knowledge about place is co-created. The young people I spoke to were frequently disengaged from more conventional research techniques. Placing young people in charge of the walks – determining where to go and what to discuss (albeit guided by my own research objectives) – offered a clearer message that they were the experts on their local environments. I am not claiming here that the approach should be considered part of a participatory research repertoire (though it could be used as such), but rather suggest that it does seek to unbalance the researcher–researched relationship. While the technique did not change in a participatory or action research vein, it did provide opportunity for participants to individually and collectively present, negotiate, and as I suggest shortly, reject, more dominant perspectives on their local experiences. Granted, the technique did not erase power differences between me and the participants. After all, I still had a job to do as a researcher, but it did offer, at least at some level, a more engaging way of getting that job done while producing grounded insights into young peoples' lives. Similarly, the use of existing groups did not eliminate power-relations between young people. Their own personalities and relationships remained evident; those who were more vocal and/or confident remained so; and the routes which were selected and followed, as well as the stories told, were in part the outcomes of how participants mediated their relationships with each other as much as through place. The neighbourhoods we walked through are thus the product of a power-laden collective decision-making process that consequently offers some reflexive insight into how groups of young people situate themselves within a neighbourhood social milieu.

Where the mobile focus group diverges from both individual walks and conventional focus group techniques can be seen in the ways in which the walks and narratives come into being. A common concern of static or room-based focus groups is that discussion may shut down opposing perspectives, either through overpowering personalities or the general tenure of debate, that may encourage less vocal or interested individuals to withdraw into reserved contemplation. In contrast, the mobile focus groups enable those not involved directly in discussion to continue to participate, as well as opening up spaces for alternative perspectives to be expressed in more private ways. The walks operated as a series of smaller or subgroups that would drop into and out of conversation as we moved. As one of these subgroups held the conversation with me, others would often be talking to the second researcher, be taking photographs, or deciding among themselves where next to direct the walk. This certainly creates difficulties for creating and recording a linear or chrono-logically coherent 'narrative' for the duration of the walk, and means that not all young people participated in all of the discussions, but these are only slight challenges. As I discuss shortly, this process of 'groups walking in groups' opened up moments when participants offered alternative interpretations and experiences away from the (potentially) charged atmosphere of direct confrontation.

Finally, some of the stories I was told appeared to be rehearsed narratives of seemingly well-known or often repeated tales involving key individuals, loca-tions and events that have become part of the common currency of neighbour-hood life. As the young people offered these stories, they presented knowledge that marked their sense of belonging or not belonging, revealing their status as 'insiders' both to me and to their peers. In doing so, the walks should be con-sidered performances of which participants were also actively aware. In telling these neighbourhood tales participants implied that they were also conscious that they were delivering a particular performance. This was most clear at times when individuals assumed the role of guide, presenting the walk as a series of 'points of interest' interspersed with narrative about why they are worth showing, frequently mimicking the gestures and tones of tourist guides. Others took fuller charge of proceedings by taking hold of the microphones and record-ing devices to engage in mock 'fly-on-the-wall' documentary style reporting, questioning each other as well as passers-by. In doing so they displayed their awareness of a visual and audio-documentary culture. As they have grown up with an environment of 'reality' media and investigative journalism, the mobile focus groups with their accompanying equipment did not appear overly strange or out of place to them. Notably, this cultural familiarity enabled some to more fully embrace the method than perhaps they would other, formal modes of data collection. It also indicates that they were reflexively aware that they were performing particular roles in a constructed interaction that was creating particular realities.

From Representing to Producing Neighbourhoods

Reflexive consideration of the active or productive capabilities of the method requires appreciation of the 'social life' of the walks (Law, 2004). The interactive qualities of the mobile focus group allows for collective insight to emerge through negotiation. In this way, the neighbourhoods I was presented with are the products of the method rather than any 'naturally occurring' phenomena and I now consider productive properties of first, talking and then, walking in this process.

The importance of talk became most apparent when there was disagreement about where to go or which stories to tell. At times, these differences were due to age, levels of independence, and parental expectations and demands about where young people could and could not go. Of course, and as we might expect, they were also due to differences in experience. In a midlands city young people debated how their neighbourhood might be perceived by non-residents:

RESEARCHER: And what's [place] like?
PARTICIPANT 1: It's alright.
PARTICIPANT 2: I think it's a dump.
PARTICIPANT 3: You do get people with knives and stuff and you do get fights. And drugs.
PARTICIPANT 2: It's a dump. Everyone says it's a dump.
PARTICIPANT 3: … You do get gangs and stuff and people hanging around.
PARTICIPANT 1: It's alright but after about nine o'clock you have to stay off the streets.

(Walk in Staffordshire town)

This interaction neatly reveals how the method provides opportunity for participants to question and clarify, as well as influence other opinion, through a reframing of experiences (Kitzinger, 1994). As Participant 1 re-appraises his views in response to being challenged, we see how participants questioned and clarified their views and reframed their experiences. A second, more troubling, example of the productive capacity of the approach emerged during a walk in a large northern city. This walk took place around a large central housing estate undergoing considerable physical regeneration. Many the properties were vacant, abandoned and boarded up, with the remaining residents (which included some participants and their families) in the process of being relocated. During the walk some participants expressed an awareness of local tensions and anxieties:

RESEARCHER: What do people think about kids round here?

PARTICIPANT 1: The elderly don't like the noise. Some of the kids are quite loud at night so the elderly do reports about noise at night [for the police]. Some adults if they hear a ball bounce on the street they come out and moan at the kids. But at the end of the day, kids will be kids, and that's more or less it, isn't it? Kids need somewhere to play. All they've got round here, when the youth groups aren't on, you've got the primary school when it's open, you've got a little five-a-side-football pitch. You've got a park, but no-one really goes in the park because it's not that good.

RESEARCHER: Why's that?

PARTICIPANT 2: Basically, we've heard that people got raped here at night time, so people get scared of going through it, but in day time it's a normal park, people go through it. It's a good place to go for chillin' [relaxing] but at night you've got to be careful because it's dangerous.

PARTICIPANT 1: Alcoholics and that.

PARTICIPANT 2: Yeah. So like, when we come home, everyone has to walk past here to come home, so [adults] tell us to, come home in like a group of people or with like two at least, so that nothing happens to us.

PARTICIPANT 1: Nothing bad's really happened here, not that we know of …

PARTICIPANT 3: And there's lots of er, like … crazy people who live round here.

PARTICIPANT 1: They're always drinking. Drinking and smoking [cannabis].

(Walk in Greater Manchester)

There is much of interest in this extract about how young people navigate and make sense of local spaces, from issues of intergenerational tension, to belonging and safety, and the workings of a localised moral panic stemming from the sorts of people who might live locally. Of relevance for my discussion here though is how interaction prompted an alternative perspective to be offered. Following this episode, the majority of the group moved away to photograph and discuss where else they could take me. As I made my way towards where the main group was waiting, one participant lingered behind for an opportunity to contribute her own perspective on the streets we were walking through:

PARTICIPANT: It was a bit awkward growing up 'cos like I was the only black kid here. And everybody used to pick on me. I had friends but they were over that side [in another part of the estate].… Round here is more of a white-based community. It is mainly white. Like you don't see many black people. And some white people, especially the older generation, they still haven't got in contact with like other ethnic people. And so some of them are still like that.… I don't like how they are, because they can be drunk at times. And like they can talk to you and like say stuff to you. Like nasty stuff. Racist stuff.… There was more like Asian and black people over there and more white people over here so you couldn't like merge. You felt it a bit hard. We didn't like interact with each other … we didn't really mix with the others that were here, we sort of went like we won't associate with them…. Our area is more like a black area, it's like more African and round here basically it's the dominance of white people. It's like territory. We didn't really, we rarely went, on the other side [of the estate].

RESEARCHER: Why was that?

PARTICIPANT: Because of racial issues. And because it was white people.

(Walk in Greater Manchester)

Such experiences resonate with the politics and morality of community (Back, 2009), and as well provide a stark reminder of everyday racism and discrimination. Emerging here then, is a very different, more sinister perspective that stands at odds to the more popular view offered by the bulk of the wider (all white) group. This participant offered away from the main group, but in direct response to what had been articulated moments earlier. It may be possible to obtain such views in static focus groups, and of course they emerge frequently in one-to-one interviews, but I contend that the method itself works to enable this perspective to emerge so quickly, and so starkly. The dynamic and fluid nature of the method thus provides opportunity for participants to respond indirectly but just as forcibly about alternative experiences. That this discussion took place outside the boarded-up properties where the protagonists in these narratives lived, in the very setting that gave rise to these experiences, also adds further weight to the claims made for situating data collection in the locations that give rise to the phenomena under consideration.

Moving beyond talk to attend to the importance of walking, I now consider the ways in which the neighbourhoods are produced through movement along, and creation of, routes and pathways (Degan and Rose, 2012; Ingold, 2007; Pink, 2008b). Walking is another way in which neighbourhoods vary for different individuals. The pace, gestures, gait and physical effort that, when done by several individuals over time, or by individuals in groups, generates a particular (walking) rhythm of the neighbourhood (Vergunst, 2010). The result are experiences and forms of place that are created by the practice of walking. On a different research project I am engaging in walking interviews with people living with dementia.[2] Although with individuals rather than groups, those walks follow a similar process to that detailed here in so far as people with dementia are asked to lead a walk around the neighbourhood where they live. In doing so, they point out the range of activities and features of neighbourhood life they find supportive and less supportive as they live with the condition. Relevant here are the differences in the pace of movement and the distances travelled. Although mindful of stereotyping or stretching the limits of generalisability, walking with people who are living with dementia, who are older, and at times physically less able, is at a more hesitant, stuttering and slower rate of progress compared to the group-walks with young people. As a result, the neighbourhood experiences that emerge differ in form and process. This is not simply because, at an empirical level, we are unable to walk far and as a result see less when accompanying people living with dementia, but because movement produces an experientially and sensorially different type of place. Older people living with dementia may thus exist in the same physical and material space as others, but they live in very different places in part because those places are produced through different rhythms of walking (Degan and Rose, 2012; Vergunst, 2010). Learning to walk together thus requires me to abandon my own rhythm and fall into step with these different neighbourhood rhythms through which people actively make their neighbourhood places.

De Certeau (1984) argued that walking is central to place-making, in part due to a walker's contact and interaction with other walkers, as well as through the embodied production and maintenance of routes. Walking also enables the appropriation of spaces through the tactical resistance of the less powerful to hegemonic strategies (in de Certeau's case, urban planners and architects). So, walking with young people offers a glimpse of how they engage in such resistance in the making of their own localised worlds. As I have noted, moving around, at times at pace rushing from one place to the next, other times more lazily, meandering in a seemingly haphazard way to spend time interacting with or avoiding others are all ways in which young people make sense of, but also shape, their neighbourhoods.

The constructivist properties of the mobile focus group enable neighbourhoods to be actualised not just in front of our eyes, but also at our feet. These neighbourhoods exist as a form of 'collateral reality' (Law, 2012). Such realities are not those that are explicitly described in the verbal exchanges that I have reported earlier and are relatively easy to hear and report on. Rather, collateral realities are those 'versions of the social that are being done quietly, incidentally, and along the way' (Law, 2012: 165). It is a glimpse into the making of these realities that, I think, differentiates mobile focus groups from static methods. The collateral realities being done by walking the neighbourhood emerge from the interplay of the conversation between environment, participants and researcher, and participants and each other, all enacted while moving along, and so remaking, habitual and familiar (as well as uncommon and strange) routes. Recalling discussion of 'doing' boredom, even this implies a restlessness that requires attention to be paid to movement: from the unremarked upon fragmented movements of fidgeting to keep warm, to the purposeful movement between locations in search of company or amusement, to the ambling around familiar places as a way of passing the time. All these movements are part of the way that neighbourhoods 'come into being' (O'Neill and Hubbard, 2010) as collective constructions, experienced at pace, multi-sensed, re-told and re-negotiated on the move.

Given that neighbourhoods are constantly being reshaped in this way, then we need research encounters that can access these fluid experiences. The neighbourhoods that emerge from the mobile focus groups may thus be the product of the method, but they are more than a methodological construct. For if young people produce neighbourhood experiences through movement and interaction, then the focus group method is not too far removed from that same process. The method should thus be considered as more than an artificially imposed attempt to obtain the empirical measures of neighbourhood life. Rather, it is a way of accessing those practices that are already producing grounded experiences

Conclusion

This chapter has outlined the possibilities for a mobile focus group method to understand young people's experiences of neighbourhood change. In common with other mobile methods, the focus groups have the potential to gain insight into grounded realities of everyday life in neighbourhoods undergoing transition, including the embodied and sensorial practices that go into the production of such places. While the chapter has presented discussion of the opportunities and challenges of the method, it should be considered as more than just another useful tool for gathering perspectives on locally lived experiences. Walking together enables a grounded insight into the histories, experiences, interactions and movements that collectively produce neighbourhood places. Paying attention to the movement, as well as the talk, that comprise the method reveals how neighbourhood life is experienced on the move. So the mobile focus group method allows for the pace of this activity to be experienced firsthand. Although the routes we follow are methodological constructs, the practices that produce them are very much part of young people's repertoire of neighbourhood life.

   Regardless of the social and economic difficulties that made up their environments, the stories young people told me are not pessimistic. They were just as proud to show us around where they live as they were to lament what could make life better for them. More than this, I was offered a glimpse of the collective acts of resistance of how young people come to negotiate and actively contest other (adult) narratives. As such, the method provides grounded insight into how people experience place, as well as the nuanced ways in which they are produced through movement.

Notes

1 This was an evaluation for Groundwork UK. The evaluation team consisted of Samantha Wright, Neal Hazel, Andrew Clark, Lindsay McAteer, Judith Renshaw and Mark Liddle. Thanks especially to Lindsay McAteer for accompanying me on many of the walks that informed this discussion. The views and ideas expressed in this chapter are my own and not necessarily those of the funders or wider evaluation team.
2 This project is being conducted with Richard Ward, Sarah Campbell, John Keady and Agneta Kullburg as part of the ESRC/NIHR-funded Neighbourhoods and Dementia research programme. John Keady is the Principal Investigator. More information is available at www.neighbourhoodsanddementia.org.

References

Anderson, Jon. 2004. 'Talking whilst walking: a geographical archaeology of knowledge.' *Area*, 36(3): 245–261.

Anderson, Jon and Kate Jones. 2009. 'The difference that place makes to methodology: uncovering the 'lived space' of young people's spatial practices.' *Children's Geographies*, 7(3): 291–303.

Back, Les. 2009. 'Researching community and its moral projects.' *21st Century Society: Journal of the Academy of Social Sciences*, 4(2): 201–214.

Back, Les. 2012. 'Live sociology: social research and its futures.' In *Live Methods*, edited by Les Back and Nirmal Puwar, 18–39. Sociological Review Monograph Series. Malden, MA: Wiley Blackwell.

Bagnoli, Anna and Andrew Clark. 2010. 'Focus groups with young people: a participatory approach to research planning.' *Journal of Youth Studies*, 13(1): 101–119.

Barker, John and Susie Weller. 2003. ' "Is it fun?": Developing children centred research methods.' *International Journal of Sociology and Social Policy*, 23(1/2): 33–58.

Brown, Donna. 2013. 'Young people, anti-social behaviour and public space: the role of community wardens in policing the "ASBO generation".' *Urban Studies*, 50(3): 538–555.

Büscher, Monika and John Urry. 2009. 'Mobile methods and the empirical.' *European Journal of Social Theory*, 12(1): 99–116.

Caretta, Martina and Elena Vacchelli. 2015. 'Re-thinking the boundaries of the focus group: a reflexive analysis on the use and legitimacy of group methodologies in qualitative research.' *Sociological Research Online*, 20(4). Accessed 22 April 2016, www.socresonline.org.uk/20/4/13.html.

Carpiano, Richard. 2009. 'Come take a walk with me: the "go-along" interview as a novel method for studying the implications of place for health and well-being.' *Health and Place*, 15: 263–272.

de Certeau, Michel. 1984. *The Practice of Everyday Life*. Translated by Steven Rendall. Berkeley: University of California Press.

Clark, Andrew and Nick Emmel. 2010. *Using Walking Interviews*, RealitiesToolkit #13. Manchester: ESRC National Centre for Research Methods. Accessed 22 April 2016, http://eprints.ncrm.ac.uk/1323/1/13-toolkit-walking-interviews.pdf.

Clark, Tom. 2008. ' "We're over-researched here!": exploring accounts of research fatigue within qualitative research engagements.' *Sociology*, 42(5): 953–970.

Degan, Monica and Gillian Rose. 2012. 'The sensory experiencing of urban design: the role of walking and perceptual memory.' *Urban Studies*, 49(5): 3271–3287.

Deuchar, Ross. 2009. *Gangs, Marginalised Youth and Social Capital*. London: Trentham Books.

Evans, James and Phil Jones. 2011. 'The walking interview: methodology, mobility and place.' *Applied Geography*, 31: 849–858.

Fincham, Ben, Mark McGuinness and Lesley Murray Editors 2010 *Mobile Methodologies*. Basingstoke: Palgrave Macmillan.

Fink, Janet. 2012. 'Walking the neighbourhood, seeing the small details of community life: reflections from a photography walking tour.' *Critical Social Policy*, 32(1): 31–50.

Goodwin, Susan and Alexandra Young. 2013. 'Ensuring children and young people have a voice in neighbourhood community development.' *Australian Social Work*, 66(3): 344–357.

Greene, Stuart, Kevin Burke and Maria McKenna. 2016. 'When words fail, art speaks: learning to listen to youth stories in a community photovoice project.' In *Youth Voices, Public Spaces, and Civic Engagement*, edited by Stuart Greene, Kevin Burke and Maria McKenna, 235–258. New York: Routledge.

Hall, Tom, Brett Lashua and Amanda Coffey. 2006. 'Stories and sorties.' *Qualitative Researcher*, 3(3): 2–4.

Hogan, Sarah. 2009. 'Images of Broomhall, Sheffield: urban violence, and using the arts as a research aid.' *Visual Anthropology*, 24(3): 266–280.

Ingold, Tim. 2007. *Lines: A Brief History.* London: Routledge.

Kitzinger, Jenny. 1994. 'The methodology of focus groups: the importance of interaction between research participants.' *Sociology of Health and Illness*, 16(1): 103–121.

Kusenbach, Margarethe. 2003. 'Street phenomenology: the go-along as ethnographic research tool.' *Ethnography*, 4: 455–485.

Kusenbach, Margarethe. 2012. 'Mobile methods.' In *Handbook of Qualitative Research in Education*, edited by Sarah Delamont, 252–264. Cheltenham: Elgar.

Law, John. 2004. *After Method: Mess in Social Science Research.* London: Routledge.

Law, John. 2012. 'Collateral realities.' In *The Politics of Knowledge*, edited by Patrick Baert and Fernando Rubio, 156–178. Oxford: Routledge.

Law, John and John Urry. 2004. 'Enacting the social.' *Economy and Society*, 33: 390–410.

Lawson, Louise and Ade Kearns. 2016. 'Power to the (young) people? Children and young people's empowerment in the relocation process associated with urban re-structuring.' *International Journal of Housing Policy*. Accessed 22 April 2016, doi:10.1080/14616718.2016.1143788.

Lee, Jo and Tim Ingold. 2006. 'Fieldwork on foot: perceiving, routing, socializing.' In *Locating the Field: Space, Place and Context in Anthropology*, edited by Simon Coleman and Peter Collins, 67–86. Oxford: Berg.

Lewis, Gail. 1985. 'From deepest Kilburn.' In *Truth, Dare, Promise: Girls Growing Up in the Fifties*, edited by Liz Heron, 213–236. London: Virago.

MacDonald, Rob, Tracy Shildrick, Colin Webster and Donald Simpson. 2005. 'Growing up in poor neighbourhoods: the significance of class and place in the extended trans-itions of "socially excluded" young adults.' *Sociology*, 39(5): 873–891.

Moles, Kate. 2008. 'A walk in thirdspace: place, methods and walking.' *Sociological Review Online*, 13(4). Accessed 22 April 2016, www.socresonline.org.uk/13/4/2.html.

Neary, Joanne. 2015. *Changing Contexts: Young People's Experiences of Growing up in Regeneration Areas of Glasgow.* PhD dissertation, University of Glasgow.

Neary, Joanne, Matt Egan, Peter Keenan, Louise Lawson and Lyndal Bond. 2013. 'Damned if they do, damned if they don't: negotiating the tricky context of anti-social behaviour and keeping safe in disadvantaged urban neighbourhoods.' *Journal of Youth Studies*, 16(1): 118–134.

O'Neill, Maggie and Phil Hubbard. 2010. 'Walking, sensing, belonging: ethno-mimesis as performative praxis.' *Visual Studies*, 25(1): 46–58.

Pickering, Jonny, Keither Kintrea and Jon Bannister. 2012. 'Invisible walls and visible youth: territoriality among young people in British cities.' *Urban Studies*, 49(5): 945–960.

Pink, Sarah. 2008a. 'Walking with video.' *Visual Studies*, 22(3): 240–252.

Pink, Sarah. 2008b. 'An urban tour: the sensory sociality of ethnographic place-making.' *Ethnography*, 9: 175–196.

Rogaly, Ben and Becky Taylor. 2009. *Moving Histories of Class and Community: Identity, Place and Belonging in Contemporary England*. Basingstoke: Palgrave Macmillan.

Skelton, Tracey and Katherine Gough. 2013. 'Introduction: young people's im/mobile urban geographies.' *Urban Studies*, 50(3): 455–466

Tuan, Yi-fu. 1977. *Space and Place: The Perspective of Experience*. Minneapolis: University of Minnesota Press.

Watt, Paul. 2013. '"It's not for us": regeneration, the 2012 Olympics and the gentrification of East London.' *City*, 17(1): 99–118.

Vergunst, Lee. 2010. 'Rhythms of walking: history and presence in a city street.' *Space and Culture*, 13(4): 376–388.

Westfield Stratford City, 2016.
Source: Alex Rhys-Taylor.

6 Westfield Stratford City

A Walk Through Millennial Urbanism

Alex Rhys-Taylor

> I first started visiting the shopping centre in 2012, months after it opened, when I became a father. After several years of internet shopping I found myself needing to see, and touch, the cots, buggies, and clothes I was buying. I also, at times, needed to get out of the house more than I had been. London's creaking retail heart – Oxford Street – is twenty-five minutes in the wrong direction and hardly worth the effort. The newly opened Westfield Stratford City shopping centre seemed a logical destination.
>
> On its way to the new mega-mall, the train trundles through a post-industrial landscape of parks and housing, punctured with dual carriageways and rail lines. The train slows as it approaches London's Olympic park: the stadia, Zaha Hadid's otherworldly swimming centre, Anish Kapoor's twisted metal tower and several blocks of newly laminated housing. It stops right beside the windowless grey cuboid of Westfield; all the greyer for the towering storm clouds out of which rain has just started to pour. I step out. The train carries on to the city's satellites.
>
> Over the canyon between train and platform, into a metallic urea-tinged lift. Out of the lift, the pedestrians flow through a tiled subterranean underpass and toward escalators that rise into the ticket hall of the mall's dedicated train station. Three police officers keep an eye on the bodies passing through the barriers.
>
> Out of the ticket hall and into the mall's entry colonnade, filled with a fog of burning tobacco and butterscotch e-cig vapour. Through the mist, past a further police officer and a private security guard, toward the automated entry doors which swing open as I approach them.

On 6 July 2005, to the surprise of many involved in the bid, London won the right to host the 2012 Olympic games. Despite revelations of skulduggery surrounding subsequent Olympic bids, it *appears* that London won that privilege fairly, on the promise of the 'legacy' that the sporting events would leave. As abstract as 'legacy' was at the time of the bid, it eventually took concrete manifestations in the form of a large municipal swimming pool, assorted stadia and a park. Less charitable evaluations of the legacy might also point to the lost industrial space, bulldozed allotments (Norman 2014a), the demolition of buildings previously incubating London's creative industries (Pappalepore 2016), and the displacement of social housing residents (Cheyne and Baxter 2008). All of which combined to catalyse the erection of numerous clusters of barely afford-able Ballardian high-rise residences around the Olympic park.

Although it had already been in the planning prior to the Olympics, by far the most frequented 'legacy building', is the retail environment that 'London 2012's' ticket-holders were channelled through on their way to the stadia. Westfield Stratford City is a 'mega-mall' in Stratford, part of the east London borough of Newham. Covering 1,905,542 square feet, the Westfield site encom-passes 70 bars and restaurants, a 17-screen cinema, bowling lanes, a gym, a casino, 3 hotels, 1,000 student flats, luxury office space and, most importantly, 250 shops. It is nothing short of a colossal cathedral of desire, consumption and pleasure.

The above is clearly not the first sentence to have compared a shopping mall to a cathedral. Carl Gardner and Julie Sheppard might not even have been the first when they formally coined the cliché in their landmark essay 'The New Cathedral: The Rise and Rise of the Shopping Centre' (Chapter 5 in Gardner and Sheppard 2012). Since then, the comparison has become hackneyed at best, readily deployed as a compact critique of consumer culture's hold over the morality, imagination, fears and aspirations of twenty-first-century cities and citizens. As tired as the analogy might seem there are, however, many similarities between cathedrals and malls. The most notable of these compari-sons are structural. Half a century before Gardener and Sheppard, Walter Ben-jamin had already noted modernity's mimesis of religious architecture in his pedestrian reflections on the public buildings and shopping arcades of the nine-teenth century (Benjamin and Tiedemann 1999: 152, 406, 541), particularly their use of glass and light, and the awe-inducing height of their ceilings. Today's multi-level shopping malls make even greater use of vertical space, large windows and cavernous acoustics. Manchester's Trafford Centre (the largest mall in the UK) even sports a giant cloudy renaissance-style fresco across its vast ceiling. It is also notable that today's malls regularly rely upon the cruciform layout commonly associated with churches (Langrehr 1991: 428; Buxton 2015: 35).

The most interesting comparisons between mega-mall and cathedral, however, lie in a more focussed consideration of the ways in which their patrons' bodies interact with the space. Consider the placement of the altar at the end of an atrium, pews either side of the nave, the choir, the organ, the pulpit, the alignment of windows and the congregation, for instance. The arrangement of these elements in the church serve to 'emplace' the body, subtly informing each individual who they are, how they should behave and where they belong. As I will discuss for the remainder of this chapter, this is also, in many ways, the case for the mega-mall. Like the cathedral, the specific arrangement of sights, sounds, smells and textures in the twenty-first century mega-mall emplace the user within a particular vision of society, history and culture (Goss 1993). Like the cathedral, this 'emplacement' is achieved not through standing, staring and contemplating. Rather, the affective qualities of the mall work best on the kinaesthetic body, through the act of moving, be it rolling, shuffling or walking, through the mall.

Perspective and Expertise

> Through the automatic doors into the yellowy white light of Westfield's ground floor atrium. A broad desk with a smartly dressed concierge who greets me as I approach. 'Good morning.' Beside the entry desk, the first kiosk, a florist.

In the case of the 'text' of the mega-mall, there are a broad range of expert readings, many of which have been used to forecast the future of cities in the new millennium (Langrehr 1991; Back 1997; Abaza 2001; Tyndall 2010; Minton 2012a). Some of these readings have been notably optimistic and affirmative. In the mid-century honeymoon period of the shopping centre, architectural historian, Reyner Banham, noted that "some of the best 'civic design' […] in the Los Angeles area is to be found in shopping centres […] the natural foci of a highly mobile population" (Banham 2009: 153–154). Another architectural historian Margaret Crawford has also been a vocal celebrant of the synthetic environs of late twentieth-century shopping centres (Crawford in Sorkin 1992).

If Banham and Crawford read a bright future in the development of the shopping centre, many other "truth sayers of the mall" (Kroker *et al.* 1989: 209) saw the late millennial shopping centre to be less auspicious (Davis 2006; Goss 1993; Kroker *et al.* 1989). We find a particularly influential, critical reading of mall-urbanism in Mike Davis's (2006) deconstruction of South Central Los Angeles: *City of Quartz.* Therein, as Davis had it, far from being designed to serve any civic duty, shopping malls were proposed as a simple, security-focussed, profit-driven solution to the scorched asphalt left in the wake of the city's race riots. Fitted with central security towers, wrought iron fences, substations of the LAPD, video cameras and motion detectors, such developments were seen as a win/win for both the municipality and property speculators. Davis, perhaps needless to say, saw all of this as a loss for any broader sense of spatial justice and dignity in the city (Davis 2006: 242–243). In 2011 an analogous reading of London's new mega-malls was undertaken by Anna Minton, whose book *Ground Control* is very much twenty-first-century London's equivalent of Mike Davis's pre-millennial overview of Los Angeles. Moving through shopping centres in post-industrial British cities, Minton traces the return of the 'shopping centre' from its 1980s suburban haunts, directly back into the urban core. Therein, Minton argues, the 'privatised' and 'securitised' realm of the US-inspired suburban mall is now replacing the remainder of urban Britain's 'public space' (Minton 2012). To qualify her point, Minton 'visits' the Westfield Group's older west-London-based shopping mall, Minton noting "lots and lots of shops, and pristine marble floors, but little to distinguish this place from any other or to remind me that I was in West London" (ibid.). Minton follows this trip up with a visit to the building site of the yet to be opened Westfield in Stratford, east London. Or rather, she views the building site and its "matchstick figures of construction workers" from the heights of a neighbouring tower block. Elevated above "the local, the body, the streetscape, pyschogeographies of intimacy, erotic subjectivities and the microworlds of everyday life" (Soja in Westwood and Williams 2003: 21) Minton claimed to see the bigger picture: the substitution of public spaces, public life and local culture, with place-less, culture-less, securitised opportunities for atomised consumption. Walking through the tea-leaves of Britain's new retail environments, Minton, like Mike Davis 20 years previously, reads off a future of increasing control, oppression, debt and disenfranchisement, ameliorated with ever-more opportunities for private consumption. What is particularly striking about both Minton's and Davis's readings of these spaces is the extent to which the critical tour of the shopping mall is conducted from a position of distant unfamiliarity, yet executed with certainty.

There are, *of course*, important truths to be garnered from such expert readings. There is no sense, however, in either of the aforementioned expert readings of malls, of how the intended users actually make sense of their environs. There is no account as to whether the mall's technologies work or fail, nor any sense of how the mall is actually experienced. Not that such accounts are to be expected. As cultural critic Richard Hoggart said once of middle-class Marxist accounts of the everyday lives of 'the masses', there is an enduring tendency to "pity the betrayed and debased worker, whose fault he sees as almost entirely the result of the grinding system which controls him, [...] part pitying and part patronizing them beyond any semblance of reality" (Hoggart 2009). This comes, as Hoggart goes on to argue, at the expense of "moving beyond habits" to an understanding of what "habits really stand for", of moving "beyond statements" to an understanding of what "statements really mean" (ibid.).

Local Experts

> Past the concierge desk and another security guard, the sheltered warm entrance area opens up onto two bright broad aisles cutting right through the length of the mall to a vanishing point in the distance. The aisles are separated by a series of kiosks selling high street staples. Belts, wallets, phone cases, body jewellery, cookies and ice cream. Either side of the aisles are a series of familiar retailers. A popular high street chemist, an international coffee franchise, a national newsagents chain, another coffee franchise, a high-street bakery, a couple of high-street banks, a betting shop, a mobile phone shop and a national optometry franchise. Familiar as they might be, each seems to be a slightly more polished version of their high street equivalent. More blue LEDs. More chrome. More exciting.

In Hoggart's work, the literary-critic-turned-cultural-theorist argued for a greater understanding of working-class culture and sociality, based not on meta-theoretical deductions, but rather on the experiences of those living behind the doors of Britain's terraced streets. Taking Hoggart's lead, it might be argued that a better understanding of the purported 'death of the city', would be gained from a closer attention to uses, and experiences, of the shopping centre. There are, of course, a range of methodological options for any researcher wishing to gauge the experience and uses of any given space. These range from questionnaires and interviews to observation-focused tracking studies. Questionnaires, however, are famously impervious to the nuances of behaviour and the idiosyncratic meaning. Post-hoc interviews, on the other hand, are notoriously unreliable methods for ascertaining detailed accounts, with significant episodes often missing from recall (Brown 1991, 1992). Brown (1992) argues that the response to such pitfalls, with regards to 'shopping mall research', lies in covert movement tracking. While such methods are sensitive to each and every movement of shoppers, like questionnaires they lack any account of the specific meaning or reason given to each action. More significantly, they are beset with a barrage of 'ethical' prohibitions on covert research (an irony given the surveillance that characterises retail spaces).

Some of these shortcomings can be partially addressed through Margarethe Kusenbach's (2003) sketch of a "street phenomenology" that taps into meaningful experience through 'go-alongs' or 'walkalongs' (Pink 2008; Clark and Emmel 2010; Degen *et al*. 2010). The mobile interview has in fact found a particular utility in the study of retail environments. For instance, a recent study by Jacqueline Kennelly and Paul Watt explicitly deployed walk-alongs to look at the ways in which a group of young people, all of whom came from temporary housing near Westfield, 'made sense' of their exclusion from the mall (Kennelly and Watt 2012; Watt 2013). While such readings are invaluable in terms of unpicking the significance of the mall for a particularly vulnerable constituency, they only offer a partial understanding of what the space is and does. There are, needless to say, many other constituencies of mall user, as well as different researchers, between whom walk-and-talks would lead to different readings again. In his study of a mall in Buenos Aries, for instance, Jacob Miller records a baby-sitter-ballerina remarking that the mall is "like a little piece of heaven in the middle of, I don't know what, a crazy place" (Miller 2015). Miller's mall-walker echoes others who have contrasted the "heaven" of the mall to the historically masculine public sphere of the high street (Valentine 1989). Another likely reading, not dissimilar to the aforementioned critics, might arise from bourgeois avoiders of the mall, perturbed by the distinction-blurring luxuries it affords the masses. Suffice to say that different biographies lead to radically different experiences of the space. And so too do different bodies. Mobility scooter and wheelchair users for instance, who are visibly drawn in numbers to the mall by its 'shopmobility' inspired 'roll-on-roll-off' design, *might* have a more positive reading of the space (Gant 2002; Gant and Smith 1998). Partially sighted individuals, on the other hand, might be perturbed by the mall's abundant use of reflective low contrast colour palettes and twinkly lights (Bright *et al*. 1999). Similarly, the sonically sensitive are likely find significant 'acoustic discomfort' (Yang and Kang 2005) in the reverberant background noise generated by the aforementioned tiles (Chen and Kang 2004). While idiosyncratic on their own, taken together, such readings say more about the role of the shopping mall, than the distant view of any expert.

This is not, however, to shun the role of critical experts in reading the deep structures of such epoch-defining spaces. Nor to suggest that 'the people' are somehow experts of their own environment, let alone the structures that lie beneath it (Duneier *et al.* 2001; Back 2007; Burawoy 2013). Moreover, even the thick data garnered through 'walk-alongs' is often littered with significant absences. Perhaps most significant in the case of the mall is the absence of conscious reflection on affects that were experienced at the level of the body but which never *quite* reached emotional awareness, let alone discursive consciousness. The inaccessibility of data on these spheres of experiences is particularly worrying in the case of the shopping mall if we acknowledge that the "sensual logic of late capitalism" (Howes 2005) involves explicit efforts to exploit the "involuntary vulnerabilities" of the "other senses" for the purposes of increasing profit (Healy 2008).

As such there is a clear need for spatial analyses that emerge from somewhere in between the perspective of critical experts – fluent in design and political economy – and the pot-holed user-generated analyses of the space. And here, I offer myself: an everyday user of the city who would rather not have to use it everyday. A "default man" (Perry 2014) who enjoys the hedonic experience of luxury consumerism, but who is aware of the profit his amusement brings others. A professional urbanist and specialist in the sensory ambiences of public space (Rhys-Taylor 2013a, 2013b) who also routinely uses the city's 'public spaces'. It is from this position that I want to present you the remainder of this walk-along.

Simulations of Place?

> It's 12.00 now, and there are two dense flows of pedestrians moving up and down on either side of the nave. Mothers with pushchairs, several walking in pairs that require conscious effort to side step. Young couples pulling each other one way or another. Large families. Dads doing the one handed pram push. A familiar face that I can't place. Four carers in head scarfs giggling as they heave wheelchairs laden with a group of portly West Ham supporters. Beards. Tunics. Pyjama suits. Niqabs. Sweaters screen-printed with Japanese signage. At least 60% in jeans. A few suits. Some startlingly flashy loafers. A handful of track suits. And so far, no fewer than 8 mobility scooters.

One of the particularly striking things about Westfield's east London site is its subtle differences with Westfield group's west London site. Far from speaking of the 'non-place-ness' of the shopping centre (Augé 1995; Minton 2012a), some of these differences genuinely help distinguish the mall from any other in the city, and the world; albeit faintly. The least effectual of these distinctions arise out of half-hearted attempts to dissimulate a 'sense of place' amidst a mixture of global brands, glass and polished floors. These include the 'Great Eastern Market', a high-end pastiche of east London's residual community of barrow boys. Only here scented candles and artisan chocolates replace the West African style fabrics, saris, knock-off trainers, rugs and jellied eels typical of the old markets. Synthesised versions of 'place' are also encountered when the walker strolls off the main thoroughfare into one of the darkened 'chill out' areas around the lifts. Each of these is kitted out with coin-operated massage chairs and hydraulic children's rides, both typical of non-places. Some of the alcoves, however, have the added flourish of carefully hung photography memorialising the locale's history with pictures of its canals and iconic Georgian and Victorian architecture. Again, like the ersatz market place, stylised photos of the 'real world' outside are not fooling anybody. They fail, in part, because, unlike Baudrillard's Disneyland (a fiction that successfully masked the actual "death of the real" outside) (Baudrillard 1983), it is well-known to the mall's visitors that the mythical old East End, memorialised by the photography and the market barrow, is long dead. That is if it ever really was alive.

For all the 'death of the real' signified by the simulations of London in the mall, a sense of place *is*, however, still tangible within its panelled walls. This sense of place derives not, however, from the effort of the mall's interior designers. Rather, the strongest sense of place experienced in the mall emerges out of the river of faces, sartorial styles and cadences that move past the walker as they enter it. It is worth noting here that Westfield Stratford City, the Westfield group's second London site, is located in Newham, the eighteenth most diverse of London wards. The area has a population claiming to be 43 per cent English born, followed by notable Bengali, Ghanaian, Indian, Nigerian and Pakistani constituents (ONS 2012). In contrast to the group's west London site, 'White City' (located in the 175th most diverse ward with 14 per cent in top managerial positions), Stratford City has 7.2 per cent in management and three times as many residents working in elementary occupations. Taking the two Westfield malls – both archetypal non-places – as an example, the differences are subtle, but unmistakeable to anybody attuned to the acuity of class and cultural distinctions carried by the bodies of Londoners.

The Essence of Local Culture

Further into the mall. Another security guard passes me with what looks like a sniffer dog. Our eyes meet as he approaches. He is the first to pay me obvious attention. Maybe he's seen me making verbal notes into my smartphone. His dog seems uninterested. He walks by. Shuffling through the mass of bodies, my walk takes me past the ground floor 'food hall', a large central seating area set to the left of the main aisle, surrounded on one side by a crescent of international burger, fried chicken and sandwich franchises. The odour that swells out from it is, precisely because of the ubiquity of these fordist food outlets, deeply familiar. There is also an unexpected whiff of faeces – perhaps from a toilet to the side of the seating area. Parents flick thumbs across smart phones while tweens fling French fries and chewed up napkins at one another. A table of young men, maybe local employees, are eating from their own lunch boxes. An elderly South Asian Londoner unwraps her own homemade sandwich from cling film. Cheese and pickle on brown bread.

As well as rendering east London's cultural heritage, and social structure, visible through clothing and bodies, it should be noted that the environment of the shopping mall also renders the area's cultural milieu very faintly smell-able. Of course, it's rude to sniff people. And genuinely dangerous to talk about the way people smell. But our nostrils are unable to close. And our emo-tional responses to smell hard to supress. It is precisely for these reasons that, for many years now, environmental engineers of capitalism have thrown every effort at producing, and controlling, aromatic atmospheres conducive to con-sumption (Baron 1997; Chebat and Michon 2003; Davies *et al.* 2003; Michon *et al.* 2005). To be fair to the aerodynamicists of Westfield, they have done a reasonably good job; with very few smells, except those deliberately placed there, actually lingering amidst its remarkable array of ducts and fans. Yet these engineers' dreams of mastery remain challenged by two key facts. The first is that shoppers stubbornly bring the odours of their own dwelling and labour practices with them, and carry them through the mall. Each of these traces is inflected by the variety of ingredients, and changes as the day passes. In the morning it's coffee and cigarette breath overlaid with the cosmetic scents that Londoners dress in: coconut oil, talcum powder, shea butter, some tiger balm. Partially reconstructed masculinities of post-industrial cockneys leave trails of vetiver and sandalwood as they lollop to work, while young women cast faint swirls of saccharine body spray, powdery perfumes and fruity scented hair. Towards the middle of the day, the smells shift toward faint hints of the food that shoppers routinely imbibe, cumin, garlic, sesame oil and fried onions. Toward the end of the day, the bodies in the mall also carry very faint olfactory traces of the work shoppers have been doing: sweat, engine oil, chlorine and baby sick. Also clearly discernible around the lower ground floor food hall on this occasion is the smell of shit. The second problem likely to thwart serious efforts to tweak the olfactory atmosphere of the shopping centre lies in the fact that as long as you have people moving through the mall, you have an unpredictably fluid movement of air. As a result of moving bodies, the scent of freshly squeezed orange juice gets relocated to just outside a shoe shop. The trail of rubber and petrol fumes of the car park drifts around the artisan chocolate kiosk. The result, for a sensitive nose at least, is a dizzying amalgam of synthetic, organic, bodily and mechanical aromas. Importantly, in its combination of diverse ingredients, the olfactory essence of the mall is like no other.

In the first instance, the sensory experience of walking through the space is significant because, despite hubristic efforts to engineer the shopping centre, the nose, eyes and ears testify to the recalcitrance of 'actual' embodied lives. The nose in particular, as Jean Baudrillard once remarked, has, as yet, been saved from the "digital metastasis" afflicting both sound and vision (Baudril-lard 2003: 103). As such the nose retains a connection with real bodies that have otherwise become entangled with the seductive simulations of late capit-alism. Beyond loosely anchoring the body in the 'real world', the assortment of smells met by the nose also provide an interesting index of the biographies unfolding within the mall's catchment area. For my nose at least, the mall's smellscape reveals enduring traces of a distinctly local, yet globally inflected, multiculture, a sensory signature of the city's everyday culture, or put otherwise, the 'sensory order', of London (Classen 1990; Geurts 2002; Vannini *et al*. 2011). In this respect, the nose picks up on a very real, and unsynthesisable, sense of 'place'.

The index of local culture, undertaken by *my* nose, offers a hint of the meaningful practices that endure within, and sometimes despite, the shadow of homogenising consumer culture. In thinking about the city's multiculture in relationship to the mall, it is also worth reflecting less on what my nose detects, than what the noses of the mall's other users are doing: in contrast to a visual encounter (mediated through photons) or the auditory encounter (mediated through vibrating air) the act of smelling is, in every respect, a direct physical encounter with another physical entity. In this respect, the sense of smell has a kinship with the senses of touch and taste. Unlike touch, however, which remains a contact between outer surfaces, the act of smelling and tasting entail the breach of the symbolic border between self, and other. Smells and tastes actually enter our body. Olfactory and gustatory disgust are, as a consequence, important mechanisms in policing both the cultural and biological integrity of the body (Rhys-Taylor 2013a). It is for this reason that 'the smelly immigrant' is such a tiringly predictable trope. Importantly at Westfield, however, the trope seems to have little purchase. Even when surrounded by a feint but undeniable fog of shit, there is notably little repulsion on show between shoppers. On the contrary, it is worth noting that each shopper – within the context of the mall at least – appears entirely comfortable inhaling low-level particles of the other.

This quiet, everyday disregard for the boundary of shoppers' own physical bodies speaks volumes of the hospitality that exists between the mall's users. This is remarkable, not least, because of the constant challenges from fascists and nationalistic xenophobes that the East End has faced over the last century (Macklin 2007). With the solidarity from local labour and religous groups, many of these struggles against racist violence were successful and resulted in migrant groups establishing small commercial hubs tailored to specific cultural needs: Bengali butchers in Whitechapel, Somali supermarkets in Stepney, Polish delis in Walthamstowe and Turkish Cypriot Cafes in Hackney. Yet despite the relative intermingling of nominally Bengali, Turkish or Polish neighbourhoods, there remained relatively few spaces in east London where one might encounter a proper cross-section of the area's cultural heritage. Parks, leisure centres, schools and the work place are all likely contenders. However, alongside these classic sites of multicultural conviviality, there is no reason not to also list mega-malls like Westfield Stratford. Therein the differences simply become what Amanda Wise rightfully describes as "part of the wallpaper" (Wise 2010). As unwelcome as the shopping centre might be amongst leftist critics, the "rubbing along" that Sophie Watson noted in London's more loveable street markets is also evident at the mall (Watson 2009).

Notable Absences

> Moving towards the middle section of the ground floor – the belly of the mall –
> the high street food brands have given way to an archipelago of kiosks between
> the main aisles. They are selling hand made cookies, gelato and donuts. The
> familiar high-street shops have also been replaced by an assortment of chil-
> dren's specialists. A toddler's trainer shop, a teddy bear factory, the Lego store,
> a party-goods store and a generic toy store. This cluster orbits around an indoor
> play area. Plastic, knee-height amusement with rounded corners.

At the most basic level, walking through the mall, reading the space and its
users, suggests that despite a century of effort to homogenise both consumers
and spaces of consumption, diversity endures. Importantly within the mall, each
user is quietly interacting with others, at the very least, through a form of culti-
vated indifference. It is the indifferent sociability of such spaces that lead some
to claim "shopping" to be the "last form of public activity" (Chung *et al.* 2001).
Certainly, if we understand 'publicity' as emerging from loose forms of co-
presence, grounded in the technologically and spatially mediated phenomenological encounter with strangers (Amin 2012: 6), the shopping mall *partially* fits
the functional bill of a 'public space'. The fact that the space operates, first and
foremost, as a space of consumption might even be said to facilitate that function, with the role of 'the shopper' acting as a weak solvent for the ethnic and
gendered hierarchies that abound elsewhere.

That the shopping mall only *partially* fills the role of public space, however,
is related to the fact that, as I am sure the reader is keen to point out, there are
still notable groups missing from the millennial retail space. Some of these
absences are entirely voluntary, such as that of London's 'super rich' who generally avoid shopping in public, save to be seen by each other in one of west London's hyper-exclusive boutiques (Atkinson 2015). At the other end of the
socio-economic spectrum there are more predictable absences. For instance,
while they are a regular presence, sat on the ground beneath London's ATMs
and outside minimarkets, there are no beggars, rough sleepers or vagrants in
either of the Westfield Group's London malls. Unlike the super rich, however,
such absences are not produced through self-regulation. On the contrary, as the
work of Hall and Smith (also featured in this volume) demonstrates, the city's
most vulnerable inhabitants routinely gravitate to the same commercial magnets
as the rest of the population (Hall and Smith 2013, 2015). Like their counterparts
in privately policed shopping malls across the world (Pospech 2014), it is the
security staff of Westfield Stratford City that work assiduously to keep "the lamentable sight of homelessness" away (Pospech 2014; Gerrard and Farrugia
2015). The exclusion, of course, seems 'logical' when remembering that the
mall's primary function is not to facilitate a 'public' but to induce consumption.
The glimpses of inequality and despair that rough sleepers present to the eyes
and noses of shoppers, obviously, present a significant obstacle to the guilt-free
embrace of capitalism's logic.

Groups of 'hoodies' (local working-class youths) constitute another predict-able absence from the mall (Kennelly and Watt 2012). I write 'predictable' because, as the reader might recall, the nationwide construction of the 'hoody' as the millennial Britain's folk-devil coincided with the 2005 ban of young men, generally dressed in CCTV-defying hooded sweatshirts, from a suburban shop-ping mall (Hier *et al*. 2011). Assiduously constructed as a folk-devil for over a decade, excluding groups of 'hoodies' provides a relatively straightforward way to address an increasingly ubiquitous, and highly mediated, sense of fear that might otherwise keep potential shoppers on their sofas. The exclusion of large groups of poor young people is also related to concerns about the crime gener-ated by the mall. Despite the banks of cameras and security staff that police the inner-city's new retail palace, the opening of Westfield Stratford saw the post-code in which the mall is located soar to the UK's number one hot-spot for reported crime (York 2013; Wheatstone 2015). Some of these crimes have been notably violent, with several stabbings and a murder taking place, generally around the perimeter of Westfield (Norman 2014b; Al-Othman 2016; Mann 2016). For the main part, however, the majority of these crimes (over 500 per annum) are shoplifting and petty theft (Martin 2013). Clearly, the mall dangles a range of temptations in front of the same hooded "defective and disqualified con-sumers" (Bauman 2011) who in 2011 elevated smash and grab to the level of riot. While there may well be "no such thing as a typical shoplifter" (Bamfield 2012), excluding the seemingly most explicable, and certainly the most vulner-able culprits, goes some way to allaying investors' concerns about Westfield's ability to convert Stratford into somewhere more profitable. Aside from merely displacing and potentially amplifying 'deviant' behaviour, such efforts *inevitably* come at the expense of a more thoroughly inclusive space.

Also notably absent from the mall are a set of 'public characters' whose appeals to the senses of passing pedestrians were once synonymous with Lon-don's erstwhile public spaces: the city's pamphleteers and trestle-table evange-lists. In contrast to London's more anarchic commercial spaces such as Ridley Road, Queens Road or Deptford street markets, at no point on a walk through Westfield Stratford City does anybody offer any possibilities or moral systems other than those fitting with advanced capitalism. No one thrusts a triple-fold invitation to the Kingdom of Heaven into your hand. Nor would the walker encounter any of the city's many table top Imams. In contrast to the city's erst-while retail destinations such as Oxford Street, there are also no Scientologists inviting you inside for a stress test, no Hari Krishna's offering free meals and books, nor megaphone laden Baptists bursting capillaries to save shoppers from sin. Nor are there any of these figure's secular analogues. No socialist paper sellers. No anti-vivisection campaigners. No 'Free Tibet'. The mall, of course, abounds with deliberate messages aimed at the walker. Treat yourself. Shop until you are healed. Be distinguished. Try to fit in. Report suspicious behaviour. People on the ground floor of the mall also interrupt walkers to palm them pam-phlets for new TV packages or mobile phone deals. In each instance, however, all that is being offered are better value versions of the same reality. Within the nave of the mall, capitalist consumerism's monopoly over the real estate of the mind is, ostensibly, unchallenged.

When it first opened in 2011 and early into 2012 the specific restrictions on what could and could not be said at the mall fitted neatly with the quasi-martial-law that engulfed east London around the Olympics (O'Sullivan 2012). For the period leading up to and during the sporting festival any hint of public protest or proselytisation within a wide circumference of the mega-event was suppressed. Since the mega-event ended, however, the Westfield Group has extended the state of exception. Notably in December 2014, when hundreds of people took part in Black Rev's die-in on the lower-ground floor of the Westfield White City shopping centre as part of a global display of solidarity against New York City Police Department, 76 protestors found themselves in a jail cell. It is worth noting that they were charged under the brilliantly catch-all offence of 'public disorder': an instructive irony given the limitations to 'public space' that the protest revealed. If you want you could certainly still buy a Bible, a Quran or a range of subversive literature at the mall. You could also buy protest music and even try on the aesthetic styles of rebellious youth cultures. But you could not use them *in situ*. For the main part, the actual walk through the mall is kept clear of any directives other than that of self-fulfilment through shopping.

If face-to-face encounters are, in any way, important for the development of a genuinely public sphere, the absence of a range of the city's constituents clearly limits the actual extent of the 'public' mediated by the shopping centre. For all of the obvious inclusivity of its main aisle, the maximisation of the mall's intended functions rest on these exclusions. But then what public space, or more general public, is not partially contingent on some sort of exclusion? The history of London's open spaces is a history of dissenters parcelled off to parts of the city wherein they can be ignored or contained. Even London's archetypal public spaces, such as Habermas' coffee houses, depended in part on the exclusion of women, or at best the delimitation of their normative roles (Clery 1991; Cowan 2001). Despite the advances, made in part through institutions such as department stores (Walkowitz 2013), women's presence in a range of 'public' spaces remains enduringly fraught (Valentine 1989). Moreover, when they emerge in locations like China, Egypt and Turkey, locations wherein public space has hitherto been controlled through degrees of gendered, sectarian and state violence oppression, the blurry lines between public and private that come with the mall place it amongst the most potentially radical of spaces (Abaza 2001; Erkip 2003; Houssay-Holzschuch and Teppo 2009; Jewell 2016). All of this to say that, while they are upheld through degrees of exclusion, the Westfield Group's malls are not alone in the selective nature of the 'public' gatherings that they curate. Moreover, the gatherings that they do convene are not as straightforwardly injurious to a healthy social sphere as they might appear.

Invisible Structures

Ahead, in the middle of the mall is a circular white island, about chest height, splashed with bright pink bubble letter words "Positivity. Vitality.

Unwind. Relax. Harmony." The island is surrounded by a circle of seven or eight white leather massage chairs. Each chair is helmed by a woman, also dressed in white. Cleanliness. Godliness.

Two of the women are busy pummelling the upper backs of their clients. One speaks for the rest, offering massages to passers by.

"A massage sir?"

"Oh. God. No. I've got this to carry." I show them my bag. "I need to be out of here soon. Thanks anyway."

"We can look after that. Take a minute for yourself."

"Er. Really. How much?"

"You pay whatever you want."

"Really?" I ache but how am I supposed to calculate the monetary value of human contact?

Beyond the masseuse cluster, a long escalator promises to take me out of the melee, to the 'next level'. I hurry towards it.

Any quasi-publicness ascribed to the mall rests on understanding public space as being grounded in pedestrian encounters with 'others'. There are, of course, many other ways of defining 'public space' that might cast the mall in an even less democratic light. Rather, for instance, than looking at who is actually using the mall, how they are using it and whom they are meeting, the political economist of public space might, instead, point to the regimes of ownership, expropriation and formal rights to participation that characterise shopping malls (Davis 2006: 240–244; Harvey 2006: 101; Minton 2012a: 15–36). More specifically, they would point to the fact that the land on which the shopping mall sits has, more often than not, been taken out of public hands and away from collective decision-making, often using state resources, before being enclosed for the interests of *private* capital accumulation. The same critics might also want to highlight the assortment of physical, mental and emotional labour that upholds the enclosed commons, work undertaken by labourers who are as alienated from the product of their labour as the shoppers are from the actual production of their 'consumer experience'.

Slight hints of the labour that goes into producing the 'shopping experience' are glimpsed when, on rare occasion, an employee from the mall pushes tiredly through a veneered wall panel to reveal breeze block walls, bare neon bulbs and rows of wheelie bins: the backstage to capitalism's star performance. The aesthetic contrast between 'front of stage' and the staff quarters is, obviously, merely the tip of the iceberg in terms of the maltreatment of labour that goes into the production of exquisite consumer experiences. But such glimpses, nevertheless, puncture the mall's performance of effortless luxury. More telling reminders of who is *really* being amused in this place of amusement lie in excavating the mall's genesis. The land on which the mall sits was bought off its previous owners (a railway company) following a mass 'compulsory purchase order' administered by the state (the London Development Agency), under the auspices of the Olympic development. Because of its centrality to the Olympic 'master plan', of which 'the public good' was thought to be self evident (Minton 2012a, 2012b), there was comparatively little scrutiny around the mall's development. As a result, while having the appearance of 'a public space', private companies hold the entire area around the mall, ultimately for private interests. Yet it also serves to recall that many of the more esteemed 'public spaces' to which the mall might be unfavourably compared – London's famous parks and squares in particular – often sit atop archaic forms of ownership and appropriation that are far from any common-sensical understanding of 'public land'. Not withstanding the recent proliferation of privately owned 'public spaces', all land in the UK is ultimately owned by 'The Crown', grounded in laws established in 1066 to assure the superiority of the monarchy. Even London's grand estates, such as the Dulwich Estate in south London, the colossal Grosvenor estate in west London, or the Benyon Estate in Hackney, are in a legal sense, merely granted revocable land rights by the monarchy. Such is the history of the city's land ownership, let alone the opacity of international investment in the city's land, that any effort to map the city according to high contrast definitions of public and private is thwarted by a murky reality. Lastly, if attempting to evaluate the tangle of public and private interests invested in the mall, consider the fact that the ownership of Westfield Stratford City is currently shared between four major owners, one of which is the pension fund for Dutch civil servants and educators. Quasi-public land enclosed for private interests, some of which include the (Dutch) public sector. None of this is to credit Westfield Stratford with undue publicity, but it is to complicate some of the definitions of 'the public' operationalised by 'truth sayers' of the mall, and to foreground the experience of 'publicness' grounded in the actual experience of walking through the mall.

All Equal Under One Roof?

Lifted by the escalator from the 'lower ground floor', straight up through the intermediary floor, now at the very upper shopping level, space suddenly opens up. The aisles feel wider. Streams of pedestrian traffic are lighter, and you can feel the proximity to the glass ceiling above. Ahead, in the distance, is the mall's terminal destination, the source of its gravity: the upper floor of John Lewis. Luxury home wear, sports gear and electronics. To the right of it, the 'Apple Store'. To the left, the second of the mall's food courts: 'World Food Hall'. No central seating area. Instead, an assortment of kiosks and small islands – a simulation of adventure-tourist friendly street food stalls – scattered across a large area of seats and walkways. Anglicised versions of Indian, Chinese, Thai, Vietnamese and Japanese food, along with Mexican and Southern soul food. I see the same familiar face I saw before, this time sitting down eating. The penny drops and we both recognise and greet each other: her, the manager of a bakery near where I live, me her weekly customer. Weaving in and out of the food stands leads toward a gangway beneath a large window, notable in the otherwise windowless space. The window has been placed here to give the walker a vista of the Olympic Park.

"Blade Runner innit?" laughs a young man to his friend, gazing over the neon rain slicked plazas below. A simulation of a simulation of a simulation of a ...

Turning back around, heading past more restaurants, back into the main isle of the first floor, through a string of boutique sports brands and mid-range shoe retailers. These are no longer the high street franchises typical of each and every small town. Instead, it's a selection of outlets, typical of a small city centre. Swaroski Crystal, an assortment of American, British and European clothing outlets (Tommy Hilfiger, Karen Millen, All Saints, Kooples, Cos, Banana Republic) and a small cluster of cosmetic and perfume retailers. I wonder around the Apple Store for a bit, fondling the newest tablets and phones. Then I visit John Lewis to pick up replacement buggy parts I had ordered from the retailer (aside from 'research' this is the reason I am here on this occasion).

In some respects, the mall is akin to the 'great equaliser' that was the medieval 'catholic' cathedral. As long as you are admitted, all are ostensibly equal under its roof. Only, as the history of schisms within European Christianity demonstrate, the church did not see all as being equal. In the cathedral, hierarchies crystallised in specific seating areas for the clergy (a gendered and classed group) and separate seating areas for the multiplicity that comprised the laity, in the nave. Until the egalitarian upheavals of the Reformation, the nave was also generally organised into a series of subdivided seating and standing areas (Brooks and Saint 1995: 4), wherein "groups" and "cliques" publically "act[ed] out differences and boundaries" (Brooks and Saint 1995: 4; Raguin and Stanbury 2005: 141). Moving through the church to one's allotted place, in a very tangible sense, offered a metaphor for one's broader biographical journey and position. And here, too, an analogy with the shopping mall resurfaces. For, while consumer citizenship clearly has an ability to reduce the potency of otherwise salient differences, the priests of the mall still see important distinctions amidst the congregation. And these differences are quite deliberately mapped out onto the space of the mall and reproduced through corporeal interactions with it.

As was the case with the cathedral, the social differences mapped on to the mall are almost entirely socio-economic (although age and gender play a part as well). This mapping is primarily achieved through the distribution of particular goods, brands and signs, according to the classed patterns of consumption they are associated with. Take, for instance, the difference between the shops that line the aforementioned main entrance to the mall, and those around the upper floor and far reaches of the shopping centre. Around the entrance area the same mix of mobile phone shops, coffee franchises, pharmacies, bakeries, card shops and bookmakers bemoaned by the middle classes as appearing on every British small town and borough high street. They sell what are tantamount to the necessities of twenty-first century living. Medicine. Caffeine. Sugar. Salt. Fats. Tobacco. Mobile communication devices. Credit. Cheap shoes. Somewhere to gamble. Basic gifts symbolising gratitude, condolence and celebration. On the top floor, however, there is a far higher ratio of retailers vending 'comparison goods' and aspirational 'lifestyle brands', the Apple Store, Adidas Store and Levis Store, for instance.

Consider also the differences between the foods sold at the mall's food halls. The ground floor is dominated by very well-known fordist burger and chicken franchises. Notably, the carbohydrate that accompanies the meals sold from nearly all the ground floor outlets is the quintessential northern European staple, the fried potato. The food hall on the upper level serves ostensibly hand-cooked post-fordist omnivore fare, each meal with a portion of rice or rice-based noodles. What these differences might signify, or the type of social configurations they reflect, can be approached through a consideration of the aforementioned carbohydrates. Per gram, rice costs twice as much compared to fried potato, while delivering up to five times fewer calories. While the clear growth in British rice consumption (Pot *et al.* 2015) was clearly buoyed by the growing number of working-class immigrants accustomed to rice, qualitative data suggests that rice's growing popularity is particularly pronounced amongst the metropolitan middle classes to whom it is marketed (James in Howes 2002: 87). At the same time, as exemplified by the chicken shops of east London (Rhys-Taylor 2017), fried potato has become increasingly popular with the under-employed second- and third-generation children of erstwhile migrants, who might otherwise have eaten rice. All of this bilateral carbohydrate osmosis is to say, the food hall on the ground floor serves little more than what a Bourdieusian would recognise as working class 'tastes of necessity', offering the most calories available in the mall, for the least money possible. The food hall on the upper floors on the other hand, like the retailers around it, offers a little bit of luxurious distinction, with more to appreciate and more to gain from that appreciation, for those able to afford it.

Of course, there's a practical logic to ways in which malls arrange their tenants (Brown 1992; Dawson and Lord 2012: 57–72). Databases and retail consultants help with the subtleties (Yuo *et al.* 2004; Shun-Te Yuo and Lizieri 2013), but the basic orthodoxy has it that the units housing 'magnet stores' be placed at the end of the mall, furthest from the primary entrance, while necessities, the high street shops selling basic daily goods and services, are placed around the most accessible (generally entrance) areas of the mall. In the space between, the accepted idea is to try and cluster particular types of shops, say menswear or children's toys and clothing. The premise behind this logic is that while shoppers might pop into Westfield for a necessity – some painkillers, a packet of sweets, or a cheap pair of flip-flops – they might be drawn towards the flagship aspirational stores (Brown 1991, 1992; Dawson and Lord 2012). Once there, relatively few people actually purchase anything compared to the ground floor shops. The hope is, however, that on their way either to or from the 'magnet stores' the masses might be enticed into another unit where they *will* buy something.

So the arrangement of shops within the mall is clearly planned according principles designed to maximise consumption. However, the way in which they are arranged also results in a subtle form of 'class zoning' based, quite literally, on the difference between class-cultural consumption patterns, distinguished between necessity and luxury. To walk into the mall from its main entrance, passing along the nave to the escalators and up to the flagship stores and lifestyle brands is, in many respects, a walk through the fine grain distinctions that fracture the middle ground of British class cultures.

Or at least it *was*. For, while the shopping centre's managers made initial efforts to fill the top floor and upper reaches with international lifestyle brands, some apparently found the units too large and rents too high. As such the 'hand' of the market has recently started to play a role in determining the position of shops. On the upper floor notable early closures included the Samsung Experience store, midrange-clothing brand Miss Sixty and exotically-American-yet-cheap clothing retailer Forever 21. New stores across the mall include a hair salon, a car dealership, a supplement and herbal medicine retailer, a high street travel agents and a handful of generic perfume and fragrance shops. Of course, some of these may well have been deliberately sought and placed according to the designs of the mall's managers. However, it is striking how some of the new additions, and their placement, are starting make Westfield look like some of the older thrown-together 'everyday' retail environments that it sought to replace.

A Brighter, If Dustier and Dilapidated, Future

Now I am tired. Rather than fighting my way through the crowds on the ground floor again, I plough along the notably less crowded upper floor, back toward the south-western end. I take an elevator down to the automatic doors, through which I exit.

Out of the exit I can see the Stratford Centre over the square in the distance, an older mall from the 70s. In the name of research, I decide to cross the square and take a walk through it. It is, in many respects, a rejuvenating experience. Much like the ground floor of Westfield, the mall is full of basic high-street retailers and international fast food franchises. It also has an indoor market. Unlike Westfield, however, there are no chocolates or hand-crafted candles on offer. Rather, the market traders vend an assortment of saris, kaftans, cheap rugs, comic t-shirts, counterfeit handbags, jellied eels, Polish style smoked meats. A traditional East London market place: dilapidated, a bit dusty, but notably convivial. Groups of young people, political pamphleteers and street drinkers, otherwise excluded from Westfield are also all here, congregating in the shopping centre yet left alone by the mall's nonchalant security guards. I sit on a bench in a central seating area for a while. As evening approaches and the shops close, the mall itself stays open and starts filling up with over a hundred skateboarders and roller skaters, drawn to the malls marbled floors and 24 hour opening. The glassy pop muzak having been turned off for the day, laughter and clattering of wheels and wood on tiles echo through the Stratford Centre late into night.

In the three decades since Carl Gardener and Julie Sheppard christened malls as the 'New Cathedrals' of the age, the comparison between these two urban institutions, the mall and the cathedral, has, in many respects, only become more striking. Beyond the economic entanglement that both institutions have with the life of their patrons; beyond their analogous impact on surrounding geography and economy, the two spaces have distinct similarities, using architectural techniques, signs, symbols and movement through space, to affect their users in profound ways. The uses of light, height, layout length, and trans-human scale, have the power to instil a sense of something bigger than the individual. Both institutions also offer a nearly hermetic sanctuary from the 'real' that exist outside. Both buildings seek to equalise those that enter them, facilitating the emergence of a quasi-public grounded in face-to-face encounters. Yet, while acting as a partial solvent for some social taxonomies, the spaces serve to spatialise others, not least through excluding some of society's most vulnerable constituencies. Both buildings also enforce a strict delineation of front and back stage, the nave and the cloisters, in an effort to sequester the machinations of their illusions. All of this, it should be said, can only really be recorded, and understood, through the experience of actually moving through the mall, be it walking, or as is the case for many in the 'shopmobility' friendly space, rolling. Not least, this is because it is precisely through the act of walking through the shopping centre that these techniques actually work, and thus potentially reveal themselves. That these techniques reveal themselves at all is testament to the fact that they do not *entirely* work.

While the aesthetic experience of Westfield Stratford City is indicative of the future that some may wish to incarnate, "nothing dates faster than the future" (Wallop 2016). It is perhaps not in the pristine spaces of New London that we find the city's futures. Rather, following Walter Benjamin's walks through century-old shopping arcades (Benjamin and Tiedemann 1999), we might understand the city better stepping away from Westfield, into the relatively older shopping centre that sits opposite it. The 'Stratford Centre' over the road from Westfield is a notably less luxurious and notably more demotic and genuinely exciting space, perhpas bordering on scary for some. But what is forgotten in the obvious comparison is that this shopping centre *too* was, at one time, exactly the type of space that the early critics of shopping malls were decrying. In 1972, the Stratford Centre was itself built atop Angel Lane, a typical Olde London street of small shops and market stores (Doubleday and Page 1973: 94). It is only today, at least three recessions and 30 years after its original construction, full of the debris that progress leaves in its wake, that this archetypal late century non-place has become one of the most remarkably convivial, and quintessentially local, public spaces in the area. Many others of London's retail centres, Elephant and Castle Centre, the Kingsland Shopping Centre and Surrey Quays, have undergone similar transformations. *Perhaps*, once the sheen of its luxury fades, Westfield might mature into something more convivial, vivacious, unpredictable and more thoroughly 'urban' than any might presently imagine.

References

Abaza, Mona. 2001. Shopping Malls, Consumer Culture and the Reshaping of Public Space in Egypt. *Theory, Culture and Society*, 18(5): 97–122.

Al-Othman, Hannah. 2016. Four Arrests after Disturbance outside Westfield Stratford. *Evening Standard*. www.standard.co.uk/news/crime/shoppers-locked-in-at-westfield-stratford-as-police-disperse-large-group-of-youths-a3216536.html, accessed 2 August 2016.

Amin, Ash. 2012. *Land of Strangers*. 1st edition. Cambridge: Polity Press.

Atkinson, Rowland. 2015. Limited Exposure: Social Concealment, Mobility and Engagement with Public Space by the Super-Rich in London. *Environment and Planning A* (August), doi:10.1177/0308518X15598323.

Augé, Marc. 1995. *Non-Places: Introduction to an Anthropology of Supermodernity*. London: Verso.

Back, Les. 2007. *The Art of Listening*. Oxford: Berg.

Bamfield, J. 2012. *Shopping and Crime*. New York: Springer.

Banham, Reyner. 2009. *Los Angeles: The Architecture of Four Ecologies*. 2nd revised edition. Berkeley, Calif.; London: University of California Press.

Baron, Robert A. 1997. The Sweet Smell of… Helping: Effects of Pleasant Ambient Fragrance on Prosocial Behavior in Shopping Malls. *Personality and Social Psychology Bulletin*, 23: 498–503.

Baudrillard, Jean. 1983. *Simulations*. Los Angeles: Semiotext(e).

Baudrillard, Jean. 2003. *Cool Memories*. Translated by Chris Turner. London: Verso.

Bauman, Zygmunt. 2011. The London Riots: On Consumerism Coming Home To Roost. Social Europe. www.socialeurope.eu/2011/08/the-london-riots-on-consumerism-coming-home-to-roost, accessed 27 July 2016.

Benjamin, Walter and Rolf Tiedemann. 1999. *The Arcades Project*. Cambridge, MA: Harvard University Press.

Bright, Keith, Geoffrey Cook and John Harris. 1999. Building Design: The Importance of Flooring Pattern and Finish for People with a Visual Impairment. *British Journal of Visual Impairment*, 17(3): 121–125.

Brooks, Chris and Andrew Saint. 1995. *The Victorian Church: Architecture and Society*. Manchester: Manchester University Press.

Brown, Stephen. 1991. Shopper Circulation in a Planned Shopping Centre. *International Journal of Retail and Distribution Management*, 19(1). www.emeraldinsight.com/doi/abs/10.1108/09590559110135935, accessed 11 August 2016.

Brown, Stephen. 1992. Tenant Mix, Tenant Placement and Shopper Behaviour in a Planned Shopping Centre. *Service Industries Journal*, 12(3): 384–403.

Burawoy, Michael. 2013. Ethnographic Fallacies: Reflections on Labour Studies in the Era of Market Fundamentalism. *Work, Employment and Society*, 27(3): 526–536.

Buxton, P. 2015. *Metric Handbook: Planning and Design Data*. Abingdon: Routledge.

Chebat, Jean-Charles and Richard Michon. 2003. Impact of Ambient Odors on Mall Shoppers' Emotions, Cognition, and Spending: A Test of Competitive Causal Theories. *Journal of Business Research*, 56(7): 529–539.

Chen, Bing and Jian Kang. 2004. Acoustic Comfort in Shopping Mall Atrium Spaces: A Case Study in Sheffield Meadowhall. *Architectural Science Review*, 47(2): 107–114.

Cheyne, Julian and Charlotte Baxter. 2008. Displaced by London's Olympics. *Guardian*, 2 June. www.theguardian.com/uk/2008/jun/02/olympics2012, accessed 19 August 2016.

124   *A. Rhys-Taylor*

Chung, Chuihua Judy, Jeffrey Inaba, Rem Koolhaas, Sze Tsung Leong and Harvard University Graduate School of Design. 2001. *The Harvard Design School Guide to Shopping*. Cologne: Taschen.

Clark, Andrew and Nick Emmel. 2010. *Using Walking Interviews*. http://eprints.ncrm.ac.uk/1323, accessed 19 March 2014.

Classen, Constance. 1990. Sweet Colors, Fragrant Songs: Sensory Models of the Andes and the Amazon. *American Ethnologist*, 17(4): 722–735.

Clery, E. J. 1991. Women, Publicity and the Coffee-House Myth. *Women: A Cultural Review*, 2(2): 168–177.

Cowan, Brian. 2001. What Was Masculine about the Public Sphere? Gender and the Coffeehouse Milieu in Post-Restoration England. *History Workshop Journal*, 51: 127–157.

Davies, Barry J., Dion Kooijman and Philippa Ward. 2003. The Sweet Smell of Success: Olfaction in Retailing. *Journal of Marketing Management*, 19(5–6): 611–627.

Davis, Mike. 2006. *City of Quartz*. London: Verso.

Dawson, John and Dennis Lord. 2012. *Shopping Centre Development (RLE Retailing and Distribution)*. Abingdon: Routledge.

Degen, Monica, Gillian Rose and Begum Basdas. 2010. Bodies and Everyday Practices in Designed Urban Environments. *Science Studies: An Interdisciplinary Journal for Science and Technology Studies*, 23(2): 60–76.

Doubleday, Herbert Arthur and William Page. 1973. *The Victoria History of the County of Essex*. Westminster: Constable.

Duneier, Mitchell, Hakim Hasan and Ovie Carter. 2001. *Sidewalk*. New York: Farrar, Straus and Giroux.

Erkip, Feyzan. 2003. The Shopping Mall as an Emergent Public Space in Turkey. *Environment and Planning A*, 35(6): 1073–1093.

Gant, Robert. 2002. Shopmobility at the Millennium: 'Enabling' Access in Town Centres. *Journal of Transport Geography*, 10(2): 123–133.

Gant, Robert and José Smith. 1998. Shopmobility, Personal Mobility and Disabled People. *Geography*, 83(3): 280–283.

Gardner, Carl and Julie Sheppard. 2012. The New Cathedral: The Rise and Rise of the Shopping Centre, in *Consuming Passion: The Rise of Retail Culture*. Abingdon: Routledge.

Gerrard, Jessica and David Farrugia. 2015. The 'Lamentable Sight' of Homelessness and the Society of the Spectacle. *Urban Studies*, 52(12): 2219–2233.

Geurts, Kathryn Linn. 2002. *Culture and the Senses: Bodily Ways of Knowing in an African Community. Vol. 3*. Oakland, Calif.: University of California Press. https://books.google.co.uk/books?hl=en&lr=&id=UiFtWXSkuwwC&oi=fnd&pg=PR7&dq=geurts+classen+%22sensory+order%22&ots=JZSTN9RIDH&sig=SFjs7lbFS-jBJar4COGchYiMf8U, accessed 23 May 2016.

Goss, Jon. 1993. The 'Magic of the Mall': An Analysis of Form, Function, and Meaning in the Contemporary Retail Built Environment. *Annals of the Association of American Geographers*, 83(1): 18–47.

Hall, Tom and Robin James Smith. 2013. Stop and Go: A Field Study of Pedestrian Practice, Immobility and Urban Outreach Work. *Mobilities*, 8(2): 272–292.

Hall, Tom and Robin James Smith. 2015. Care and Repair and the Politics of Urban Kindness. *Sociology*, 49(1): 3–18.

Harvey, David. 2006. *Spaces of Global Capitalism*. London: Verso.

Healy, Stephen. 2008. Air-Conditioning and the 'Homogenization' of People and Built Environments. *Building Research and Information*, 36(4): 312–322.

Hier, Sean P., Dan Lett, Kevin Walby and André Smith. 2011. Beyond Folk Devil Resistance: Linking Moral Panic and Moral Regulation. *Criminology and Criminal Justice*, April, doi:10.1177/1748895811401977.

Hoggart, Richard. 2009. *The Uses of Literacy: Aspects of Working-Class Life*. London: Penguin.

Houssay-Holzschuch, Myriam, and Annika Teppo. 2009. A Mall for All? Race and Public Space in Post-Apartheid Cape Town. *Cultural Geographies*, 16(3): 351–379.

Howes, David. 2002. *Cross-Cultural Consumption: Global Markets, Local Realities*. Abingdon: Routledge.

Howes, David. 2005. Hyperaesthesia, Or, the Sensual Logic of Late Capitalism, in D. Howes (ed.), *Empire of the Senses*, pp. 281–303. Oxford: Berg Publishers.

Jewell, Nicholas. 2016. *Shopping Malls and Public Space in Modern China*. Abingdon: Routledge.

Kennelly, Jacqueline and Paul Watt. 2012. Restricting the Public in Public Space: The London 2012 Olympic Games, Hyper-Securitization and Marginalized Youth. *Sociological Research Online*, 18(2): 19.

Kroker, Arthur, Marilouise Kroker and David Cook. 1989. *Panic Encyclopedia: The Definitive Guide to the Postmodern Scene*. 1st edition. New York: St Martins Press.

Kusenbach, Margarethe. 2003. Street Phenomenology: The Go-along as Ethnographic Research Tool. *Ethnography*, 4(3): 455–485.

Langrehr, F. W. 1991. Retail Shopping Mall Semiotics and Hedonic Consumption. *Advances in Consumer Research*, 18: 428–433.

Macklin, Graham. 2007. *Very Deeply Dyed in Black: Sir Oswald Mosley and the Postwar Reconstruction of British Fascism*. London; New York: I. B. Tauris.

Mann, Sebastian. 2016. Police Hunt Four Teens over Double Stabbing at Westfield in Stratford. *Evening Standard*. www.standard.co.uk/news/crime/police-hunt-four-teens-over-double-stabbing-at-westfield-in-stratford-a3148511.html, accessed 2 August 2016.

Martin, Emer. 2013. Westfield Stratford's Postcode Is the Country's Worst Crime Hotspot. *Evening Standard*. www.standard.co.uk/news/crime/westfield-stratfords-postcode-is-the-countrys-worst-crime-hotspot-8756741.html, accessed 22 July 2016.

Michon, Richard, Jean-Charles Chebat and Lou W. Turley. 2005. Mall Atmospherics: The Interaction Effects of the Mall Environment on Shopping Behavior. *Journal of Business Research*, 58(5): 576–583.

Miller, Jacob C. 2015. The Critical Intimacies of Walking in the Abasto Shopping Mall, Buenos Aires, Argentina. *Social and Cultural Geography*, 16(8): 869–887.

Minton, Anna. 2012a. *Ground Control: Fear and Happiness in the Twenty-First-Century City*. London: Penguin.

Minton, Anna. 2012b. London 2012: The Real Winners *The Occupied Times*. https://the-occupiedtimes.org/?p=2584, accessed 10 August 2016.

Norman, Zachary. 2014a. Former Olympics Minister Accuses Legacy Bosses of 'Broken Allotments Promise'. *East London and West Essex Guardian Series*. www.guardian-series.co.uk/news/11124606.Former_Olympics_minister_accuses_legacy_bosses_of_broken_allotments_promise_, accessed 19 August 2016.

Norman, Zachary. 2014b.Teenager Handed Life Sentence for Westfield Murder. *East London and West Essex Guardian Series*. www.guardian-series.co.uk/news/wfnews/11131501.Teenager_handed_life_sentence_for_Westfield_murder, accessed 2 August 2016.

ONS (Office for National Statistics). 2012. *London Datastore: 2011 Census Diversity*. http://data.london.gov.uk/dataset/2011-census-diversity, accessed 7 July 2016.

O'Sullivan, Feargus. 2012. The Two Towers of London's Olympic Misgivings. *CityLab*. www.theatlanticcities.com/neighborhoods/2012/05/two-towers-londons-olympic-misgivings/2012, accessed 25 July 2016.

Pappalepore, Ilaria. 2016. Going, Going, Gone: How Olympic Legacy is Killing London's Creative Culture. *The Conversation*. http://theconversation.com/going-going-gone-how-olympic-legacy-is-killing-londons-creative-culture-63791, accessed 19 August 2016.

Perry, Grayson. 2014. Grayson Perry: The Rise and Fall of Default Man. *New Statesman*. www.newstatesman.com/culture/2014/10/grayson-perry-rise-and-fall-default-man, accessed 18 August 2016.

Pink, Sarah. 2008. An Urban Tour: The Sensory Sociality of Ethnographic Place-Making. *Ethnography*, 9(2): 175–196.

Pospech, Pavel. 2014. Out of Control and out of Sight: Defining Deviance in Czech Shopping Malls. *ISA World Congress of Sociology*. https://isaconf.confex.com/isaconf/wc2014/webprogram/Paper41962.html, accessed 22 July 2016.

Pot, G. K., C. J. Prynne, S. Almoosawi, D. Kuh and A. M. Stephen. 2015. Trends in Food Consumption over 30 Years: Evidence from a British Birth Cohort. *European Journal of Clinical Nutrition*, 69(7): 817–823.

Raguin, Virginia Chieffo and Sarah Stanbury. 2005. *Women's Space: Patronage, Place, and Gender in the Medieval Church*. New York: SUNY Press.

Rhys-Taylor, Alex. 2013a. Disgust and Distinction: The Case of the Jellied Eel. *The Sociological Review*, 61(2): 227–246.

Rhys-Taylor, Alex. 2013b. The Essences of Multiculture: A Sensory Exploration of an Inner-City Street Market. *Identities*, 20(4): 393–406.

Rhys-Taylor, Alex. 2017. *Food and Multiculture*. London: Bloomsbury Academic. www.bloomsbury.com/uk/food-and-multiculture-9781472581181, accessed 10 August 2016.

Shun-Te Yuo, Tony and Colin Lizieri. 2013. Tenant Placement Strategies within Multi-Level Large-Scale Shopping Centers. *Journal of Real Estate Research*. http://aresjournals.org/doi/abs/10.5555/rees.35.1.d378883835h75176, accessed 11 August 2016.

Sorkin, Michael. 1992. *Variations on a Theme Park: The New American City and the End of Public Space*. New York: Farrar, Straus and Giroux.

Tyndall, A. 2010. 'It's a Public, I Reckon': Publicness and a Suburban Shopping Mall in Sydney's Southwest. *Geographical Research*, 48: 123–136.

Valentine, Gill. 1989. The Geography of Women's Fear. *Area*, 21(4): 385–390.

Vannini, Phillip, Dennis Waskul and Simon Gottschalk. 2011. *The Senses in Self, Society, and Culture: A Sociology of the Senses*. 1st edition. Abingdon: Routledge.

Walkowitz, Judith R. 2013. *City of Dreadful Delight: Narratives of Sexual Danger in Late-Victorian London*. Chicago, Ill.: University of Chicago Press.

Wallop, Harry. 2016. Brent Cross Is Now 40-Years Old: Will Shopping Centres Be Here in Another 40? *Telegraph*, 18 March. www.telegraph.co.uk/business/2016/03/01/brent-cross-is-now-40-years-old-will-shopping-centres-be-here-in, accessed 19 August 2016.

Watson, Sophie. 2009. The Magic of the Marketplace: Sociality in a Neglected Public Space. *Urban Studies*, 46(8): 1577–1591.

Watt, Paul. 2013. 'It's Not for Us': Regeneration, the 2012 Olympics and the Gentrification of East London. *City*, 17(1): 99–118.

Westwood, Sallie and John Williams. 2003. *Imagining Cities: Scripts, Signs and Memories*. Abingdon: Routledge.

Wheatstone, Richard. 2015. A Crime Happens Every 15 Minutes in UK's 50 Problem Postcodes: Are You near One? *Mirror*. www.mirror.co.uk/news/uk-news/britains-crime-hotspots-revealed-50-5852573, accessed 10 August 2016.

Wise, A. 2010. Sensuous Multiculturalism: Emotional Landscapes of Inter-Ethnic Living in Australian Suburbia. *Journal of Ethnic and Migration Studies*, 36(6): 917–937.

Yang, W. and J. Kang. 2005. Acoustic Comfort Evaluation in Urban Open Public Spaces. *Applied Acoustics*, 66(2) (Special Issue 'Urban Acoustics'): 211–229.

York, Melissa. 2013. Stratford Is the Crime Hotspot of the UK, Police Figures Reveal. *Newham Recorder*. www.newhamrecorder.co.uk/news/crime-court/stratford_is_the_crime_hotspot_of_the_uk_police_figures_reveal_1_2332786, accessed 2 August 2016.

Yuo, T. S.-T., Neil Crosby, Colin Martyn Lizieri and Philip McCann. 2004. Tenant Mix Variety in Regional Shopping Centres: Some UK Empirical Analyses. http://centaur.reading.ac.uk/21650, accessed 11 August 2016.

A Walk in Wales.
Source: Mike Michael.

7 Walking, Falling, Telling

The Anecdote and the Mis-Step as a 'Research Event'

Mike Michael

Introduction: Three Anecdotes about Mis-Stepping

In October 2014 I was moving out of my apartment in Rushcutters' Bay in Sydney and into a new house in Newtown in the Inner West. My partner and daughter would be joining me for the coming year and I needed more space. I also needed more furniture – or rather, I just needed furniture, given that my apartment had been fully furnished. After a feverish couple of weeks of buying IKEA furniture and assembling it, the house was heading toward being ready. On the occasion in question, I had just finished assembling the beds and was going about removing the packaging from the bedrooms. This consisted mainly of large cardboard panels and thin plastic sheeting. As I made my way down the stairs, laden with cardboard and plastic I fell at about the mid-point of the staircase. I bounced to the bottom, hitting heavily each of the ten or so step-edges on the way, stopping in a bundle where the stairs curved toward the living room. Perhaps less gingerly than I should have, I jumped up and checked nothing was broken. Certainly I felt sore (my bottom hurt, and my left elbow too where it had hit the bannisters). Still, I gathered the now scattered rubbish and put it out for eventual recycling. Then I noticed that my watch was missing. At first I wasn't sure that I had had it on in the first place. But on reflection I was pretty certain I had been wearing it throughout this bout of bed-building. I began to search for it, worried that it had been damaged beyond repair (it was a birthday present from my partner). As it turned out I quickly found it across the room, under the living room table, though there was only one half of the strap still attached. After some more searching around I found the other half of the strap with the pin (which attached the strap to the body of the watch) still lodged in place. I checked that the watch was still working and, satisfied, re-attached the strap, and put the watch back on.

Around 15 years ago (it's hard to be more precise), we were spending New Year with friends in North Wales. This had become something of an annual trip, one which usually involved a visit to the local mountain, Cadair Idris. On most occasions, because we had young children accompanying us, we would only go as far as the lake. However, on this occasion it was agreed that a friend and I could carry on, climbing along the ridge of the mountain, over its crest and down the other side through some pretty steep terrain. This was generally grassy, with a few small rocks scattered about, and one or two little streams to negotiate. As we were going down – quite quickly as I recall (in order to get back to the farmhouse before it got dark) – I tripped and landed awkwardly on my right hand. I say 'awkwardly', but this is only insofar as I put my hands out to break my fall and managed to hurt my right hand. I looked around to see what had made me trip, there were no rocks in the vicinity and I put it down to catching my right foot on a clump of grass. Testing for damage in my hand, I found that when I tried to make a fist the palm hurt, as if the bones inside had been shifted out of place and were grinding against each other. I identified a small rock as the culprit but couldn't really be sure that that was where my hand had landed. Anyway, I assumed that with time, all would settle back into normality, which it more or less did. My hand stopped hurting and it seemed to function normally. Except for one particular category of actions. If I shook hands and the other person's grip was particularly forceful, then I felt a dull but intense pain in my palm – a pain as if an underlying soreness or fragility had revealed itself. This is still the case.

I don't really recollect this particular slipping or its circumstances, but I think it was winter about a couple of years ago, we were in a city, we were walking along and I slipped over. I vaguely remember there being some slimy leaf litter on a pavement which I stepped on and lost my footing, and my feet went from under me and I landed on my bottom with such speed that I didn't have a chance to respond by putting my hands out. What makes this memorable was my son's – who witnessed the fall – subsequent reaction. Later in the day my partner told me that my son had been quite upset at my slipping over (he was nearly twenty at the time), saying that it was the first time he had seen me so vulnerable. We've since spoken about it and though he can't remember the circumstances or the details of the slipping either, he certainly recalls his feelings about it and me.

I have presented these stories in order to explore what the processes of mis-stepping – and its related effects and affects – can tell us about the unfolding of world, or what Connolly (2011) calls a 'world of becoming'. As interruptions in the trajectory of walking, I want to treat these events as 'research events' that become so through their telling as anecdotes, while recursively shaping the process of anecdotal telling. This requires thinking about the relation between a number of concepts – becoming, event, anecdote, and speculation and the possible – but all of them mangled (Pickering, 1995) through the specificities of walking and mis-stepping.

In what follows, I set out my conceptual stall by discussing the particular notion of event that interests me, and the ways in which this links to becoming and speculation, and especially to that of the process of telling in the form of making anecdotes. I then apply this broad schema to the anecdotes presented above – in each case seeking to speculate about how we might understand the possibilities that attach to a number of elements that contribute to social life (such as embodiment, technology, ageing, temporality, status, masculinity, nature). However, I also discuss how the specificities of the mis-stepping shape how the analytic schema itself comes to unfold.

Becoming, Event, Speculation and Anecdote Too

Deleuze famously shifted his initial view of the event from a 'singularity', that is, a turning point or a juncture where 'difference' takes place (1990), to a more Whiteheadian formulation where the event is characterized by, amongst other things, the mergence of diverse elements (the concrescence of prehensions – see Whitehead, 1929) whose completion (or satisfaction) punctuates the flow of becoming or change (Deleuze 1993; also Shaviro, 2007; Livesey, 2007). More recently, Mariam Fraser (2010) has crystallised two views of the event. As with Whitehead, she regards the event as an occasion in which heterogeneous elements come together and combine, whether these be macro and micro, cognitive and affective, human and nonhuman, or social and material. Crucially, for Fraser, as these entities come into relation with one other, they mutually change, they co-become, or become-together. Because of this mutual change, it would seem that the event itself becomes obscure: if we are unclear about its components, how can we be sure about its character? Under such circumstances, we need to engage with the possibilities entailed in such events (Stengers, 2010), that is to say, speculatively pursue not a solution to 'what the event is', but use the event as an opportunity for asking 'better questions', and crafting 'more inventive problems'. This applies no less to 'research events'. Often, research events entail a co-becoming of elements (researcher, researched and recording technology – see Michael, 2004, 2012a) that transform the meaning of the research event, allowing us to ask questions about, for instance, the nature of the research programme, or the role of discipline in rendering nonhumans docile and social data gatherable.

However, how do we know that an event has reached completion (or satisfaction, as Whitehead would call it)? How do we know it has become a punctuation in the flow of worldly becoming? Or, to draw on Deleuze's earlier formulation, how do we know that an event has occurred, precipitating some sort of change? If we take the examples of walking and mis-stepping in the foregoing, it is partly in their telling that these happenings become events (although as we shall see their meaning, or significance, is by no means straightforward). I say 'partly' because these telling are themselves shaped by the events of which they speak. After all, telling is itself an event. To follow Whitehead (1929), this means that, on the one hand, the event of telling is comprised of previous events (such as that of a mis-step), but, on the other, only some of those prior events are 'welcome' into a telling event (i.e. can be 'satisfactorily' combined with other events). In other words, in telling an event, we are affected by a previous event (the mis-step, in this case), but in its telling we are also reformulating it (entertaining some elements, 'othering' others).

It is at this point that we can introduce the notion of the anecdote. The anecdote has a number of features: it is often personal to the speaker; it is a part of the historical record and can impact on the unfolding of historical events; it marks a notable or extra-ordinary incident; it is a mixture of factual reportage and fictional creation; it might allow us to draw out 'broader lessons' beyond its specificity (Michael, 2012b; see also Thompson and Adams, 2013). However, key for present purposes is the idea of 'anecdotalization'. By this is meant that we do not treat anecdotes as a way of accounting for, or describing, an empirical reality (the social-world-as-a-social-scientific-object-of-study). Instead, anecdotalization connotes one means of doing social scientific research which at once acknowledges the contingency of the event of accounting (its complex grounding in – the pattern of inclusion and exclusion of – prior events), and pursues the speculative potential that inheres in such an event. Put bluntly, the aim here is to try, in some small way through the anecdotalization of the mis-step, to operationalize Connolly's 'exquisite sensitivity to the world of becoming'.

Another way of framing this is in terms of John Law's (2004) concept of a method assemblage. The method assemblage can be understood as a way of engaging with a 'world of becoming' through technique (which includes both formal methodology and informal encountering) which is no less a part of that 'world of becoming'. It is a point of articulation between two worlds in flux that generates contingent accounts that are also performative (in that they are necessarily a partial rendering of the world that is being studied). Anecdotalization is simply one version of a method assemblage – an interface between researcher and researched in which each enacts the another, or, put otherwise, an occasion in which research, researched and researcher are 'co-eventuated'.

Needless to say, this is a rather abstracted account of the present methodological frame, and we shall work through it in detail when we return to the anecdotes of mis-stepping with which the chapter opened. However, before this, I want to go think about walking and mis-stepping through some more traditional sociological categories (by way of further differentiating the present chapter).

The Mis-Step as a Social Scientific Object of Study

The artwork 'Doomed' by Tracy Moffat is a video montage of film clips in which people perish in various disasters. Drawn from across cinematic history we see people falling again and again (down cracks in the earth, or off collapsing buildings, or under panicked crowds), and yet recognize different styles – what Mauss (1985) famously called body techniques – of falling. To this modern eye, the fall of the silent movie era is particularly noteworthy, marked by a throwing up of the arms. This seems to lessen as we move into the contemporary period: indeed to throw one's arms upwards as one fell would nowadays be either ridiculous or ridiculing.

Arguably, there are certain common corporeal mechanisms which need to come into play in order to slip, fall or trip (and some of these are elegantly described by Vergunst, 2008). However, the point here is that how one mis-steps and the meanings that attach to a mis-step are historically contingent. Sociology (along with several other disciplines, most obviously anthropology) is particularly attuned to such shifting styles and significations.

- For instance, we can imagine that falling, tripping or slipping can be more or less 'civilized' in Elias' (eg 1994/1939) terms: that is to say, in those periods in which violence is much more of a chronic feature of a society, mis-stepping might simply be another manifestation of the relative 'lack of control'. Accordingly, it is with increasing civilité that the slip, the fall, the trip come to seen as faux pas, or at least in need of explanation, or accounting.
- In relation to Goffman's (1959) dramaturgical model, one might imagine that the fall comprises a sudden and unexpected exposure of the 'back' of a role where the control needed to perform that role suddenly deserts one. In my case, the role of competent handyman was undermined when I fell down the stairs – I suspect the over-enthusiastic getting up had much to do with re-installing that role.
- In the context of Bourdieu's theory of practice (e.g. 1977, 1984), we can suggest that an individual's habitus (loosely, the dispositions that shape people's situated practices and understandings), derived as it is from a particular class position (however, see Skeggs, 2004), will affect how one does falling, slipping or tripping, both on the way down (how limbs are used) and on the way up (how one repairs the situation by displaying humour, or exasperation, or seeking an element of the environment to blame).

In all three cases one might be on display and thus subject to social judgement: a fall might be a lapse in civilité, a fissure in the presentation of self, or the expression of a particular class position. However, the mis-step might also precipitate a more assiduous form of what Goffman (1972) calls 'civil inattention' – the seeming lack of attention paid (which ideally removes any social threat) to mis-stepping others, while actually taking note of them.

Finally, we might also mention those approaches that focus on the riskiness of walking and mis-stepping and the processes of governance that are put in place in order to 'deal with' those risks. For instance, falling, tripping or slipping as a failure of 'discipline' in which the routine comportment of individuals is disrupted, might require interventions which re-assert such discipline (e.g. Foucault, 1979). These might take material-semiotic forms, such as the multitude of warning signs that co-habit many urban spaces with us, or colonize such spaces, especially where a new danger appears (I'm thinking of those small yellow signs that are placed near a spillage in public spaces such as transport hubs or supermarkets and which as often as not pose as much of a danger as the spillage itself). Or, in a more neo-liberalist mode, we can point to the various ways in which people are 're-made' so that they take more responsibility for their careful walking. (e.g. Hacking, 1986; Dean, 1999: cf. Woolgar and Neyland, 2013). For instance, Michael (2009) notes how tourists are responsibilized by various agencies (rescue services, hiking clubs, the media) in terms of their possession of the right equipment for, and attitude toward, hill-walking and the risks of mis-stepping intrinsic to hill-walking.

Of course, these are superficial sociological renderings of falling, tripping and slipping. The aim has not been to discuss in detail how these events might be analysed sociologically, not least because this would mean treating falling, tripping and slipping as 'objects' of study, that is as topics that can be put through a sociological analytic mill to illustrate existing social scientific framings. The aim of this chapter, in contrast, is to consider how falling, tripping and slipping might be treated as methodological resources. In other words, can they serve as means by which to explore how we come to grasp the world, and how to grasp that grasping?

Having drawn this distinction, we must not forget that walking has already played a part in recent methodological innovations in sociology. For instance, Sarah Pink (2007, 2009) has used walking while videoing with participants in the exploration of elements of everyday life. However, it is not clear how a fall or stumble could be integrated into such a method. One can imagine that for some (researchers and participants), this might need to be edited out of the empirical record or sidelined from the final account. For others, such an incident might serve an occasion for further explorations (for instance, one can imagine a discussion about the complex role of clutter – see Cwerner and Metcalfe, 2003; Michael, 2006). Nevertheless, as an occasion for reflection, under the circumstances the fall or stumble is at best an opportunistic moment, and one in which the opportune-ness of the occasion remains unreflected-upon. In the next sections, we return to the anecdotes of mis-steps presented in the introduction and begin to unpick in detail (some of) their analytic implications.

Anecdotalization

As I proceed through the following analyses, it will not be lost on the reader that some aspects of the analyses – the anecdotalizations – can be shared across the three cases. The differentiated accounts are thus a reflection of the process of writing analytically, of focusing on difference, in this instance for the purpose of showing how different types of mis-step and their anecdotalization can yield, hopefully, different sorts of insight into 'the world of becoming', and distinctive 'more interesting questions' about walking as a method. In other words, the event of the writing a chapter such as this entails particular anecdotalizations that might have, in a different sort of setting, eventuated a different sort of 'world of becoming'. For example, one can imagine an ironic conversation with friends where these three stories merge into a cumulative narrative about Mike's general incompetence and lack of awareness of his surroundings – an evocation of the stereotype of the cloistered and un-dexterous academic. The point is that these anecdotalizations need to be treated with circumspection insofar as they are events shaped by current elements, not least that of writing a chapter in a book about walking and methodology. Having said that, the choice of the mis-step reflects in part the 'ingression' (as Whitehead would put it) of a different set of elements, namely that of falling, slipping and tripping. In other words, these events are themselves also central to the pattern of anecdotalizations that are presented here ...

a ... Falling Down the Stairs ...

The anecdote about falling down the stairs can be unraveled in relation to a number of themes. First, there is the theme of skill. Prior to the fall, I had spent time successfully assembling a queen-sized bed, a job for which, the instructions insisted, two people were required. There was therefore some not inconsiderable self-satisfaction (especially intense because I had for a long time thought of myself as constitutionally incapable of DIY – an echo of the relationship with my father). With the 'falling down the stairs', there was a sort of sudden unskilling, made worse because the skill was 'walking down the stairs'. After picking myself up, noticing the missing watch, and looking for it, I managed to find it and reassemble it. Here, there is, arguably, a re-assertion of skillfulness. To be sure, this is a different type of skill (putting a watch back together and assembling furniture require different parts of the body, different sorts of hand-eye co-ordination), but it is a skill nevertheless and a re-establishment of a sense of skill-in-general, or, one might say, an adaptability to the practical task at hand.

In this anecdotalization, we see how 'a fall down the stairs' in its specificity (and peculiarity of circumstance in which it is topped and tailed by specific skilled performances of assembling a bed and re-assembling a watch) raises interesting questions about the relation between 'general' and 'specific' skills. On the one hand, there are the specific skills and indeed 'craft' (see Sennett, 2008) in which bodily capacity is 'tied' to particular affordances (Gibson, 1979; Ingold, 1992) and objects (e.g. Akrich, 1992; Latour, 1992). On the other, there is a generic adaptability to a range of objects/affordance – what (and here there are masculinist overtones – see below) might be understood in terms of an ability to 'turn one's hand to anything' (or being a 'handyman'). Needless to say, there are limitations to this adaptability (placed by anatomy and physiology) but also enablements and enhancements (mediated by other technologies – see Michael, 2000). However, what this contrast raises is a question about how to imagine the shifting configuration of body parts as they more or less skillfully interact – one might say intra-act (Barad, 2007) – with the shifting configuration of things (bed, stairs, watch). There are resources to be had in the recent work of Ingold (2007, 2008), of course – not least in terms of how this is all an unfolding of the world in what he calls a 'line' and a 'meshwork' in which 'stuff' moves forward (in a line) all the while enmeshing itself in a situated and contingent way with other sorts of stuff which is itself on a similar trajectory, such that the property of this stuff is varied and varying. But under such circumstances what does it mean 'to fall down the stairs'? Can this be seen as a mistake or a problem – or is it simply more 'unfolding'. Here, we might be able to draw on Bennett's (2010) notion of 'thing power' in which the liveliness of stuff can manifest as recalcitrance, or a reversal of the idea of affordance in which people 'afford' particular possibilities for objects ('falling down the stairs'). Now, at stake here is not the 'viability' of these rough analyses (or rather, speculations), but the illustration of how a mis-step (that of 'falling down the stairs'), and its particular anecdotalization (that of the skill lost and regained) opens up a line of thought that facilitates an engage-ment with 'the world of becoming'.

Here is another anecdotalization of the 'falling down the stairs'. This con-cerns a longer timeframe of events – or rather an extended sequence in which the fall fits in between the several years of living in Sydney alone and the imminent arrival of my family. To recall, after falling, on coming to rest I did not lie there quietly, checking to see if I was still in one piece. Instead, I immediately jumped up, assuming I was more or less intact. Of course, this is not an uncommon feature of a mis-step, or general mishap for that matter. Probably, such a speedy and automatic bodily 'correction' signals an immediate recovery of self and bodily control. However, in relation to the sequence of events mentioned above, there are other ways of understanding this reaction. Namely, the clambering quickly back to my feet is as much a 'hopeful' reaction as a response to the momentary lapse of control. To have injured myself would have had all sorts of more or less disastrous ramifications. At the milder end, the seamless transfer of my family to Australia would have been complicated had I broken a bone or twisted an ankle. At the extreme end, my family would have had to spend much of their time in Australia helping me to recuperate or providing long-term care. To 'find my feet' again was a matter of re-asserting control of myself but also a putting back in sequence – or rather, a desperate testing of – a presumed train of events that had momentarily been derailed.

In this anecdotalization, there is a series of becomings (my family coming to, and immersing themselves in, Australia) that my building of furniture (along with many other events such as finding and renting a house in a specific suburb, making the arrangements for school registration, utility payments, etc.) was meant to ensure. All of this might have been unraveled by a simple fall, and a different trajectory set in motion. What this opens up is a sense of the 'crux event' that interrupts an unfolding world of becoming, that bifurcates it and sends it off in a different direction. But then, it also alerts us to the fact that this is a crux event only in relation to a sequence of events that has been planned. Had I been someone with a history of falls, then this would be not such a 'crux event': indeed the planned sequence would probably have been very different. The more general point, however, is that what counts as a pivotal event – an event that 'makes a difference' – rests on the presumed sequence of events, the tacit narrative of occasions. The inverse to this account is, we might say, that any event can be a 'crux event' if we choose the appropriate sequence of events in which it is embedded. So, for instance, if the visit to Australia turned out to be disastrous anyway, then the event of 'surviving intact a fall down the stairs' becomes, potentially, a 'crux event'. The corollary point is that anecdotalization implicates a 'point' to the anecdote; but the 'point' can change and, thus, so too can the event that is the object of the anecdote. Put another way, to the extent that an event 'causes' an anecdote, that event only ever exercises, to borrow from Bennett (2010), 'emergent causality'. That is to say, causality can only be identified and attributed retrospectively in light of a given narrative end-point (rather than in light of an effect): should such a 'point to the story' change, so would the distribution of causes and causal agents.

b ... Tripping on a Mountain Slope ...

In this anecdote, the 'trip on a mountain slope' connotes a number of things. First, there is the challenge to masculine competence again – this time that entailed in the process of negotiating rough-ish terrain. My companion was (and is) altogether more accomplished as an 'outdoors-man'. In the immediate circumstance, there was the embarrassment of failing to meet the 'standards' of a certain masculine skillfulness, or more academically, of hegemonic masculinity (Connell, 2005). However, treating this incident as a 'research event' we can see how masculinity is played out in its specificity, through the intersection of bodies, activities, technologies and environments. Thus, rather than a 'structural' notion of masculinity that affects behaviour, we can conceive of masculinity as both a matter of complex embodiment (Connell and Messerschmidt, 2005), or bodily performativity (e.g. Butler, 1993) but all conducted through an embroilment with the nonhuman, whether that be everyday technologies (Lie and Sorensen, 1996) or, as in this case, the 'natural' nonhuman. The anecdotalization of this event therefore opens up the possibility of an exploration of how 'gender' is enacted through masculinized outdoor pursuits and male companionship, but mediated and translated through technologies (e.g. boots, gloves) and 'natural' environmental elements (which might themselves be gendered – see MacNaghten and Urry, 1998; Michael, 2000).

In some ways, there is nothing especially surprising or enlightening about the preceding anecdotalization. As even this very light engagement with the relevant literatures suggests, there is a wealth of argument addressing the relationship of the enactment of gender in relation to the nonhuman. Perhaps more intriguing is a second anecdotalization that focuses on 'loss of strength of the handshake'. Here, the 'tripping on a mountain slope' and the injury to my right hand attaches to an anxiety about the loss a firm (and manly) handshake (see Schrock and Schwalbe, 2009). Indeed, every time I shake hands with someone whose handshake is firmer, I am reminded of the 'trip on a mountain slope': it is a corporeal spur to the anecdote. Having said that (see below), the anecdote takes on a different tenor – in relation to an exchange of manly greetings, it serves as an 'excuse' for the lack of a sufficiently firm handshake. Of course, where those handshakes don't generate pain in my hand, then it is less likely that the event 'of the trip on the mountain slope' be reanimated, that is, to have that anecdote come to mind.

On the one hand, this simply evokes the fact that every anecdotalization is itself an enactment – an event – that can be rolled into subsequent anecdotalizations (and in some ways the present recounting is just such a subsequent – or *n*th

order – anecdotalization – about the coming to presence, or absence, of an anecdote). On the other hand, there is the issue of the meaning of a handshake as a
performance of masculinity. While this is certainly what is immediately trig-
gered (for me) through the experience of a firmer handshake, it also open up the
possibility of becoming sensitive to the becoming of 'the handshake'. For
example, there is much popular and professional literature on business greetings
(the importance of a firm handshake), on cultural responsiveness (e.g. in the
Philippines, the preferred handshake is a limp one), on alternative greetings to
the handshake. And, of course, given that I can no longer produce a 'sufficiently'
firm handshake, what does that say about the shifting parameters of 'disability' –
would a more 'overtly disabled' hand have served to diffuse the 'masculine disability' of a less firm handshake?

   However, over and above these reflections on how pain affects the meaning
of a handshake, there are other ways of thinking about pain in relation to anecdotalization. In particular, one can think of pain as, in Michel Serres' terms
(1982), a 'parasite'. According to Serres, the parasite can be understood as
something that disrupts and in the process generates more complex orderings.
So in one of his most famous scenarios, he describes a guest who arrives unin-
vited at a house and joins the hosts at their dinner table. The guest is disruptive insofar as their unexpected arrival and request for food unsettles the
normal sequence of events that take place at the dinner table – the serving of
food, the polite conversation. In return for the food, the guest is willing to
exchange stories, however – in payment for sustenance, therefore, they offer
narrative entertainments. For Serres, this narrative (derived from a fable)
addresses the ways in which the material and the semiotic flip between one
another: the food generates stories; stories re-introduce order around the
dining table, as well as gain food and shelter for the visitor. However, it also
show how the disruptions of the parasite open up the possibility of more
complex orderings. The visitor's disruptions generate stories which lead to
more stories, more food and drink, more layered and inter-connected relations.
In the context of the 'trip on the mountain slope' – that trip was a material
happening that led to the complex ordering of the subsequent anecdote even
as, conversely, the anecdote served in complexifying the meanings of the 'trip
on the mountain slope'. Similarly, the pain felt in a handshake is an intervention in a greeting that serves to complexify that greeting from a simple
communicative exchange to a nexus of acountings around masculinity, multiculture and shifting notions of 'ability'.

c … Slipping on the Pavement …

In this final anecdotalization, we shift tack somewhat, in the main because so
few details about the event of 'slipping on the pavement' can be recalled. In
some ways the anecdote barely exists in narrative form. What does persevere,
however, is a sequence of affects, linked by a storying of the response to the
event. As mentioned in the opening section to this chapter, I certainly could

remember very little of the incident, nor could my son even when I quizzed and prompted him. What turned this into an event was my son's shock at my apparent vulnerability, which clearly affected my partner so that she had to relay it to me, and my subsequent shock of being seen as vulnerable (as opposed to someone who happened to slip in what was a rare and insignificant incident). Put simply, there was a sort of circulation of affect that seemed to 'pin down' this incident as an event (for important writings on affect, see, for example, Massumi, 2002; Clough, 2009; Wetherell, 2012).

However, for me, there as an additional affective element that allowed this event to take hold. Of course, there is the shock of being seen as vulnerable, ageing, losing taken-for-granted capacities – and having to confront this external perception, contrasting it to my own self-perception as a physically adept young-ish middle-aged man. But there was also a resonance with a different set of affects, where I was the son being confronted with my own father's increasing infirmity. This occurred when I was in my early thirties and was told by a cousin, in an offhand, matter-of-fact, way that my father was becoming an old man (this at the age of around 65 – he died at 67). First, there was outrage that this could be said in such a casual way – as if it was of no consequence. Second, there was the sudden realization that my father was indeed 'getting on': his increasing difficulties in walking, his frequent bouts of breathlessness, his constant sleeping – all these were indicative of his 'decline' (at least in my eyes). Now, I was in my father position ... in my son's eyes.

So, the 'slipping on a pavement' event serves, in the specificity of this case, to evoke an affect (being seen as a vulnerable father) that 'latches onto' a prior affect (seeing a vulnerable father) which in turn further crystallizes the later affect. The resonance set up between these can perhaps be thought in terms of a topology. Topology, for present purposes, can be understood as a way of conceptualizing time and space that does not assume external indices or parameters (such as the x/y coordinate system) but sees any such indices as emergent. Thus points seemingly at a 'distance' (according to one set of parameters) might be much 'closer' according to others, and vice versa (Mol and Law, 1994; Lash and Lury, 2007; Lury *et al.*, 2012). As topology is used here, 'close' and 'distant' might refer to meaning as well as space and time. As such, the event of 'slipping on a pavement', as we have anecdotalized here, ties together – knots – a sequence of events distributed in space and time (my son's and partner's 'subsequent' accounts, my cousin's throwaway comment) and an array of meanings (meaning of my son's and my own reactions) which allows for a re-visioning of the 'originary event' (of my 'slipping on a pavement') which is, of course, anything but 'originary'.

Concluding Remarks

In the last three sections, we have addressed three events of mis-stepping and their respective anecdotalizations with the aim of exploring how the mis-step – in its specificity – might serve in the methodological engagement with a world of becoming. We saw how 'falling down the stairs', 'tripping on a mountain slope' and 'slipping on a pavement' open up different ways of thinking about accessing the possibilities of a world that is unfolding. Let us briefly summarize these. In the first case study of 'falling down the stairs' we saw how the anecdotalization of 'falling down the stairs' could illuminate, for example, potential family trajectories, but also how the particular event that comes to anecdotalized takes on its significance depending on the peculiar sequence of events in which it is situated: its impact is thus contingent (or, its causality is emergent). In the second case of 'tripping on a mountain slope' we considered how a corporeal condition might trigger the anecdote in the service of excusing a compromised masculinity, for instance. However, we also examined how the event of 'tripping on a mountain slope', as well as the consequent pain during handshaking, served as parasites that disrupted a sequence of happenings (walking down a mountain slope, shaking hands in greeting), in the process complexifying the possible meanings that attach to these (or that can be derived from them). And in the third case of 'slipping on a pavement' we traced how a barely articulated event triggers a sort of migration of affect across son, partner, father that facilitates the possibility of a series of anecdotes (about the affects connected to the shock of the slip, about paternal vulnerability). At the same time, we proposed that such anecdotalization (about affects) topologically brought together a number of 'distant' events, that is set up a set of new (affective) parameters in which new associations could be rendered 'across space and time'.

Hopefully, the anecdotalization of the mis-step has yielded some insight into certain empirically substantive concerns (the performance of family and skill, the doing and undoing of 'masculinity', and the interlacing of affect and account). But further, perhaps it also offered some potentially useful conceptual themes in relation to the methodological implications of the mis-step. Specifically, anecdotalizing the mis-step in its specificity suggests particular conceptualizations of 'walking as a method' in terms of its 'emergently causal', 'parasitical' and 'topological' possibilities.

Needless to say, this all remains rather tentative and in need of further detail and nuance, but with any luck, the foregoing has at the very least been suggestive. There is one final reflection that needs to be made. This chapter has proposed the mis-step and its anecdotalization as one means to realizing – operationalizing, even – Connolly's idea of an 'exquisite sensitivity to the world of becoming'. What has emerged does not seem very much like 'exquisite sensitivity'. Rather, the three cases we have discussed have entailed moments of, let us call it, 'inexquisite vulnerability' (and there are plenty of other terms one could coin) where the mis-step is an event marked by an accidental openness. The value of this in part lies in how the walking of which it is an interruption is framed. Walking down the stairs, walking down a mountain slope, walking in the street, were in all cases expanded beyond their immediate circumstances and situated within particular narrative trajectories (the significations of family arrival, masculine comportment, waning paternal capacities). But, we might also ask, how does the mis-step serve in re-purposing the walk, as it were. The proposition here is that by paying specific attention to the mis-step (as opposed to neglecting or ignoring or marginalizing it) we can invest new meanings and orderings in the 'walk' and 'walking' and thus open these out to speculative exploration.

References

Akrich, M. (1992) The de-scription of technical objects. In W.E. Bijker and J. Law (eds), *Shaping Technology/Building Society* (pp. 205–224). Cambridge, MA: MIT Press.

Barad, K. (2007) *Meeting the Universe Halfway*. Durham, NC: Duke University Press.

Bennett, J. (2010) *Vibrant Matter*. Durham, NC: Duke University Press.

Bourdieu, P. (1977) *Outline of a Theory of Practice*. Cambridge: Cambridge University Press.

Bourdieu, P. (1984) *Distinction: A Social Critique of the Judgement of Taste*. London: Routledge.

Butler, J. (1993) *Bodies that Matter*. New York: Routledge.

Clough, P. (2009) The new empiricism: affect and sociological method. *European Journal of Social Theory*, 12(1), 43–61.

Connell, R.W. (2005) *Masculinities*, 2nd edn. Berkeley, CA: University of California Press.

Connell, R.W. and Messerschmidt, J.W. (2005) Hegemonic masculinity: rethinking the concept. *Gender and Society*, 19(6), 829–859.

Connolly, W.E. (2011) *A World of Becoming*. Durham, NC: Duke University Press.

Cwerner, S.B. and Metcalfe, A. (2003) Storage and clutter: discourse and practices of order in the domestic world. *Journal of Design History*, 16, 229–239.

Dean, M. (1999) *Governmentality: power and rule in modern society*. London: Sage.

Deleuze, G. (1990) *The Logic of Sense*. New York: Columbia University Press.

Deleuze, G. (1993) *The Fold: Leibniz and the Baroque*. Minneapolis: University of Minnesota Press.

Elias, N. (1994/1939) *The Civilizing Process*. Oxford: Blackwell.

Foucault, M. (1979) *Discipline and Punish*. Harmondsworth: Penguin.

Fraser, M. (2010) Facts, ethics and event. In C. Bruun Jensen and K. Rödje (eds), *Deleuzian Intersections in Science, Technology and Anthropology* (pp. 57–82). New York: Berghahn Press.

Gibson, J.J. (1979) *The Ecological Approach to Visual Perception*. Boston: Houghton Mifflin.

Goffman, E. (1959) *The Presentation of Self in Everyday Life*. Harmondsworth: Penguin.

Goffman, E. (1972) *Relations in Public*. Harmondsworth: Penguin.

Hacking, I. (1986) Making up people. In T.C. Heller, M. Sosna and D.E. Wellberg (eds), *Reconstructing Individualism* (pp. 222–236). Stanford, CA: Stanford University Press.

Ingold, T. (1992) Culture and the perception of the environment. In E. Croll and D. Parkin (eds), *Bush Base: Forest Farm – Culture, Environment and Development* (pp. 39–56). London: Routledge.

Ingold, T. (2007) *Lines: A Brief History*. Cambridge, MA: Harvard University Press.

Ingold, T. (2008) When ANT meets SPIDER: social theory for arthropods. In C. Knapepett and L. Malafouris (eds), *Material Agency* (pp. 209–215). New York: Springer.

Lash, S. and Lury, C. (2007) *Global Culture Industry: The Mediation of Things*. Cambridge: Polity.

Latour, B. (1992) Where are the missing masses? A sociology of a few mundane artifacts. In W.E. Bijker and J. Law (eds), *Shaping Technology/Building Society*, (pp. 225–258). Cambridge, MA: MIT Press.

Law, J. (2004) *After Method: Mess in Social Science Research*. London: Routledge.

Lie, M. and Sorensen, K.H. (1996) Making technology our own? Domesticating technologies into everyday life. In M. Lie and K.H. Sorensen (eds), *Making Technology Our Own? Domesticating Technologies into Everyday Life* (pp. 1–30). Oslo: Scandinavian University Press.

Livesey, G. (2007) Deleuze, Whitehead, the event, and the contemporary city. https://whiteheadresearch.org/occasions/conferences/event-and-decision/papers/Graham%20Livesey_Final%20Draft.pdf. (accessed 23 November 2015).

Lury, C., Parisi, L. and Terranova, T. (2012) Introduction: the becoming topological of culture. *Theory, Culture and Society*, 29, 3–35.

MacNaghten, P. and Urry, J. (1998) *Contested Nature*. Sage: London.

Massumi, B. (2002) *Parables of the Virtual*. Durham, NC: Duke University Press.

Mauss, M. (1985) A category of the person: the notion of person; the notion of self. In M. Carrithers, S. Collins and S. Lukes (eds), *The Category of the Person* (pp. 1–25). Cambridge: Cambridge University Press.

Michael, M. (2000) *Reconnecting Culture, Technology and Nature: From Society to Heterogeneity*. London: Routledge.

Michael, M. (2004) On making data social: heterogeneity in sociological practice. *Qualitative Research*, 4(1), 5–23.

Michael, M. (2006) *Technoscience and Everyday Life*. Maidenhead, Berks.: Open University Press/McGraw-Hill.

Michael, M. (2009) 'The-cellphone-in-the-countryside': on some ironic spatialities of technonature. In D. White and C. Wilbert (eds), *Technonatures* (pp. 85–104). Waterloo: Wilfred Laurier University Press.

Michael, M. (2012a) Toward an idiotic methodology: de-signing the object of sociology. *The Sociological Review*, 60(S1), 166–183.

Michael, M. (2012b) Anecdote. In C. Lury and N. Wakeford (eds), *Inventive Methods: The Happening of the Social* (pp. 25–35). London: Routledge.

Mol, A. and Law, J. (1994) Regions, networks and fluids: anaemia and social topology. *Social Studies of Science*, 24(4): 641–671.

Pickering, A. (1995) *The Mangle of Practice: Time, Agency and Science*. Chicago: University of Chicago Press.

Pink, S. (2007) *Doing Visual Ethnography: Images, Media and Representation in Research*. London: Sage.

Pink, S. (2009) *Doing Sensory Ethnography*. London: Sage.

Schrock, D. and Schwalbe, M. (2009) Men, masculinity, and manhood acts. *Annual Review of Sociology*, 35, 277–295.

Sennett, R. (2008) *The Craftsman*. New Haven: Yale University Press.

Serres, M. (1982) *The Parasite (Posthumanities)*. Minneapolis; London: Johns Hopkins University Press.

Shaviro, S. (2007) *Deleuze's Encounter with Whitehead*. www.shaviro.com/Othertexts/DeleuzeWhitehead.pdf (accessed 23 November 2015).

Skeggs, B. (2004) *Class, Self, Culture*. London: Routledge.

Stengers, I. (2010) *Cosmopolitics I*. Minneapolis: University of Minnesota Press.

Thompson, T.L. and Adams, C. (2013) Speaking with things: encoded researchers, social data, and other posthuman concoctions. *Distinktion: Scandinavian Journal of Social Theory*, 14(3), 342–361.

Vergunst, J.L. (2008) Taking a trip and taking care in everyday life. In T. Ingold and J.L. Vergunst (eds), *Ways of Walking: Ethnography and Practice on Foot* (pp. 105–121). Abingdon: Routledge.

Wetherell, M. (2012) *Affect and Emotion: A New Social Science Understanding*. London: Sage.

Whitehead, A.N. (1929) *Process and Reality. An Essay in Cosmology (Gifford Lectures of 1927–8)*. New York: The Free Press.

Woolgar, S. and Neyland, D. (2013) *Mundane Governance: Ontology and Acounability*. Oxford: Oxford University Press.

Air Walk.
Source: Citizen Sense.

8 Air Walk

Monitoring Pollution and Experimenting with Speculative Forms of Participation

Jennifer Gabrys

Life is in the transitions as much as in the terms connected;
often, indeed, it seems to be there more emphatically …
(William James, *Essays in Radical Empiricism*, 87)

The sites and sources of air pollution in London include automobile exhaust and building heating, construction debris and factory emissions, as well as pollution drifting in from neighboring European countries and fine particles from sandstorms in the Sahara. Settling and mixing in the lived atmospheres of this conurbation are the debris of local, distant, present and inherited material processes as they are worked through and form the city's heady exhaust. While on one level a tale of urban activity could be extracted from the circulations of these chemical residues, on another level the very practices by which the composition of the air and its pollutants come to be identified are also of relevance, for they extend toward bodily and environmental effects, institutional mechanisms for measurement and regulation, as well as infrastructures of instrumentation that settle into a set of standards for assessing air pollution over time.

Air pollution has emerged as an environmental problem with considerable negative impacts. The EU designated 2013 as the 'Year of Air,' and the World Health Organisation (WHO 2006) has issued recent reports indicating that urban air pollutants give rise to extensive health concerns. Yet unlike the smoky skies that plagued London in the 1950s, the air pollution of today tends to be odorless and colorless, as it forms not through sulfur dioxide (SO_2) from burning coal, but rather from nitrogen oxide (NO) and nitrogen dioxide (NO_2) and particulate matter ($PM_{2.5}$ and PM_{10}), primarily emitted from combustion engines. These pollutants are known to impair pulmonary, cardiac and respiratory health, so much so that air pollution has become one of the leading causes of death worldwide (Lim *et al.* 2012). Distinct social formations concretize through the distributed and lived experiences of air pollution, and through public health attempts to mitigate and address it. However, air pollution and its effects have not (until recently) registered as an environmental problem since these pollutants tend to be less evident.

The monitoring of air pollution also unfolds within the not-quite-evident spaces of registering emissions levels. In multiple locations across London, official monitoring infrastructures keep track of concentrations of recognized air pollutants in order to meet national and international air quality objectives. At the same time, practices for monitoring air quality are migrating from primarily 'official' modes of detection and regulation to a number of 'citizen' initiatives for assessing air pollution emissions and exposure. Since air quality is now typically assessed through numerous instruments that measure and monitor particular pollutants, any discussion of what is in the air becomes entangled with the technologies used to monitor air quality.

These technologies are not just making air pollution legible and evident, but also could be said to *experiencing* the air by processing and transforming particles of air into measurements that become legible within wider institutional networks (Gabrys 2016). The sites, practices and objects of measurement within air monitoring are continually shifting arrangements of pollutants, bodies, environments and monitoring technologies. This chapter asks: What are the ways in which experiences of air and air pollution are generated through different and speculative modes of monitoring and detection? What new and possibly collective environmental and participatory practices concretize along with sensing devices, and in what ways might these sensors also delimit environmental practice within specific ways? And how might walking give rise to particular encounters and experiences of air pollution, particularly as an experimental and speculative form of participation that is distributed across multiple sites and subject?

In order to address these questions, I discuss an 'Air Walk' held in the south London neighborhoods of New Cross Gate and Deptford as part of the International Visual Sociology Association conference hosted at Goldsmiths in July 2013. The walk was held as part of the Citizen Sense research project, which studies citizen-based practices and technologies of environmental monitoring. The 'Air Walk' was undertaken as a pilot study examining how environmental sensing is practiced through multiple modalities, and how DIY citizen-sensing devices inform environmental practice. The walk was also developed as a process for testing how it might be possible to experiment with the experiences of air and air pollution by setting in motion the sites, participant encounters, monitoring kit, infrastructures, urban situations and speculative practices as they come together in this context. In part, the 'social' worlds that the 'Air Walk' traversed then came into being through lived and live encounters with air pollution (cf. Back and Puwar 2012), and were not entirely pre-constituted. In another sense, as a form of 'collective experimentation' (Gabrys and Yusoff 2012), the walk set speculative encounters into play so that new social formations were also concretizing through this event. The walk was then a mode of experimentally composing different experiences of urban air.

Analysis of Walking: Forms of Participation

This investigation of the walk as an experimental form of participation draws on and responds to literature and research that investigates the broad range of public participation to consider how it might variously be more constructive, open-ended and experimental, and potentially less normative and scripted (Bogner 2012; Delgado *et al.* 2011; Lengwiler 2008). In dialogue with these investigations, I consider what an experimental approach to the *speculative forms* of participation might offer. As a pilot, the 'Air Walk' was not a fully fledged unfolding of 'publics'. Instead, it was an experiment with the forms and processes of engagement, and a specific consideration of Felt and Fochler's (2010) suggestion that *more experimentation* is exactly what is needed when investigating public engagement.

In this sense, this chapter is also not making grand claims for citizen science, but rather is suggesting that as a form of participation walking – and citizen monitoring – might be approached as generative and speculative rather than prescribed processes. Citizen science and citizen sensing are practices that could – or could not – 'empower' participants, and which potentially could lead to forms of political intervention and realignment. But these capacities are largely dependent upon the communities, contexts and environmental problems to be addressed, and are not a de facto attribute of citizen science or citizen sensing – just as many citizen science projects could be characterized as rote tasks contributing to distant scientific problems, or as public-relations exercises in obtaining citizen 'consent' for technoscientific developments (cf. Felt and Fochler 2010). My focus here is to consider how citizen sensing as a practice *could* activate environments and environmental concerns, and thereby give rise to new possibilities for experimental forms of participation and public engagement through inventive experiences.

But by experience I do not mean simply human bodies sensing air, since this would suggest a mediatory way of how subjects feel the object of air. Instead, I am interested to think through how air is experienced and encountered on this walk across and by a distributed range of entities, from institutional monitoring networks to air apps to pamphlets and organisms, busy streets and active incinerators, auto exhaust and lorries, mobile kits and DIY practices, as well as human and more-than-human bodies. All of these entities, I suggest, sense and experience air in actual occasions (Whitehead 1929), of which this walk might serve as one instance.

By experimenting with ways of experiencing air pollution, the walk becomes a process for testing speculative forms of participation, not just with human participants, but also with the multiple distributed entities that are involved in experiencing the air. On this walk, we attended to the infrastructural monitoring networks in place in this one area of London, together with the more mobile technologies increasingly available for assessing air quality, and the DIY sensing kits assembled for the event that were tuned to NO_2, $PM_{2.5}$ and 'other gases.' The ways in which the walk experimented with sensing and monitoring the air then included the use of DIY sensors, GPS devices, black carbon meters, pamphlets and maps, existing air monitoring infrastructure, roadsides and industrial sites, as well as human and nonhuman bodies that were variously incorporating the effects of urban air.

The walk attempted to *tune in* to these experiences and entities (James 1912, 126; Stengers 2008; Gabrys 2012b), as actual and speculative encounters with air pollution. Walking can be seen as a speculative form of participation since it is not possible to know how the experience will unfold – in other words, it is an always-experimental form of encounter (O'Rourke 2013). The walk was then an attempt to work through – in practice – the contours of *experiencing* air quality, and through experience consider what forms of participation are generated in this actual occasion. In thinking of the air walk in this way, I am influenced by the work of James (1912), Whitehead (1929) and Stengers (2002), who variously suggest that experience serves as the critical modality for considering how speculative encounters might give rise to engagements – or relational articulations – that recast not just what counts for participation, but also what counts as the subjects, objects and sites for experiencing air quality. Air and air pollution are not fixed entities, but rather are concrescences that are drawn together and inflected across multiple experiences. 'The Air' is not an absolute point of reference, but rather forms through drifting and atmospheric experiences in and through which distinct moments and materialities of air register. This is not to say that everything is constructed in the old sense of the social construction of technology, but rather that particular constructions of air *matter*, since these are distinct ways in which the feeling for air is expressed – across instruments, geographies, bodies, policies, more-than-human organisms – and sedimented into future a/effects of air (cf. Suchman 2007).

Further to this, walking could be seen as a *transition* in experience that, following James in the epigraph to this chapter, puts emphasis on the connections and disconnections made through processes of relating. This emphasis on transition makes 'the distinction between knowing as verified and completed, and the same knowing as in transit and on its way' (1912, 67–68). As a transitional experience, walking unfolds as an experiment with knowing in passage, and with connections made through processes as they unfold. Such transitions are, as James notes of experience, 'speculative investments' that draw together the actual with the more-to-come (ibid., 88). Even if mapped in advance, a walk does not allow one to know what will be encountered during the walk itself, what relations will emerge or what exchanges will occur. Walking draws together some entities, milieus and experiences, while excluding others. It develops as a speculative grammar of movement and pause, of attention and inattention.

This chapter is organized as a series of five transitions made across the trajectories and stopping points, as well as subjects and milieus, encountered along the walk. These transitions provide the radical empirical material under discussion, and are points at which the walk is considered as potentially generative of distinct forms of participation and experience that provide different entry points to the problem of urban air pollution. Through recounting the process of the walk as a series of transitions, this chapter further considers how it might be possible to switch the emphasis on monitoring technology as the usual site of invention to consider how the relations and practices that are put in motion are sites of invention as well. Walking decenters the apparent thingness of an object of technical invention. In this radical empirical approach, rather than focus attention on a fixed thing or location, emphasis is instead brought to bear on the animating relations and things that concretize *across* speculative forms of participation. In the text that follows, I explore how walking as an experimental form of participation unfolded through these different experiences of urban air in south London.

Transition 1: Walking and Multiplying Forms of Monitoring

Reflecting the interdisciplinary character of this conference event, our walk was made up of architects and artists, sociologists and policymakers, as well as public health researchers and practitioners. We began the 'Air Walk' in the campus green at Goldsmiths, a space removed from the busy streets of New Cross yet full of activity from the conference. New Cross as a whole is an area that regularly exceeds NO_2 levels set in place by the EU, and has recurring high levels of $PM_{2.5}$ as well. The walk was situated within this set of concerns about air quality, and considered how to experiment with environmental engagement in air quality.

Walking can be articulated through multiple modalities, from protests and parades to flâneurie and botanizing on the asphalt, as well as moving experiments with locative media, art and geography, which have variously tested and worked with walking as a form of engagement (Gabrys 2012a). This particular walk could on one level be characterized as a sort of 'walking seminar,' following Annemarie Mol (n.d.), which undertook a walk as a way to bring together experiences of and discussions about air pollution along with the instruments and environments in which these technical alignments might be put to work.

As a pilot walk for eventual engagement with citizen-sensing communities, the walk tested the coming together of kits and practices in situ, and to understand the types of encounters that might unfold through real-time monitoring. The route was planned in advance in order to make visits to official air quality monitoring infrastructure, and to visit key sites of industrial activity and urban development in the area. Prior discussions had taken place in order to plan for the walk, including interviews with local borough air quality officers, meetings with urban planning and design firms, and collaborating with the King's Environment Research Group (ERG) that runs the official London Air Quality Network. We were also accompanied by researchers working on public engagement at the NHS, who brought a micro-aethalometer and GPS – devices loaned to us by the King's ERG – to monitor and locate black carbon levels, which is emitted from combustion activities but is most common in diesel exhaust.

Even though the route was planned in advance, at the same time it was not possible to know what would occur along the route as we walked, testing monitoring equipment in the heat of the day, traversing crowds and traffic, bringing together questions and encounters: specific experiencing entities would inevitably still form and erupt in this actual occasion. In the process of beginning and introducing the walk to participants (many of whom were not familiar with south London), there was an inevitable gathering and assembling of cameras and pamphlets, maps and monitoring equipment, notebooks and backpacks, as well as sunscreen and water bottles, which made this a heterogeneous research undertaking that was neither too orderly nor too contained. At the same time, researchers on the research project were a part of this experiment, not standing outside observing from a singularly authorized position (cf. Haraway 1997), but moving along with this rolling kit of parts, and attempting to make sense of air pollution along this particular trajectory.

After a brief introduction to the walk and to each other, we then made our way from Goldsmiths down New Cross Road. Our first stop took place at the New Cross Road monitoring station, located adjacent to the Rose Pub and directly across from the New Cross Gate train station. This monitoring station is one of four in the Borough of Lewisham, and one of nearly 100 stations in the London Air Quality Network (LAQN), which includes council-owned stations and Automatic Urban and Rural Network (AURN) national stations (cf. Barry 1998). There is a wide array of instruments and methods for measuring air quality, from hand-held personal air monitors to diffusion tubes and badges, as well as spot-checking devices and mobile laboratories, but when it comes to monitoring air in response to and to influence environmental policy in a widespread and systematic way, fixed monitoring stations within government networks tend to be the most common technology and infrastructure used for regulation and enforcement.

Air monitoring stations are part of the urban infrastructure that typically recedes into the background. Yet as part of this walk we made a more deliberate encounter with this infrastructure, while standing on a busy roadside in the heat and thick air of numerous automobiles rushing by. We asked how the station is managed, how the data is processed, and the responses that arise to exceedances of air pollution levels. These questions about the governance and logistics of monitoring cannot always be answered in situ, but as part of this encounter we discuss how stations are typically owned by councils, which also decide where to locate stations.

We consider the particular pollutants captured at this station. NO and NO_2, as well as SO_2, and PM_{10} and $PM_{2.5}$ are monitored here. The pollutants monitored within the LAQN are set in relation to EU-led policy that is developed in response to health research on the damaging effects of air pollution (European Commission 2008). The measurements obtained from this station and the many others across the network are compared and managed (or ignored) against European standards for acceptable emissions of certain pollutants. Yet as we investigated this grey box, we had little sense of the measurements or modes of governance that converge into this and the multiple other stations across London. Different modalities of measurement might even be said to generate different experiences of pollution, which take hold in distinct environments of relevance (Gabrys 2016; Stengers 2002).

To give a somewhat more immediate sense of air pollution, King's ERG has set up the London Air app, which we looked at on several smartphones brought along on the walk. This app allows the general public to look at maps and specific locations in London to receive a relatively near-time reading of air pollution levels. The bandings on the app indicate whether air pollution is low, moderate or high according to the daily air quality index. This app also sends air pollution alerts for specific locations, and includes a record of air pollution episodes. Yet the 'low' or the 'high' readings of the app do not always seem to correspond to the microclimate in which we are standing, and the readings within any given hour may not reflect the longer-term air pollution exceedances that occur.

At the same time that we are considering the measurements taken or expressed by the air quality station, the diffusion tubes at this site, and the London Air app, we are taking measurements with the micro-aethalometer, which measures black carbon but does not have a real-time display (and so the comparative data will have to be gathered after the walk has taken place), and we are also carrying DIY environmental sensors measuring NO_2, PM and 'other gases.' Traversing and transitioning past one air quality station, we encounter multiple forms of monitoring that parse the experience of air pollution differently. Participation does not settle into a singular engagement with a device, in this sense, but rather opens up into a series of questions about how air pollution is captured, measured, communicated and experienced across a range of sensing instruments.

Transition 2: Exposure and Embodiment along Mercury Way

As we make our way from the New Cross Road monitoring station to a less busy residential street, we stop to consider the ways in which embodied experiences might enable distinct experiences of air quality, while potentially not capturing others, by testing our sense of the smell of the air just beyond the busy road and just before approaching the nearby incinerator and waste yard. Even though the 'official' readings suggest we are experiencing low levels of air pollution, and the low-cost devices flickered in and out of zones of safety and toxicity, on our walk we were pointedly experiencing the effects of air that felt quite burdensome, as scratchy throats and watering eyes indicated. Our experience in this moment was then intersecting with this range of technologies that differently articulated air and pollution – across bodies, technologies and environments.

As Debaise (2014) has suggested, bodies-subjects are not the 'ground' of experience, but rather are a node within a process of experience, a node that 'polarizes' the datum in particular ways. Bodies, in this sense, are diffractive vectors, capturing and transforming air while also being made and remade by these same hazy currents. The process of accessing the distributed and polarized experiences of what is in the air becomes a project that is contingent and imperfectly constituted, traveling across DIY devices, monitors without displays, tubes without immediate analysis and monitoring stations that are more or less opaque, save for the data linking up through a one-hour delay to an air quality app that gives notional qualitative bandings of how high or low air pollution for select pollutants was at any given time.

On one level, it is evident that these multiple monitoring practices are productive of different engagements with air quality and pollution. But beyond the multiplicity of these practices, what also stands in relief are the ways in which these encounters give rise to different relations. We could say that the New Cross Road monitoring station is *experiencing* the multiple forces that inform the type of air quality assessment that actually goes on here, in a way that differently compares with the attempt to smell the air or register air pollution through different sensors. The monitoring station is an active distribution of experience that works through, processes and prehends the 'datum' that is air quality, and which contributes to the potential for further experiences to arise, since social environments are comprised of 'mutual prehensions' (Whitehead 1929, 230).

The different ways in which these technologies *experience* air by monitoring and measuring pollutants begin to inform the types of work that can be done with them, and what our experience might be as citizen scientists and citizen sensors, attempting to understanding and potentially intervene in the space of urban air quality. As should be clear by now, moreover, this is not a phenomenological rendering of experience, since a human decoding subject is not at the center of these experiences. Rather, experience is distributed across and expressed by entities that form societies of actual occasions. Our attempt to monitor, experience and understand pollution emissions and exposure at this moment of the walk inevitably intersected with multiple other 'bodies' that were processing, distributing, remaking and analyzing air quality on this afternoon and across longer durations.

Bodies also become sites where the experience of air pollution is taken up as a sort of constructive and constitutive function (cf. Shaviro 2014). These bodies are not just of the human sensing type, rather, they form as experiencing entities sloughed off from multiple pollution processes. Combustion and suspension of pollutants forms across the burning of fossil fuels, the circuiting of motor vehicles, the friction of urban spaces, the scattering and gathering of crowds, the channeling of buildings as street canyons, the flowing of pedestrians and passersby, and the absorbing by lungs and hearts, soils and trees, an assortment of dusts and gases that drift in and out of a zone of reactivity, bonding, lighting up, amplification, local weather, multiplying and transforming in and through urban air.

An Incinerator and the Absence of Monitoring

In the heat and grit of this rather hot 27°C July day in London, we then walk to the Mercury Way monitoring station at the intersection with Cold Blow Lane, which is adjacent to a waste transfer site, and nearby the Southeast London Combined Heat and Power (SELCHP) incinerator. The Mercury Way monitoring station, which has only been in operation since 2010, is one of the four stations operated by Lewisham Council and managed within the LAQN by King's ERG. This site is classed as an industrial monitoring station, which only monitors for PM_{10} and weather data, and does not have NOx or other sensors. As an industrial monitoring station, data from this site is also not included in the Department for Environment, Food and Rural Affairs (DEFRA) air quality reports to the EU as constituting relevant exposure. Although housing surrounds this site, the *industrial* classification of the monitoring station (one of only seven in the LAQN) designates the data from this site as less relevant in comparison to hotspots such as New Cross Road.

While at this site, we noted that the street on which we stand, 'Mercury Road,' seems to be a monument to this and any number of toxic chemicals. We considered what types of dust the PM_{10} instrumentation is monitoring, and whether it would also be relevant to monitor $PM_{2.5}$ and NOx in this site of intensive heavy vehicle traffic and industrial activity. We examined how the monitoring station is situated and if it was downwind or upwind of SELCHP, and as we inspected the monitor more closely, we saw that the anemometer at the top of the station was jammed and was catching on the protective grating over the weather sensors. Since part of what would make the monitoring data from this site relevant is whether and how emissions might be travelling from the industrial sites to residences, this jamming of the anemometer interrupts this understanding of emissions and their trajectories.

As we move from the Mercury Way monitoring station around the waste transfer yard to the SELCHP incinerator, we consider the long-standing environmental justice issues related to where industrial infrastructures such as incinerators are sited. This particular structure was located in an immigrant community that at the time of its construction was seen to pose less resistance to this development (Parau and Wittmeier Bains 2008). Incinerators were at one time considered a useful form of infrastructural investment, and these developments at times receive subsidies for generating 'renewable energy' and for diverting waste from landfills.

We considered the uncertain relationship between monitoring and emissions, and the ways in which incinerators were perhaps less frequently addressed as environmental matters of concern (cf. Corburn 2005). At one time, the looming chimneys of incinerators and factories were icons of environmental harm, but attention has increasingly shifted to automobiles and individual consumption. The environmental impacts of these more collective infrastructures can still be felt, however, and the absence of certain regulatory types of monitoring and attention to sites such as incinerators are often what spur interest in citizen-led monitoring.

Transition 3: 'Instruments for a Speculative Cartography' at Deptford Park

What's in the air? What is monitored? How is it monitored? How is this information acted upon or otherwise influence environmental politics and

practice? As we walk and visit different monitors and different sites of pollution, we are repeatedly testing these questions about what monitoring makes
evident, and how monitoring is located and operationalized. We next walk
past Sir Francis Drake Primary School at Grinstead Road and Trundley's
Road, as well as Deptford Park Primary School at north-east corner of park at
Evelyn Street to Deptford Park, a large green field surrounded by plane trees
and offering welcome relief from the full blaze of the sun. Here, in the
shadow of the SELCHP incinerator, we consider in more detail how the rise
of citizen science and citizen sensing activities attempt to democratize
environmental monitoring and data collection, while addressing the specificities of individual exposure as distinct from the fixed sites of emissions monitoring. These citizen sensing practices are often what might be referred to as
'instruments for a speculative cartography,' following Guattari (1989, 5),
which test out new technical arrangements without having any guaranteed
outcome. There is no guarantee that the data gathered by citizens will make
sense, that the instruments will work or that evidence will concretize in such
a way as to generate political change. Yet these speculative practices still
create a lure toward expanded ways of understanding the experience of
environments and environmental pollution.

While the LAQN captures air quality data at points throughout London for
generating legally admissible data, and DEFRA and EA monitors captured data
at points of distinct land use, and models and emissions inventories various
project and forecast pollutants across London and the UK, now more monitoring
projects are emerging that are related to community engagement with air quality.
The King's ERG that runs the LAQN has also been involved with the Southeast
NHS public engagement group to study how air pollution data might be used to
improve health. With us on our walk are several researchers from the Southeast
NHS group, who are carrying a micro-aethalometer, which has also previously
been used in a study of personal air monitoring of journeys (Brannon 2012). The
point with many of these mobile and individual monitors is that individual exposure may vary widely from the emissions captured at fixed monitoring stations,
and so exposure studies can provide a much different picture of what is in
the air.

The micro-aethalometer is far from a low-cost or DIY device, however, and
we have along with us a set of Grove Seeedstudio sensors alerting us to the relative 'freshness' of the air, and at one point recording NO_2 levels as high as
$76 \mu m/m^3$. From backpacks and balloons to wearable sensors and sensors on
drones, from handheld sensor prototypes to smartphone apps, and even from
lichens to strawberries, a number of air monitoring kits are currently under
development, in use, and being tested in the field in order to give indicative
assessments of air quality in finer-grain spatial and temporal detail.

The data that these devices generate, however, are typically less relevant
for the absolute number produced and more relevant in relation to indications
of activity or changes in pollution patterns over time (cf. Gabrys and Pritchard
2015). Tuning citizens into exposure patterns, filling in the spaces between

monitoring sites, generating a sense of shifts in urban activity over time: these are different types of insights that might emerge from the use of DIY sensors. Sensors are often presented as participatory technologies, yet there is a considerable amount of expertise needed to code and assemble this kit for monitoring. And different sensors can provide distinct experiences air, given that some sensors used in DIY electronics are manufactured for monitoring Boeing jets or lavatory air freshening, rather than urban air quality.

On this walk, we then explore the rise of personal and DIY environmental monitoring as a way in which air quality data is made intimate and immediate to lived urban experiences. The assumed immediacy and directness of what is being sensed inevitably influences the experience of environments. The monitoring that generates air pollution data is meant to provide a direct route to action, even though it is somewhat unclear how forms of participation that make pollution visible facilitate action. Indeed, strategies of visibility through data might potentially elide other influences within the problematic of urban air pollution. As experiments with forms of participation, these monitoring practices arguably unsettle some (regulatory) engagements while solidifying others. In this sense, monitoring is not just an epistemic consideration, but also an ontological one, where distinct relations are put in place in order to identify, monitor and potentially even act upon that which is detected.

Transition 4: Anticipating Pollution at Sayes Court and Convoys Wharf

Moving north-east from Deptford Park, we then crossed Evelyn Street to Oxestalls Road, taking a right on Grove Street past the Deptford Park Primary school located next to a petrol station and the Veolia Environmental Services yard to our next stop, Sayes Court. Standing here in the ward of Evelyn, in the district of Deptford in the Borough of Lewisham, we encounter a park and relic of sorts of John Evelyn, who was author of *Fumifugium* (1661). This text is often referred to as one of the first treatises on air quality, which considered the relationship between urban industry and air.

Why refer to this text besides the fact that it seems to be a curious accident that Evelyn once lived on a site that is now immediately downwind from the SELCHP incinerator? Not only was *Fumifugium* one of the first texts on air quality, it was continuously recycled and reprinted in the context of air quality discussions, including by the National Smoke Abatement Society in 1933 and 1961, and by the National Society for Clean Air in 1944. The basic gist of the text was an appeal to Charles II to control the 'smokes' in London. Because people were unable to adapt to the extreme London air pollution, there was a high incidence of death due to London air, and people who had the means often repaired to the countryside. Evelyn argued that breathing was an indispensible process, and that poor air quality had a harmful affect on the body.

Evelyn's argument not only addressed the 'aesthetic' appeal of better air quality – that air has a spiritual quality, but also that London did not have air befitting a world capital city. He made a series of proposals for remedying air pollution, including moving industry and the 'vile' working cottages out of London, or at the very least beyond the 'mountain' of Greenwich; planting sweet-smelling flowering trees and shrubs, including lavender, rosemary, hops, bay, woodbind, musk and roses. Merchant has suggested in the *Death of Nature* (1980) that Evelyn's approach to the environment was fundamentally flawed as it was organicist and managerial (and classist), yet his proposals continue to provoke considerations about how urban air and urban development swirl together in the same smoky broth.

With Evelyn's text in mind, and the murky commons that are made in urban air, we move toward the final stopping point on the walk, Convoys Wharf in Deptford. This 46-acre site on the Thames was currently in the planning stages for a major urban development by Hutchison Whampoa. The site had previously been owned by News of the World, and had become a site primed for redevelopment, including high-density housing of approximately 3,500 new units along with commercial and cultural units. Inevitably, such a development would produce air pollution, both in the construction of the site (anticipated to last 15–20 years), and in the increased traffic and building use that would generate common urban pollutants.

Planning regulations typically require strategies to be in place for mitigating or abating anticipated pollution from new developments. Planning proposals are also required to submit air quality assessments and models as part of the planning package outlining the current state of the air, along with anticipated forecasts of air quality in 4–5 years if no development were to occur, and anticipated forecasts of air quality in 4–5 years if development were to occur. These planning documents form the basis for mitigation and reduction measures that Lewisham Council would then work with the developer to put in place. Yet as often as not, development unfolds without such oversight, and the city absorbs the new sources of pollutants, with or without an air quality strategy.

As we stand at the Convoys Wharf site discussing the imminent development, momentary readings of NOx spike and then fall. We speculate whether this is due to the wind from the river, passing ships, or some other airborne event. And we wonder how accurate this momentary reading is, since this site is currently far less overloaded with traffic and industrial activity than many of the other sites we have passed through. We also conjecture how this site will look in ten years time when, planning permission having been granted, 40-story residential towers with boilers, and buses and lorries ferrying people and goods, amplify the pollutants here.

Inevitably, new development projects generate additional environmental impacts that require assessment, as well as monitoring and mitigation. New densities and transport configurations, as well as construction and heating, change the environmental conditions of sites and bring new requirements for ensuring air quality. Citizen sensing that focuses on real-time environmental pollutants could respond to and anticipate these future pollution events. But at the same time, these citizen-sensing practices could also occlude other types of urban political engagement, such as addressing gentrification or housing crises.

Transition 5: Alternative Exposures Along Douglas Way

Nearing the end of the walk, we finally made our way back to Goldsmiths along Douglas Way, an alternative walking route along a greenway that Lewisham Council had promoted as a way to minimize individual exposure to air pollution that one might otherwise experience if walking along New Cross Road. Emissions and exposure are two aspects of air quality management. While practices can be developed for abating air pollution and so controlling emissions, the reduction of emissions remains a politically complex project, and so managing one's individual exposure is often seen to be a more expedient approach to the problem of air pollution. The practice of taking alternative walking routes is then frequently suggested and adopted as a way to minimize individual exposure to air pollution.

By this point of the walk, we had engaged with official LAQN monitoring stations located to comply with EU air quality objectives, apps designed to give publics some sense of the quality of air, and apps designed to make explicit the connections between air quality and health, as well as bodily engagements with air pollution and DIY sensing devices. Across this array of kit, infrastructure, bodies, organisms, places and digital platforms, the ways in which we experienced and monitored air pollution became not only multiply constituted, but also provided ample space for considering how we develop practices in and around these sites of engagement.

Fast-forwarding several months from the end of this walk, we received a map of the GPS-located micro-aethalometer data from King's ERG. Here was another dataset that mapped exposure during the two-hour walk on a hot day in July. As if the intersecting experiences of monitoring infrastructures, bodies, DIY devices, health research and EU policy, as well as diffusion tubes and anecdotal tales were not enough to trouble the contours of environmental monitoring, this map provided us with minute-by-minute data at each site along the walk that at times corresponded with our DIY readings, at other times wildly contrasted, and in most cases provided a much different picture than the hourly averages communicated through the qualitative bandings of the London Air app. Different experiences of one itinerary showed up in different data sets and across different technologies.

While we were standing at the New Cross Road monitoring station, this app indicated emissions of NOx and PM_{10} and $PM_{2.5}$ to be low, while here black carbon readings indicated emissions were high. This minute-based reading of air quality was a further point of contrast, since health research and policy objectives indicate that hourly readings are sufficient for understanding and responding to air quality. On the other end of the spectrum, diffusion tubes provide averages usually on a monthly basis, depending on how long they have been placed in the field. The temporality of monitoring and exposure, of regulation and experience, then wavered in and out of focus, where official measurements might contrast with citizen data, and where individual exposure might not readily align with the averages provided through public health guidance and air quality objectives.

Conclusion

How does the experience of emissions and exposure unfold across kits, infrastructures and bodies? How do we differently participate in environmental monitoring through these diverse and distributed ways of experiencing air quality, and what consequences does this have for the human, more-than-human and environmental health? Part of the objective of the 'Air Walk' was to consider how air is experienced, whether through visual, embodied or informational registers. The walk further experimented with speculative forms of participation that concretize through encountering air pollution in process. Through experimenting with air pollution sensing kit, we tested how environmental sensing enables certain types of monitoring, and yet at the same time generates questions about the limits and possibilities of these monitoring practices.

Low-cost sensor devices not only relocate the sites of monitoring from scientific and governmental to everyday spaces, but also raise multiple questions about what is being monitored, and how environmental harm may be identified. Delineations of low or high air pollution imperfectly correspond to on-the-ground measurements, bodily experiences and accumulated effects. Environmental sensors appear to measure and record the 'facts' of air pollution, but actually give rise to new questions and matters of concern about how air pollution is monitored.

This is an extended way of saying that sensing kit is just one small part of the provocation for working through how the experience of air quality is distributed, and what the practices of reworking air might consist of. Monitoring and citizen sensing are emerging as new modes of environmental participation. We sought to investigate the ways in which these practices enable new ways to engage with and address air pollution, and to address and change environmental politics.

The walk raised many questions about how DIY sensors travel through environments, multiplying the experiences and data points gathered in monitoring activities, while also creating a new set of issues with which to grapple in order to have the kit work and be legible as a site of environmental practice and politics. But a key concluding point is that this walk mobilized speculative and experimental forms of participation that reorient research engagements. Rather than undertake an ethnographic and descriptive-based account of the walk, I have instead sought to emphasize the multiple vectors of experience that were animated and brought together in this event.

And rather than collapse this discussion into creating a typology of participation or outlining how walking might become a method, I have sought to articulate how the singularity of walking might be a way to rethink and rework forms of participation mobilized for environmental and public engagement. It is the very liveness and relationality of these encounters that might potentially contribute to new ways of unfolding engagements with air pollution. Distributions of experience actively inform the entities that are made and sustained in order for particular practices – here of environmental citizenship – to occur. From the events encountered on the route of the walk, to the air, the weather, the traffic, pedestrians, participants and monitoring kits, the 'outcomes' of the walk-as-research might prove to be somewhat unpredictable. Yet the trajectory of the walk can animate these speculative encounters, and create radical forms of pedagogy that might contribute to more generative – and collective – forms of environmental politics.

Acknowledgments

Thanks are due to Citizen Sense researchers Helen Pritchard and Nerea Calvillo for contributing to the organizing of the 'Air Walk,' as well as to the IVSA conference participants who undertook the walk. Thanks to King's Environment Research Group, especially Andrew Grieve and Benjamin Barratt, for providing information, equipment and data analysis, as well as to Laura Brannon and colleagues at the Patient and Public Involvement Project Manager with the NIHR GSTFT/KCL Biomedical Research Centre in the R&D Department at Guy's and St Thomas' NHS Foundation Trust. Thanks are due to Lewisham Borough for discussions on air quality, and to Phil Hayden at Hutchison Whampoa Properties for arranging access to Convoy's Wharf. The research leading to these results has received funding from the European Research Council under the European Union's Seventh Framework Programme (FP/2007–2013)/ERC Grant Agreement n. 313347, 'Citizen Sensing and Environmental Practice: Assessing Participatory Engagements with Environments through Sensor Technologies.'

References

Back, L. and Puwar, N. (2012) 'A Manifesto for Live Methods: Provocations and Capacities,' *Sociological Review*, 60(S1), 6–17.

Barry, A. (1998) *Motor Ecology: The Political Chemistry of Urban Air*. Critical Urban Studies: Occasional Papers. New Cross, London: Centre for Urban and Community Research at Goldsmiths College.

Bogner, A. (2012) 'The Paradox of Participation Experiments,' *Science, Technology, and Human Values*, 37(5), 506–527.

Brannon, L. (2012) 'South East London Air Pollution Community Project,' NHS National Institute for Health Research, www.londonair.org.uk/london/reports/South-East-London-Air-Quality-Community-16-01-13.pdf (accessed April 30, 2016).

Corburn, J. (2005) *Street Science: Community Knowledge and Environmental Health Justice*, Cambridge, MA: MIT Press.

Debaise, D. (2014) 'Possessive Subjects: A Speculative Interpretation of Nonhumans,' in N. Gaskill and A. J. Nocek (eds), *The Lure of Whitehead*, 299–311, Minneapolis: University of Minnesota Press.

Delgado, A., Lein Kjølberg, K. and Wickson, F. (2011) 'Public Engagement Coming of Age: From Theory to Practice in STS Encounters with Nanotechnology,' *Public Understanding of Science*, 20(6), 826–845.

European Commission (2008) 'Directive 2008/50/EC of the European Parliament and of the Council of 21 May 2008 on Ambient Air Quality and Cleaner Air for Europe,' *Official Journal of the European Union*, L 152/1.

Evelyn, J. (1661) *Fumifugium*, reprint, University of Exeter: The Rota, 1976.

Felt, U. and Fochler, M. (2010) 'Machineries for Making Publics: Inscribing and Describing Publics in Public Engagement,' *Minerva*, 48(3), 219–238.

Gabrys, J. (2012a) 'Becoming Urban: Sitework from a Moss-Eye View,' *Environment and Planning A*, 44(12), 2922–2939.

Gabrys, J. (2012b) 'Sensing an Experimental Forest: Processing Environments and Distributing Relations,' *Computational Culture*, 2, http://computationalculture.net/article/sensing-an-experimental-forest-processing-environments-and-distributing-relations (accessed April 30, 2016).

Gabrys, J. (2016) *Program Earth: Environment as Experiment in Sensing Technology*, Minneapolis: University of Minnesota Press.

Gabrys, J. and Pritchard, H. (2015) 'Next-Generation Environmental Sensing: Moving beyond Regulatory Benchmarks for Citizen-Gathered Data,' in A. J. Berre, S. Schade and J. Piera (eds), Draft conference proceedings for 'Environmental Infrastructures and Platforms 2015 – Infrastructures and Platforms for Environmental Crowd Sensing and Big Data Proceedings of the Workshop,' 57–65, Barcelona, Spain.

Gabrys, J. and Yusoff, K. (2012) 'Arts, Sciences and Climate Change: Practices and Politics at the Threshold,' *Science as Culture*, 21(1), 1–24.

Guattari, F. (1989) *Schizoanalytic Cartographies*, A. Goffey (trans.), reprint, London: Bloomsbury, 2013.

Haraway, D. (1997) *Modest_Witness@Second_Millennium. FemaleMan©_Meets_Onco-Mouse™*, New York: Routledge.

James, W. (1912) *Essays in Radical Empiricism*, reprint, Lincoln, NE: University of Nebraska Press, 1996.

Lengwiler, M. (2008) 'Participatory Approaches in Science and Technology: Historical Origins and Current Practices in Critical Perspective,' *Science, Technology, and Human Values*, 33(2), 186–200.

Lim, S., Vos, T., Flaxman, A. D. *et al.* (2012) 'A Comparative Risk Assessment of Burden of Disease and Injury Attributable to 67 Risk Factors and Risk Factor Clusters in 21 Regions, 1990–2010: A Systematic Analysis for the Global Burden of Disease Study 2010,' *Lancet*, 380(9859), 2224–2260.

LAQN (London Air Quality Network). www.londonair.org.uk (accessed April 30, 2016).

Merchant, C. (1980) *Death of Nature: Women, Ecology and the Scientific Revolution*, reprint, New York: Harper Collins Publishers, 1990.

Mol, A. (n.d.) 'The Walking Seminar,' http://walkingseminar.blogspot.com (accessed April 30, 2016).

O'Rourke, K. (2013) *Walking and Mapping: Artists as Cartographers*, Cambridge, MA: MIT Press.

Parau, C. E. and Wittmeier Bains, J. (2008) 'Europeanisation as Empowerment of Civil Society: All Smoke and Mirrors?' in W. A. Maloney and J. W. van Deth (eds), *Civil Society and Governance in Europe: From National to International Linkages*, 109–126, Cheltenham, UK: Edward Elgar Publishing.

Shaviro, S. (2014) *The Universe of Things: On Speculative Realism*, Minneapolis: University of Minnesota Press.

Stengers, I. (2002) *Thinking with Whitehead: A Free and Wild Creation of Concepts*, M. Chase (trans.), reprint, Cambridge: Harvard University Press, 2011.

Stengers, I. (2008) 'A Constructivist Reading of *Process and Reality*,' *Theory, Culture and Society*, 25(4), 91–110.

Suchman, L. (2007) *Human-Machine Reconfigurations: Plans and Situated Actions*, 2nd edition, Cambridge, UK: Cambridge University Press.

Whitehead, A. N. (1929) *Process and Reality*, reprint, New York: The Free Press, 1985.

WHO (World Health Organization) (2006) 'WHO Air Quality Guidelines for Particulate Matter, Ozone, Nitrogen Dioxide and Sulfur Dioxide: Global Update 2005,' Geneva: World Health Organization.

The Listening Walk Takes a Detour Through a Graveyard Near the Royal Mile.
Source: Michael Gallagher.

9   Listening Walks

A Method of Multiplicity

Michael Gallagher and Jonathan Prior

Introduction: Listening and Sensory Walking

The concept of the 'soundwalk' emerged in the 1960s and 1970s through the work of the World Soundscape Project, and was first described by R. Murray Schafer, one of the key members of the project, as: 'an exploration of a sound-scape of a given area' (Schafer, 1994: 213). Hildegard Westerkamp, another member of the project, only slightly embellishes on this when she states that a soundwalk is: 'any excursion whose main purpose is listening to the environment' (Westerkamp, 2007: 49). We find it helpful to distinguish between two types of soundwalks, while acknowledging that there is significant overlap. First, there are technologically mediated walks, which involve the use of microphones, personal stereos, MP3 players and so on, either to listen to the live soundscape in novel ways, or to layer pre-recorded music and sounds onto the experience of walking (Gallagher and Prior, 2014). Such mediated forms of soundwalks have been embraced to a certain extent by geographers (Butler, 2006 and 2007; Butler and Miller, 2005; Gallagher, 2015; Pinder, 2005), and by artists such as Janet Cardiff and Christina Kubisch.

The second type of soundwalk – the listening walk – is the focus of this chapter. Once again, listening walks were first described by Schafer as 'simply a walk with a concentration on listening' (Schafer, 1994: 212). Since their emergence in the 1960s in North America, these types of soundwalks have been developed as a creative practice by experimental musicians and sound artists. The impetus for these developments can be traced to John Cage's ideas about sound and silence, most famously expressed in his 'silent piece', 4′33″. In this work, a performer or ensemble of musicians plays no music, thereby drawing attention to the ambient sounds of the setting, usually a concert hall (Drever, 2009). Drever writes about the listening walks of composers Philip Corner and Max Neuhaus, who both led groups of listeners through urban environments in an attempt to take attentive listening beyond the confines of the concert hall, aes-theticising 'everyday' sounds. While some of these walks were about chance experiences with sounds, others were undertaken with an idea of the sounds to be encountered, such as Max Neuhaus' listening walks inside industrial locations normally inaccessible to visitors (Drever, 2009), making these types of listening walks akin to compositional pieces rather than completely unstructured improvisations.

Over the past 10 to 15 years, such sonic perambulations have flourished under the auspices of arts and experimental music festivals in cities such as New York,[1] Oxford,[2] Edinburgh[3] and Brussels.[4] To take just one example, the arts duo Sans façon led a listening walk entitled *Odd sympathies* through Cardiff city centre in Wales, as part of the 2008 Artes Mundi art exhibition. The walk, which makes direct reference to the work of John Cage,[5] was repeated 27 times along the same route, again with the expectation of encountering particular sounds at specific points along the route. This expectation is made all the more apparent as the leader (or 'conductor') of the walk used a graphical score to time the appearance of particular sonic features of the landscape, including traffic, fountains and the sounds of walking over different surfaces, across each walk's 30 minutes and 33 seconds duration.[6]

Listening walks have also – at least tentatively – started to appeal to academic researchers in search of a method that can be applied to help understand people's in situ experiences of different sound environments. Often this has taken the form of interrogating people's valuations of the quality of sound environments from an environmental psychology or landscape design perspective. Research in this area has instructed participants to rate the positive and negative characteristics of such sound environments, through questionnaires and surveys in which participants are asked to rank positive and negative sonic qualities of walked environments using predetermined numerical or semantic scales (most often from 'noisy' to 'quiet'), rather than providing descriptive accounts (see Berglund and Nilsson, 2006; Jeon *et al.*, 2010, 2011, 2013; Liu *et al.*, 2014). In their version of a listening walk, Adams *et al.* (2008) modified this approach slightly. Semi-structured questions were posed at different stopping points along a walked route, including questions about what sounds dominated, what was liked or disliked about the soundscape, and how participants thought the physical qualities of the built environment impacted upon the soundscape (see also Adams, 2009; Bruce and Davies, 2014).

As listening walks have made the transition from being a musical practice or experimental artistic intervention to acquiring the status of an academic research method, their meaning and intent have been transformed. First, listening walks as research method are no longer about the implicit didacticism of opening the ears of walkers to everyday sound events ('what happens when we listen to the world as a musical composition?'), but instead about a group of listeners (some 'expert', others not) acting as producers of data. Second, the type of listening judged to be of value has changed. Listening walks in their musical or artistic form tend to focus on what is termed 'reduced' listening. This type of listening involves directing attention to the aesthetic qualities of sounds – such as their texture or timbre – independent of either the cause or the meaning of those sounds (Chion, 1994: 29–33). Take, for example, the sound of someone pulling a wheeled suitcase along a cobbled pavement that is out of sight but in earshot during a listening walk. Rather than listening to the scraping and rattling to discern what is producing them or what information these sounds may convey, reduced listening will instead focus on the sonic qualities of the scraping and rattling: the pitch of these sounds, their rhythm, how they reverberate along a narrow street, and so on. As an academic method, by contrast, there is a tendency to reduce listening walk data to categories of soundscape judgements. Third, researchers to date have assumed that listening begins and ends with the human auditory system and associated cognitive processes, leading to a rather disembodied conception of listening. There has been little consideration of the inter-modality of the senses when walking and listening (though see Adams, 2009; Jeon *et al.*, 2011).

In this chapter, we argue that listening walks can perform a wider range of functions than is allowed for by a focus on aesthetics and reduced listening, a focus on value judgements of soundscapes, or a focus on auditory perception and cognition. A single listening walk can cross all of these registers and more. Consequently, listening walks are not tied to specific topics or modes of enquiry. They can simultaneously function as an aesthetic performance and a method of enquiry, a form of intensified human sensory perception and a way of connecting to the more-than-human world, a meditative experience-in-the-moment and a participatory pedagogy. They are not tied to a particular epistemology, and are applicable to all kinds of topics in all kinds of places: investigating architecture, landscape architecture and urban planning, including informing the redesign of spaces through new building or landscaping projects; exploring environmental change, such as the effects of conservation or gentrification, through 'before' and 'after' walks; mapping the rhythms and patterns of movement in a particular place; examining relations between humans and non-human species; and so on. This multiplicity is, for us, the central attraction of the method. It enables the method to be adapted to many different purposes, but also means that a listening walk can elicit wide-ranging responses that exceed any prescribed purpose. This open-ended, emergent quality produces unexpected encounters, feelings, thoughts and analyses. Though both of us have been involved in many listening walks over the years, they retain an alluring ability to surprise.

To demonstrate this argument, the following section presents a first-person autoethnographic narrative, written by Michael, about a single listening walk. Our aim is to show some of what listening walks can do, through consideration of a specific example, before we turn to analysing some of what the walk revealed. Jonathan led the walk, in connection with research that Michael undertook in 2013 to develop methodologies for sonic geography. It took place one evening in September 2013 and lasted a little over an hour. The route was planned in advance to weave around Edinburgh's historic Old Town. Participant numbers were limited to 12 to keep the walk manageable and avoid the group fragmenting. We invited colleagues and friends by email and allocated places on a first-come first-served basis. Despite our interest in audio recording methods (Gallagher and Prior, 2014), the walk was not documented with sound recordings since our aim was simply to listen, avoiding the distractions of too much equipment. However, a few photographs were taken during and after the walk by Michael.

We are aware that narrating a listening walk in text cannot capture or (re) present the multi-sensory qualities of the walk itself (Westerkamp, 2005: 34). Our aim is rather to evoke something of the sense of movement and multiplicity that characterises listening walks, and to offer examples of the kinds of affects, observations and thoughts afforded by the method. In doing so, we hope to demonstrate that listening walks hold much potential beyond how they have so far been framed as a research method.

A Listening Walk in Edinburgh

We are being issued with instructions, gentle but insistent. Please follow me, walk in single file, keep quiet. Please turn off mobile phones, put electronic devices away, focus on listening to the city. Mildly theatric in our little procession, we string out along pavements. There are pedestrian sounds: pelican crossing beeps, a rattle that sounds like the vibration of roller luggage, soft placking of footsteps on stone slabs. Across the cobbles of the Royal Mile, Edinburgh's main tourist thoroughfare, a snatch of conversation is audible. A small group stands gathered outside a café, and a male English voice says, '… the gay, balding, state-educated northern scientist …' followed by an eruption of laughter. Australian accents, American accents, unidentifiable foreign languages. Then onto a busier road and traffic noise bears down, almost overwhelming when listened to so closely. This blanket of low to mid frequencies, fuggy and cloying, is punctuated by the jarring spike of a bus clattering over a maintenance hole cover – the collective obsession with vehicular mobility is unavoidably audible.

A tourist tat shop blares out bagpipe music. The shrieking recedes rapidly as we enter the Scotsman steps, a staircase spiralling down towards the railway station. Inside its tile and stone enclosure, the chug of traffic washes out to a hollow drone. For many years these steps were used by rough sleepers and as a toilet by drunks, but in 2011 they were renovated with a public art commission, couched in the familiar terms of art-as-regeneration:

> Before restoration by Edinburgh World Heritage and City of Edinburgh Council, [the steps] were extremely dilapidated, and vulnerable to misuse. The Fruitmarket Gallery suggested commissioning a public artwork for the Steps as part of the renovation, to help change the public perception of them.
>
> (Fruitmarket Gallery, 2011)

Martin Creed, the commissioned artist, had each of the 104 stairs covered with a different kind of marble from a different part of the world. 'Whatever I did had to be functional…. But I also wanted it to be beautiful. In the past it was used as a toilet, and in fact marble is used in toilets a lot…. So I thought I'd try and make a beautiful toilet' (*The Scotsman*, 2011: unpaginated). The result is 'a staircase fit for kings' (Jones, 2011: unpaginated) but in an everyday location.

New gates now enable the council to shut off the steps at night, a securitisation of space that has both restricted usage and helped to make the place appealing for a wider public. The grime and the stink of piss have disappeared. As we tramp down, the soft flip-flop of 24 feet on polished stone reverberates around us, creating a peaceful, almost stately ambience.

Down at the bottom we pop out onto the street and things get louder again. On entering the railway station, out of the ether comes a clipped, automated announcement instructing us not to smoke. The voice is Scottish, female, middle-aged, polite but cold, with a schoolteacher-ish tone that is intensified by the boxy acoustics of the public address system. Inside we linger to take in the reverberating bustle of the main concourse, then leave by a rear exit to the same voice incanting its regulatory message, now insistent to the point of being invasive and almost sinister. These increasingly ubiquitous cyborg ladies mobilise the affective qualities of femininity as a form of soft power, with a gentle-but-firm persuasiveness that provides

> a central asset in the continued securitisation and control of contemporary space, cutting across what little is left of the public realm and providing the appearance and the illusion of efficiency and calm in commercial environments. It is estimated that 70 per cent of recorded voices in the UK are female or female-sounding.
>
> (Power, 2013: 37)

The Orwellian mood is broken abruptly by a polar opposite gender stereotype: a bloke belching, beer can in hand, as he leans against the Ingleby Gallery, a contemporary fine art space nestled behind the station. The loutish burp sounds a cheeky echo of local history. From the 1980s until 2006, this building was home to The Venue, one of Edinburgh's best-loved live music and club spaces. With the subsequent conversion to gallery, its boozy atmosphere has been scrubbed up and quietened down for a more refined clientele.

We continue walking, beneath the booming arches of a rail bridge and past a redevelopment site still in progress. Another fondly remembered nightclub once occupied an old bus depot here. As in many UK cities since the 2008 financial crash, its demolition proved premature, leaving a yawning gap site. There is a quietness here, a sense of empty space. Graffitied hoardings fence off five acres of crushed rubble with vegetation sprouting higher each year. During the Edinburgh festival, the area was used by Snoozebox, a pop-up hotel company offering temporary accommodation in modified shipping containers – hutches for humans. It's a herald of things to come, since the Caltongate development proposed for this site – a bland mix of leisure facilities, retail outlets and offices – includes three hotels, one of which will be part of Premier Inn's new 'hub' brand, with high-tech but ultra-tiny rooms designed to squeeze maximum revenue from premium real estate.

Caltongate stalled for over a decade in the planning process due to the bankruptcy of its first developer in 2009, vocal local opposition to the insertion of

generic corporate architecture into a picturesque World Heritage Site, contro-
versy over the threatened demolition of listed buildings, the meagre provision of
affordable housing and a host of other issues. However, capital usually gets its
own way in the end, and at the time of writing, the scheme's new South African
investors have finally been given the go-ahead, a decision reportedly greeted by
a chorus of boos from the public gallery in the City Council Chamber.

Back on the Royal Mile, we take a short detour through a graveyard, where
my attention is drawn to the sight of a blood-red leather glove impaled on a
black iron railing. Then the concrete façade of the Scottish Parliament comes
into view, and again we are immersed in heavy traffic drone. A narrow cul-de-
sac leads us towards the grassy sweep of Holyrood Park. I hear what Augoyard
and Torgue (2006: 29) term 'the cut out effect':

> a sudden drop in intensity associated with an abrupt change in the spectral
> envelope of a sound or a modification of reverberation…. This effect is an
> important process of articulation between spaces and locations; it punctuates
> movement from one ambience to another.

The soundscape changes gradually but radically, from rumbling main road to
small enclosed cobbled street to wide open field, with crows cawing in the trees,
the odd dog bark, and a male voice in the middle distance shouting instructions
for what might be some kind of sports match or training session just out of view.
It has been argued that urban parks are constructed through photographs, with
governmental power exercised through images depicting 'park space as distant,
and conceptually separate, from urban space' (Gabriel, 2011: 125). But landscape architecture can have strong aural effects too. Here the bustle of the city is
palpably distant, screened out by the surrounding trees and buildings. I feel an
expansive sense of space stretching away from me.

The walk ends, and for a moment we all just stand together listening. Jonathan
hands out short questionnaires to gather some written responses, and then we
form a circle to discuss our experiences. For my own part, the walk led me to
listen to my own listening. At times I could sense myself relaxing into listening,
enjoying it. At other points I could hear myself becoming impatient, exasper-
ated, not wanting to listen but to look or to touch the city instead. Listening func-
tioned as a provocation, a challenge, something to push back against rather than
a straightforward sensory orientation.

Analysing Spaces

Michael's autoethnographic account narrates one person's experience of a single
listening walk, and as such can only hint at the range of functions such walks
can perform. Nevertheless, it is possible to make some observations about what
the listening walk revealed about Edinburgh, as compared with what might be
expected from other modes of enquiry. One striking feature is that listening
walks are not only about sound, though sound is their primary concern. As

Drever (2009) argues, they are a means of engaging with the geographies of everyday life in a participative and non-hierarchical way. The instruction to listen and not talk might seem didactic, but in practice the informality of a group walk in unremarkable surroundings undermines any such tendencies. Instead the focus on listening is a provocation that unsettles sensory habits. The result is not only that people listen differently, but that in listening differently they also see, feel, smell and move differently. Listening walks invite attention to wander across different senses, provoking listening to slip between different modes, as listeners tune in to various aspects of the environment, their own bodies and listening practices. It is precisely this movement between different registers that, for us, makes the listening walk such a lively and versatile method. Requiring listeners to focus on just one of these aspects, such as judgments about noise or soundscape quality, risks restricting this liveliness.

Thus in practice, listening walks are always multi-sensory, multi-modal methods, whose relevance goes far beyond enquiries into the soundscapes of places. The walk narrated above, for instance, produced heightened awareness of incessant road traffic, the local tourist industry, urban regeneration, the securitisation and control of space, and the demarcation of parks, with these issues coming in and out of focus over the duration of the walk. At certain points one or other of these issues came to the fore; at other points multiple issues were juxtaposed, playing in counterpoint to one another or jarring in dissonance.

Nancy suggests that 'to be listening is to be straining toward a possible meaning, and consequently one that is not immediately accessible' (Nancy, 2007: 6). During the walk, this straining stretched attention to its limits, raising questions, dredging up old memories, setting up new associations, sparking off unexpected trains of thought and opening lines of enquiry to be followed up later. The city, with its many flows and sedimented accretions of materials, culture, capital and power, began to flake apart. Listening walks can thus be theorised in Lefebvrean terms as analysing the many superimposed layers of space. There is also a resonance with Lefebvre's rhythmanalysis, because so many of the rhythms of spaces are articulated sonically, in the tempo of pelican crossing beeps, the incessant hum of air conditioning, the diurnal flux of traffic noise or the seasonal variation of the dawn chorus for example. Listening walks can draw out how spaces are composed of what Lefebvre identified as 'semi-autonomous elements with distinct rhythms that co-exist without being subsumed by one another' (Karaman, 2012: 1292–1293). Crucially, the walker, as rhythmanalyst, also sets his or her body in rhythmic motion, participating in the flows of space, joining in with the improvising ensemble of the city. Analysis is produced from within the rhythms, rather than from a static or exterior position. This kind of analysis is participative, like the uniquely situated knowledge of a symphony that is produced by playing it in an orchestra.

De Certeau famously argued that visuality proceeds from a voyeuristic abstracting impulse, whereas walking in the city generates more grounded, embodied understandings of everyday urban spatial practices (de Certeau, 1988). Listening adds another dimension to walking as an embodied, situated way of knowing. It can generate knowledge about spatial elements that are often over-looked, such as the sonic by-products of other processes: construction noise, reverberations from stone, concrete and glass façades, echoes in subways and staircases, the sounds of animals, plants and weather, unexpected moments of quietness. Listening to such sounds reveals the unconscious life of spaces, a jumbled-up mass of vibrations, the flipside of the smooth logics of architecture, planning and design. There are also many deliberate and designed sounds in the world – alarms, announcements, music – and listening walks tune into these more conscious aural aspects of space too.

While embodied, multi-sensory experience is central to the affective potency of the method, listening walks are not only an in-the-moment experience. In many cases, Michael's account is embellished with additional details from sub-sequent investigations sparked off by the walk. For example, Michael had been aware of the Caltongate gap site for many years, recording some video footage of it on one occasion, and on another venturing inside to explore when some of the hoardings had been blown down. The listening walk, however, gave him a new sense of the silence of the site, and the local history and politics that might be hiding within that silence. The old Bongo club could almost be heard as a spectral presence. Further investigation revealed the fraught, noisy struggles sur-rounding the redevelopment. Likewise Michael had used the Scotsman steps on many occasions, both before and after Martin Creed's refurbishment, but the lis-tening walk prompted more in-depth exploration of the background to this public artwork and the discourses surrounding it. Listening walks can therefore act as a catalyst for further investigation; they can be particularly useful in the early, exploratory stages of research, as a way of identifying issues to pursue, perhaps in concert with other types of methods.

Listening walks also lend themselves to repetition and so can be productive in investigating the nature of spatial experience across time. To give an example, between June 2011 and May 2012, Jonathan was invited by two arts organisa-tions to lead what amounted to three listening walks along the same route in a north-west district of Brussels. Starting from near the Brussels–Charleroi Canal, each walk took the listening group (comprised of members of the public partici-pating via an open invitation) to an area called Tour and Taxis. Historically, this area was dominated by a grand postal sorting building, and a network of railway lines carrying mail in and out of Brussels. At the time of the first walk, the area had been left largely unmaintained for some time; where the train tracks used to be, a diverse brownfield grassland habitat had matured. By the third walk, a development project of Tour and Taxis had started in earnest. Diggers and bull-dozers had silenced the birds and insects, as they progressively carved out prime real estate. While clearly less rigorous than the analytical tools used in the emerging field of soundscape ecology (see Pijanowski *et al.*, 2011), the repeti-tion of the walk nonetheless starkly revealed the changing constitution of the walked route through sound; this consequently initiated discussions amongst the participants about the broader political, social and ecological implications of brownfield development and urban gentrification.

Conducting a Listening Walk

We want now to step away from these two particular walks, and offer a basic general procedure for undertaking a group listening walk. We do so because the literature that has reflected upon listening walks as a research method has not detailed in any precise manner how these are actually conducted. The procedure we offer is influenced in part by the suggestions made by Schafer (1994: 212–213), but in the main is based upon our own experiences of leading and participating in successful (and not so successful) listening walks. We wish to emphasise that the procedure is very flexible and does not need to be conducted in the manner we state. Our advice here is therefore offered as a starting point, to be adapted by other researchers for their own projects and purposes.

Before the listening walk commences, we first plan an approximate route around the chosen location, bearing in mind the desired duration, the intended participants, and any access and safety considerations (for example: will sections of the route be dark, steep, slippery, wet underfoot, cross busy roads? Will that cause any problems given the ages and abilities of the likely participants?) The route can be sketched onto a map if need be. A print out from an online map can be useful for this purpose. We usually aim for routes that pass through a variety of different spaces and ambiences, taking particular account of acoustic variations. Typically, we include both busy and quiet spaces, and both larger open spaces and smaller enclosed ones. The Edinburgh listening walk, for example, created an interesting contrast between the acoustics of the enclosed Scotsman steps and the larger railway station concourse.

Walks can be of any duration, but between one and two hours allows for immersion in the soundscape without becoming too tiring; it takes a little time for the body and ears to sensitise to the soundscape. We tend to favour routes that do not involve doubling back, although this depends on the location and aim of the walk. A circular route looping back to the starting point can work well, but equally ending in a different place can provide a transect through space. The Edinburgh walk cut through the city's Old Town, roughly following the line of the Royal Mile, with some deviation, and in this case following an established line through the city seemed to work well. Participants can be involved as co-researchers in the planning of a route and invited to lead the walk too, particularly if they are more familiar with the area than the researcher.

It is a good idea to choose a starting point that is easy to locate, relatively open, and large enough to accommodate the whole group without blocking pavements, entrance-ways and other busy areas. Some shelter in case of inclement weather can also be an advantage. Examples include public squares, road junctions, or the foyer of an easily accessible building. Transport hubs such as railway stations can be convenient, but can also be crowded, so if using one of these be sure to identify a particular place within them so participants will know where to go.

Once a rough idea for the route has been generated, the next stage is to try it out. Usually we do this as a solo exercise to allow us to concentrate and observe the route without distractions, but you might prefer to take a colleague or friend for company. The most important thing at this stage is to listen intently to the environment, shaping the route around the soundscape. If you struggle with this aspect, it might be worth seeking out a local sound artist, soundscape researcher, or someone else who has a keen ear for environmental sound, to help plan a route. It makes sense to do the trial at a similar time of day and season to when you expect to do the walk. During the trial walk, make a note of timings, precise route details, possible changes, and any particularly interesting sounds, spaces or atmospheres where the walk might stop for a few moments to enable greater immersion. It is advisable to walk slowly when testing timings, to calibrate the pace for slower walkers. The route can be tweaked to make it shorter or longer as required, perhaps doing a second test run to check timings again if necessary.

Potential participants can then be provided with information about the time, date, location and approximate duration of the walk. It is worth bearing in mind, however, that in our experience listening walks have worked best when the exact route or destination is not revealed, as this prevents participants from prejudging what they are likely to encounter. It is also worth considering weather and terrain, and advising participants on clothing and footwear if necessary. A contingency plan for bad weather, such as a shorter route with more shelter, can be useful. Alternatively you could inform participants that the walk will take place whatever the weather and ask them to prepare accordingly. Such considerations depend on your location – many of the walks we have led have been in the UK, where rain is always a possibility.

We have found that a group size of around 10–12, including the walk leader(s), is optimal, being large enough to make for a good discussion afterwards, but not so large as to be unwieldy. With larger group sizes, there is a danger of the group fragmenting or people getting lost. If many people are interested or you have a large pool of potential participants, multiple walks can be organised on different occasions, or places can be allocated on a first-come-first-served basis, keeping a reserve list of names in case anyone drops out.

Once everyone has arrived at the start point, we introduce ourselves and make some introductory remarks. One of the most important elements of the method, in our experience, is to politely ask participants to refrain from talking during the walk, to not externally document it in any way (no written notes, no photographs) and to turn off all mobile devices – not to a vibrate or silent setting, but fully off. We usually explain to participants that observing these rules will help them concentrate on listening.

The walks also seem to work best when participants are asked to walk spaced apart in single file; a little distance between each walker means that the sounds of those in front or behind will not be the only focus of the sonic environment, and prevents interactions between walkers causing a distraction from the wider environment. When leading the walk, it is best to walk at a relatively slow but steady pace, so that walkers can focus on listening, rather than trying to keep up with the person in front of them. If you cross roads or other obstacles, wait quietly at the other side to let everyone cross safely; you can inform participants about these temporary pauses before you set out.

These rules may seem prescriptive, but in our experience they help to produce distinctive sensory experiences. Participants often comment afterwards on how walking in this way, spaced apart and listening without talking, produces interesting affective states such as meditative calm, a sense of being unsettled or provoked, or a heightened awareness of their surroundings or their own bodily presence. Both of us have experienced listening walks in which these rules were not observed, where people walked alongside each other chatting casually, like an ordinary ramble, or where the walk was periodically interrupted by the leader to discuss notable features or invite responses from the group. There is nothing wrong with such activities per se, but we find them unsatisfying as listening walks because they do not create enough sustained, intensified auditory attention to disrupt usual sensory habits, which for us is central to how the method functions.

Debriefing and discussion can take place afterwards, and is often fascinating. As is evident in the Edinburgh walk narrative, Jonathan hands out short paper questionnaires immediately after a walk to gather individual responses, before breaking into group discussion. The theme of the research being undertaken will dictate the precise nature of the questions posed, but we have generally found it best to use a short number of open-ended questions using non-technical language ('Write down any unexpected or unusual sounds'; 'What changes to the sound environment did you experience as you walked?'). Ending the walk in a relatively quiet space helps to facilitate a group discussion on participants' responses to the questions; it may be of use to document these discussions on an audio recorder.

Such a qualitative form of debriefing allows participants to raise all manner of ideas and chains of association that cannot be presupposed. The following extract, from a participant on the first of the Brussels listening walks, illustrates the types of intersections between sound, space and body that can be revealed when both listening *and* walking – rather than disembodied, cochlear listening – are the focus:

> The noise from the busy street was very loud and oppressive. As we approached the open grassland [at Tour and Taxis] the noise dropped, and it became clear to me how big the influence of sound is on your state of mind. I'm constantly (subconsciously) trying to keep out the noise. This means you can't open up and relax. Entering the grassland changed this and I could feel myself again. Hearing the rustle of plants and the sounds made by the surface I walked on felt like coming home. An intimacy returned, I could reconnect with the environment.

After the Edinburgh walk, one participant described it as Wagnerian in its range of dynamics and timbres, while someone else remarked on the gendered qualities of certain sounds. Another found that traffic noise predominated, with few distinctively local sounds: a kind of aural non-place. Some said that they heard the sounds of the group, of their own footsteps, their own bodies. Several remarked on how gentle and peaceful they had found the city as a whole, to their surprise. As a group, we talked about the interaction of listening and other senses, and how the focus on sound made for a particular kind of multi-sensory awareness, invoking a different sort of seeing, a new sense of one's body in the city, even a heightened sense of smell.

The Potential of Listening Walks: Some Concluding Thoughts

We have seen that within the extant literature listening walks have been presented as a means to collect data about the sonic quality of different types of spaces. The primary intention of such walks is for research participants to provide soundscape judgements at particular moments on a walked route, and at least some information about what it is that constitutes a positive or negative sonic experience. By contrast, we have offered a descriptive account of a listening walk, pointing towards the broader potential of the method, and drawing particular attention to its multiplicity.

Listening walks can act as an analytical tool in the investigation of different spaces. Such investigations need not be confined to examining the sonic pleasure or displeasure that moments along a route may bring (important and worthwhile though this may be), but also provide a means to explore, amongst other things: (1) how a listening body, or group of bodies, affectively and emotionally respond to sounds along a particular route; (2) the production of spaces, as different modes of listening generate particular analytical insights, which are often different and complementary to those produced through visual and textual method; (3) the multiple layers of spaces – listening, for example, to the political economy of a given space, or its material constitution, or its cultural, social or ecological attributes. Listening walks can also be used as a starting point for other strategies of knowledge production, such as 'counter mapping' (Wood, 2010: 182), in which individual or inter-group sonic representations of spaces are produced, either textually or graphically.

Listening walks are endlessly adaptable and repeatable across all types of terrain, and require no special equipment, technical facilities, budget or venue. For this reason, listening walks hold great potential as a pedagogic tool for a wide range of age groups and disciplinary specialisms (and, indeed, none, given that we have used them as such a tool outside of educational institutions). We have both used listening walks in a teaching capacity with groups of students on social science, arts and humanities courses, and with practitioners. Michael, for example, recently organised a listening walk as part of a continuing professional development course for a group of early-years educators, to help them to reflect on the nature of listening in their own practice. Afterwards, some said that they had done sound walks with young children, but always with the adult professionals directing the children to listen to certain sounds; the more open-ended, uninterrupted listening walk led by Michael, with its absence of talk, enabled them to hear in a deeper and more expansive way.

Similarly, in 2009 soundscape composer John Drever ran a listening walk for acousticians and noise control experts attending the Euronoise conference, as a way to gently unsettle their more usual technocratic, normative focus on noise reduction. We see no reason why listening walks could not be similarly used with other groups, such as natural scientists interested in particular ecological systems and environments. The method would be well suited to teaching on courses concerned with the sensory and phenomenological experience of spaces, transport and mobility issues. It also has obvious relevance for professional practices that shape the sounds of environments, such as engineering, planning, design, architecture and acoustics. As a form of participatory pedagogy, listening walks can be used together with other types of sonic methods (see Gallagher and Prior, 2014) to act as a catalyst for a range of discussions about sound, listening and space.

Finally, given that the listening walk we have outlined is a group endeavour, it is useful in offsetting the individualism that often arises with other types of phenomenological accounts of spaces, or indeed the notion that 'listening' is a solitary act. Listening walks can instead contribute to the development of listening practices that are engaged, collective, participatory and inclusive. We also think that listening walks are well suited to research and teaching where sound per se is *not* the focus; in such scenarios they can act as a provocation to experience spaces differently (quietly, in a group), or invite different kinds of attention to spaces that other teaching methods would struggle to accommodate.

Notes

1 www.elastic-city.org/about.
2 http://consumerwaste.org.uk/audiograft/walks.html.
3 www.deveron-arts.com/urbanscape-ruralsprawl-project.
4 www.tunedcity.net/?page_id=3858.
5 See www.sansfacon.org/odd-sympathics.
6 For the graphical score, see www.inspiringcities.org/odd-sympathies-2008-orchestrated-sounds-of-a-city.

References

Adams, M. (2009) Hearing the city: reflections on soundwalking. *Qualitative Researcher*, 10: 6–9.
Adams, M., Bruce, N., Davies, W., Cain, R., Jennings, P., Carlyle, A., Cusack, P., Hume, K. and Plack, C. (2008) Soundwalking as methodology for understanding soundscapes, in *Proceedings of the Institute of Acoustics*, 3, Institute of Acoustics Spring Conference 2008, 10–11 April 2008, Reading, UK.

Augoyard, J. F. and Torgue, H. (2006) *Sonic Experience: A Guide to Everyday Sounds.* McGill-Queen's University Press, Montréal.

Berglund, B. and Nilsson, M. E. (2006) On a tool for measuring soundscape quality in urban residential areas. *Acta Acustica United with Acustica*, 92: 938–944.

Bruce, N. S. and Davies, W. J. (2014) The effects of expectation on the perception of soundscapes. *Applied Acoustics*, 85: 1–11.

Butler, T. (2006) A walk of art: the potential of the sound walk as practice in cultural geography. *Social and Cultural Geography*, 7: 889–908.

Butler, T. (2007) Memoryscape: how audio walks can deepen our sense of place by integrating art, oral history and cultural geography. *Geography Compass*, 1: 360–372.

Butler, T. and Miller, G. (2005) Linked: a landmark in sound, a public walk of art. *Cultural Geographies*, 12: 77–88.

Chion, M. (1994) *Audio-Vision: Sound on Screen.* Columbia University Press, New York.

de Certeau, M. (1988) *The Practice of Everyday Life.* University of California Press, Berkeley.

Drever, J. L. (2009) 'Soundwalking: aural excursions into the everyday', in Saunders, J. (ed.), *The Ashgate Research Companion to Experimental Music.* Ashgate, Aldershot.

Fruitmarket Gallery (2011) 'Martin Creed Work No. 1059, 2011. New Commission for The Scotsman Steps'. http://fruitmarket.co.uk/exhibitions/scotsman-steps.

Gabriel, N. (2011) The work that parks do: towards an urban environmentality. *Social and Cultural Geography*, 12: 123–141.

Gallagher, M. (2015) Sounding ruins: reflections on the production of an 'audio drift'. *Cultural Geographies*, 22(3): 467–485.

Gallagher, M. and Prior, J. (2014) Sonic geographies: exploring phonographic methods. *Progress in Human Geography*, 38(2): 267–284.

Jeon, J. Y., Hong, J. Y. and Lee, P. J. (2013) Soundwalk approach to identify urban soundscapes individually. *Journal of the Acoustical Society of America*, 134(1): 803–812.

Jeon, J. Y., Lee, P. J., Hong, J. Y. and Cabrera, D. (2011) Non-auditory factors affecting urban soundscape evaluation. *Journal of the Acoustical Society of America*, 130(6): 3761–3770.

Jeon, J. Y., Lee, P. J., You, J. and Kang, J. (2010) Perceptual assessment of quality of urban soundscapes with combined noise sources and water sounds. *Journal of the Acoustical Society of America*, 127(3): 1357–1366.

Jones, J. (2011) 'Martin Creed's stairway to heaven'. www.theguardian.com/culture/2011/aug/01/edinburgh-art-festival-martin-creed.

Karaman, O. (2012) An immanentist approach to the urban. *Antipode*, 44: 1287–1306. doi:10.1111/j.1467-8330.2011.00961.x.

Liu, J., Kang, J., Holger, B. and Luo, T. (2014) Effects of landscape on soundscape perception: soundwalks in city parks. *Landscape and Urban Planning*, 123: 30–40.

Nancy, J.-L. (2007) *Listening.* Fordham University Press, New York.

Pinder, D. (2005) Arts of urban exploration. *Cultural Geographies*, 12: 383–411.

Pijanowski, B. C., Villanueva-Rivera, L. J., Dumyahn, S. L., Farina, A., Krause, B. L., Napoletano, B. M., Gage, S. H. and Pieretti, N. (2011) Soundscape ecology: the science of sound in the landscape. *BioScience*, 61(3): 203–216.

Power, N. (2013) Cyborg manifestos. *The Wire*: 352–370.

Schafer, R. M. (1994) *The Soundscape: Our Sonic Environment and the Tuning of the World.* Destiny Books, Rochester.

The Scotsman (2011) Stepping out: the Scotsman Steps get a new lease of life. www.scots-man.com/news/stepping-out-the-scotsman-steps-get-a-new-lease-of-life-1-1701558.

Westerkamp, H. (2005) Soundwalking: Willow Farm Nursery. *Soundscape*, 6(2): 34–35.

Westerkamp, H. (2007) 'Soundwalking', in Carlyle, A. (ed.) *Autumn Leaves: Sound and the Environment in Artistic Practice*. Double Entendre, Paris.

Wood, D. (2010) *Rethinking the Power of Maps*. Guilford Press, New York.

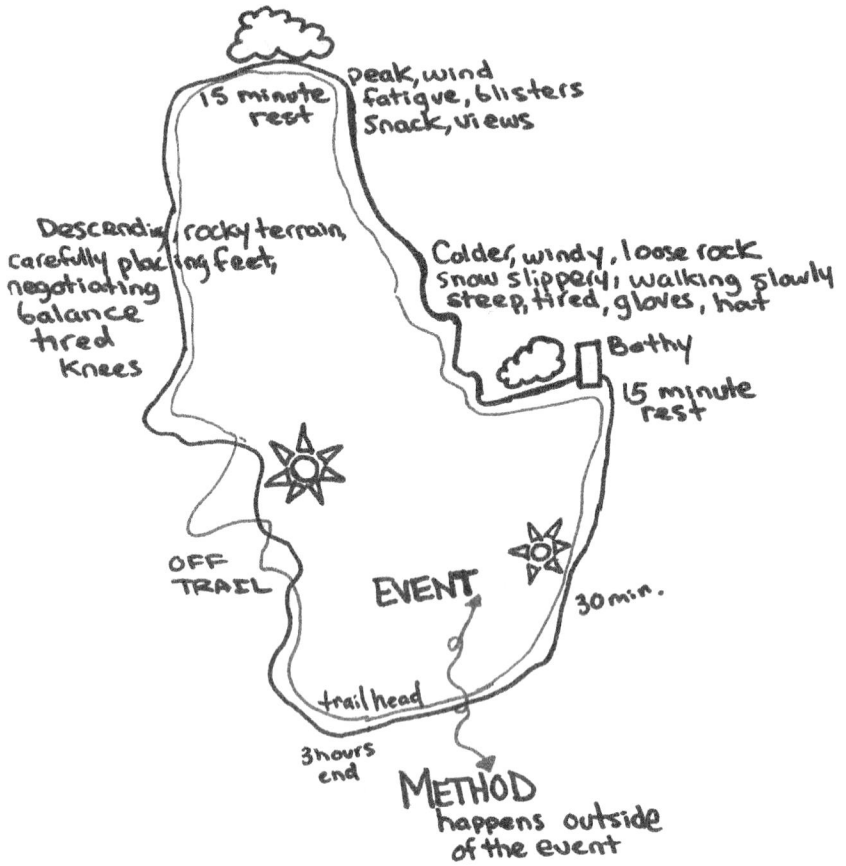

Mapping the Walk.
Source: April Vannini.

10 Wild Walking

A Twofold Critique of the Walk-Along Method

Phillip Vannini and April Vannini

Over the last decade the mobile research method known as the "go-along" (in its various manifestations such as the "ride-along" and the "walk-along") has become increasingly popular. The popularity of the go-along makes great sense in light of evolving theoretical and substantive agendas across the social sciences toward embodied, sensory, and mobile ways of knowing (e.g. see Büscher *et al.* 2010). Walking has a tremendous potential to animate spatial and sensory dynamics which static modes of inquiry cannot quite scrutinize. Nevertheless, not all is well and right with walk-alongs.

As we will argue in this chapter, much of the methodological literature on walk-alongs and a great deal of the actual research conducted through walk-alongs still suffer from many of the same ailments that go-along methods were devised to cure. Walk-alongs, by and large, are still too often informed by textualism, cognitivism, and representationalism. Walk-alongs are too often not sensuous enough, not spatialized enough, not mediated coherently enough, and not imaginative enough. Walk-alongs are also often too methodical, systematic, and pre-determined by a priori research agendas. Take, for example, this excerpt from the method section of a recent walk-along study which we reproduce nearly in full to evidence the style and orientation of the research approach:

> Three researchers conducted the walk-along interviews: a faculty member and two graduate assistants. Each graduate assistant received instruction and shadowed before conducting an independent one-to-one go-along interview. The interviews lasted an average of 48 minutes (range = 24 to 88 minutes). [...] Each interview began with an exercise that included "warm-up" questions about where to find a snack on campus; this was done to familiarize participants with the format of a go-along interview. The interview guide comprised four primary questions for the go-along interview on sexual health resources: [...] (d) You've given me a lot of examples of sexual health resources at [name of college]. Can you tell me what your top five most important or helpful resources on campus would be, including what is actually here and any other ideas you might have? When the participant named a specific resource, the researcher asked to be

shown it, and the two walked to the physical resource or went to a computer for online resources.

(Garcia et al. 2012, 1397–1398)

In this chapter we present a twofold critique to the walk-along method. Because we believe that walking is an embodied way of knowing, in what follows we each speak from our own embodied perspective, voice, and viewpoint. Thus, following this introduction we each follow a trail of our own in developing our own individual critiques of the walk-along method. Phillip's critique focuses on enlivening the kinesthetic and cinematic potential of the walk-along method, whereas April's critique concentrates on rethinking the very notion of walking as method. Regardless of our individual perspectives, we write our reflections on the basis of a shared event: a walk in Scotland's Cairngorms National Park together with Chris Townsend, a British walker known worldwide for his multi-day walks. Though our arguments and critiques are distinct, they are similarly inspired by that walk with Chris and similarly motivated by our will to rethink the nature of walk-alongs and to reimagine walking as a "wilder" way of knowing.

CINEMA = MOVEMENT

Phillip Vannini

Show, Don't Just Tell!

A few years ago I found out about Munro bagging[1] through the fieldwork of Hayden Lorimer and Katrin Lund (Lorimer and Lund 2008). I found this practice fascinating. Driven by a desire to learn more about it, and by the intention to learn more about "wildness" in the context of Scottish hillwalking together with April, I thought of asking Chris (and later two other hillwalkers, Mike and David) to go for day-long walks on the Highlands. Moreover, in an attempt to sense the world of hill-walking differently than Lund and Lorimer had, and in the hope of acquiring a new skill, I brought along video gear.[2]

The notion of "wildness" is a tricky one and we ought to be as careful stepping over it as if it were a treacherous and exposed mountain path. In Western culture, notions of the "wild" and "wilderness" have long been reputed to refer to "empty" spaces devoid of culture, signs of civilization and development, and human presence. Yet, as critics have pointed out, these notions are nothing but political myths that have regularly resulted in erasing "Others" (e.g. indigenous people) and in blindly reinforcing an artificial nature–culture binary (for a review, see Vannini and Vannini 2016). Peak-bagging, like many other ways in which people strive to "conquer" wild natural environments, is an activity underscored by colonial, androcentric, and anthropocentric ideologies that risk perpetuating the perilous idea that nature is an inert object waiting to be possessed, tamed, and classified (Lorimer and Lund 2008).

Nonetheless, mountains and similarly "wild" places around the globe continue to exercise a powerful pull over the popular imagination (MacFarlane 2008, 2009). Whether or not places like the Scottish highlands and their tallest hills and mountains can be objectively considered wild or not is truly not the important point for the throngs of walkers and tourists seduced by their awe-inspiring appeal. As MacFarlane puts it, it is less about the presence of social development and the clear absence of humans and their history and culture from these places, and much more about the subjective feeling of being alive in a place animated by at least a modicum of self-will (the idea at the etymological root of the words "wild") that wildness – as a process rich with vitality and unpredictability – depends. It is in this sense that we set out for a walk in a "wild" place.

Cameras, lenses, filters, field recorders, shotgun microphones equipped with wind screens, and related technologies are increasingly becoming recognized as essential tools of the walk-along method. Technologies such as these, as well as GIS, GPS, and other tools which blur the boundaries between arts and sciences are now starting to become incorporated into mobile approaches with promising results (e.g. Evans and Jones 2011; Jones *et al.* 2008). These tools have all been used with different intents by different researchers.

For my part I view video as a way of sensing the lifeworld[3] differently. Differently, that is, than the typical mode of academic apprehension of the lifeworld: writing. Writing demands a logocentric way of knowing. Writing asks you to search for *words:* experiential traces that are spoken, felt, or thought. Writing forces you to learn about the lifeworld in a way that can be subject to description and abstraction, to data analysis and interpretation, to literature accumulation and theory.

Filming, as an aesthetic practice, works differently. Filming demands a different sensuous way of knowing than writing does. Filming asks you – indeed it can do nothing else – to tune your attention to bodily and material surfaces that can be seen or heard. Filming pulls you into a lifeworld that does not think; a lifeworld that can only *move* in myriad ways and *speak* in a cacophony of sounds and languages. Cameras and microphones are therefore potentially able to teach us to feel something different about a place. And herein lies the premise of my main critique of the walk-along method as is most often practiced within the social sciences today. But to be clear, I am not necessarily going to argue for the need to utilize video cameras *more* as part of a walk-along. Video-recording a walk-along is in fact not at all an unprecedented strategy.

The best known practitioner of this approach is Sarah Pink, who a few years ago referred to the practice of filming walk-alongs as the "video tour." In 2008 she described it as such:

> The video tour is a collaborative method that involves walking around a specific place with a research participant. The research encounter is video recorded, by the researcher, and amongst other things might focus on

aspects of the physical and multisensorial environment as ways of exploring material/sensorial practices and meanings, and place-making.

(Pink 2008a, 7)

After images from a walk-along are video-recorded there are two options available to a researcher. And it is at this junction where my true critique comes into play.

Sarah Pink's words (Pink 2007, 2008a, 2008b) can be used to describe the first direction one may take. "In this context," Pink (2007, 243) observes with regard to the act of walking with a video camera,

> video is not merely a method of audio-visually recording people and physical settings. Rather ... walking with video provides ways of (to paraphrase Feld and Basso 1996, 91) sensing place, placing senses, sensorially making place and making sense of place.

Reinforcing this point, elsewhere, Pink (2008a, 2) writes:

> the method of video recording research participants while "walking with" them creates place on different levels: in a phenomenological sense during the research encounter; in the form of the video representation of that encounter; and again through the subjectivity of the viewer of that video.

Now, the trouble with this approach is that there is way too little emphasis on what *video does*, and not enough emphasis on *doing video*, that is, on editing and sharing video recorded as part of walk-alongs.

In fact, despite the use of a video camera during data collection, rather than cinematic representations *it is most often soundless and still photographic representations that such walks seem to yield in the published literature.* For example, in Pink (2007) we get just four still frames from the video clips shot in the field. In Pink (2008a) only one color photograph is shown, whereas in Pink (2008b) only four black and white photographs are available. Others follow a similar path. Witmore (2004) has a few more photographs, a total of ten, but no video either. More recent studies seem to go down the same road of turning cinematic recordings into static representations. For example, Yi'En (2014), despite using video while on the field, releases only photographic stills and sets of video frames. The list could go on, but the point would remain the same: in spite of all the recorded walking, only frozen visual depictions are made public. And in spite of all the talking, it is soundless textual transcriptions that can be found in the literature. And this, for me, is a serious problem.

This is where a second course of action appears to be necessary. The alternative to the textualization of video is rather simple: if video of a walk is taken, video should be edited and shown. Cinema evokes movement, rhythm, and tactile contact with the ground (e.g. terrain and landscape surfaces) and with the air (e.g. changing light and weather) in a way that photographs and writing cannot. Moreover, cinema (except for silent versions) includes sound-recording and therefore gives off a sonic impression of places and voices, with their unique texture, pitch, volume, intonation, cadence, grain, and rhythm. Cinema, in short, allows for a richer – modally speaking – apprehension of what it is like to "walk with" someone, somewhere.

Though I am confident in the value of my opinion I am not so naive to think that producing, editing, and publishing video from walk-alongs is an invariably "better" option than writing or displaying photographs. Yet, having experienced first-hand what it is like to walk with a camera, and what it is like to narrate a tale from the field through video editing, I am certain in the value of this strategy of knowledge generation. To be sure, video is difficult to shoot and edit, yet it is getting easier and easier every day, and perhaps it is not more difficult than writing clearly and evocatively. Video and editing equipment can also be expensive. Yet it is not just as expensive as travelling to an international conference or two. Video production is time consuming as well, but so is doing ethnography as a whole. And certainly video is hard to publish and distribute widely, even though all that it really takes to make it accessible is uploading it on the internet to a website like Vimeo or YouTube, copying a URL, and pasting that URL somewhere on the pages of an article or a chapter (not to mention that more and more journals nowadays actively solicit video content for their websites and are all too happy to embed Vimeo or YouTube content). In sum, taking video, and actually editing it and showing it in the shape of a narrative seems like a feasible way to evoke sensations of movement.

Walking with a Camera

To deepen my argument I want to reflect on what it is like to actually walk with a camera for the sake of recording footage editable into a short documentary. Walking with a camera is like walking with an extension of your body and of your senses (as countless people have observed). A video camera can apprehend movement differently than any other medium. Video has the potential to animate the experience of place, an encounter with a person, and the sensations unfolding throughout the act of walking in a richly sensuous way. Video – I should note – is not intended to mimic or faithfully represent the experience of being there. Because video and film are an impression of movement – based on the playing back of still images at high speed (24, 25, or 30 frames per second, normally) video is an illusion, not a copy, of movement and rhythm.

Let us focus a bit longer on the issue of rhythm. Each walk has its distinct rhythms. Cold legs at the start of a walk will slow you down and force you to fight against the ideal pace you should be keeping. Later, a fully warmed-up body will allow you to settle into a comfortable rhythm. Then there are the many breaks you end up taking: moments when you will find yourself struggling between the need to rest and the urge to go on before your legs go cold again. And then there are the last miles of the day, when your feet, knees, and back will start to feel pain and fatigue.

Add to all this the rhythms of your mental wanderings, which often seem to have a will of their own. As Edensor (2010, 70) finds: "the rhythms of walking allow for a particular experiential flow of successive moments of detachment and attachment, physical immersion and mental wandering, memory, recognition and strangeness." Walking, therefore, consists of weaving a spatial as much as a temporal path, a path contingent on both the physical characteristics of a place and the rhythmic and durational intensities in which it is kinesthetically stitched together. These are the rhythms evoked through the short video filmed throughout our time in Scotland.

Walking with a video camera has its own unique rhythm, however, rhythms that are distinct from the act of walking without a video camera. When filming I – normally a slow but steady kind of linear walker – have to walk like a yo-yo: one moment ahead of everybody to take a shot from the front, the next moment lagging behind, slowed down by having to record a vista or a minute detail of the landscape.

The camera has a rhythm, too, one that is not necessarily the same as the one preferred by its operator. Cameras do not like to move very much. This is ironic for a cinematic medium (let us remember that the word "cinema" originates from the Greek word for movement). Camera movement causes shakiness and possibly loss of focus, which in turn cause viewers dizziness and headaches. The irony is double: when a camera represents movement faithfully (albeit with ugly results), a viewer will perceive the movement as unfaithful to the conventions of good cinema, of good movement. When a camera represents the movements of walking artificially (for example, while gliding on a dolly), a viewer will perceive that movement as faithful. So once again, video works as an illusion.

For the video camera walking unfolds as constant up and down motion that throws foreground and background out of sync. As a result walking with a video camera in order to shoot steady and editable images is taught to novices as a movement unlike normal walking: a movement more or less locked in at the hips, with the buttocks carrying the center of gravity low and even, and with both feet moving forward sideways out like a goose in order to avoid the springing up and down caused by the cyclical action of left and right calf muscles.

Largely inimical to normal pedestrian rhythms, cameras generally like to rest on comfortable tripods whence they can gaze at the movement unfolding before them just like a spectator safely removed from the scene. And this intermittent positioning in turn forces their human operators to engage in the constant back-and-forth on a trail described above, interspersed with bouts of awkward hip-locked walking, and occasionally having to run in order to catch up. My point is that none of this, absolutely none of this important experience of the walk-along with a video camera, will be communicated if video is not edited and shown, and turned instead into still frames.

Weathering Whether

Something else happens when you walk outdoors with a camera with the intent of editing a short narrative video, something that can profoundly challenge your walking rhythms: weather. The methodological literature on walk-alongs is teeming with warnings about the vagaries of weather. Exposure to the elements – rain, wind, heat, cold, snow, and ice – are anathema to a systematic and efficient interview, it seems. These factors are undoubtedly some of the biggest "con's" to a method that is otherwise rich in "pro's." Carpiano (2009), for example, writes that weather can present serious obstacles to the conduction of a good walk-along interview both during winter and summer. Garcia and colleagues (Garcia *et al.* 2012) point out that the weather can present "environmental limitations" and "disruptions," which can make the walk-along method "vulnerable" and "susceptible" to challenges (ibid., 1400). As challenging as weather may be, to think of it as a limitation and a disruption is to entirely miss the point of a walk-along. While it is true that we ourselves postponed our initially scheduled walk with Chris due to a massive snowstorm – which would have made walking in the mountains very dangerous – in the end the story told by our video would not have been the same without the wildness of Scottish weather.

While reflecting on the temporalities of walking, Edensor (2010, 72) argues that walkers "attune themselves to the rhythmicity of the moment through breathing, gestures, pace of movement, speech." Those who experience walk-alongs with a video camera – as explained in the paragraphs above – also need to attune themselves to the rhythmical exigencies of their recording technologies. Of course in a weather-less space there would be little need to continuously adapt. But on a mountain, and a fickle-weather Scottish mountain to boot, the necessities of maintaining such flow by recording successive movements have clear impacts upon the walking body. Changing weather demands stopping to dry and clean lenses and filters. Tricky passages on uneven trails and icy terrain require a camera be sheathed away for safety. Cold temperatures compel the use of gloves – though operating a zoom lens with manual focus demands bare-handed tactile precision. Scrambling on rocks and unstable paths means needing both hands for safe gripping, which means stopping once again to store away a camera or perhaps swap a handheld one for a head- or chest-mounted GoPro. It is in this way that "the specific affordances of place," "the variability of the surface underfoot, the unevenness of the fixtures blocking a seamless path," and the moods of weather push the body (of both human and camera) "along certain routes, disrupt and facilitate its progress, cajole it into certain gaits and manoeuvres and in other ways produce a particular rhythmic or arrhythmic beat" (Edensor 2010, 73; also see Vergunst 2008).

In simple words, weather is not a limitation of the functionality of the walk-along method. Weather is part and parcel of the walk-along method. And walking with video with the intent of editing it and sharing it magnifies even more the importance of weather in the context of the walk-along. The sound of wind or footsteps on snow, raindrops or snowflakes touching the lens, and fog banks shifting before the eye of the camera are all movements of the lifeworld that cinema – over photography, and over still frames – is remarkably well-equipped to evoke.

"We cannot see things unless we first can see," Ingold (2005, 99) reminds us, "and we cannot see unless we are immersed, from the start, in what Merleau-Ponty calls 'the soil of the sensible' – that is, in a ground of being in which self and world are initially commingled (Merleau-Ponty 1962, 160)." We cannot film things, we might say, unless we can first see and hear, and we cannot see and hear unless we are aware of being immersed in a ground of being, moving, and becoming in which self, other, and world are commingled – indeed a *life*world. This ground is nothing more and nothing less than the spaces and places where we walk with others. The filmed walk-along is nothing more and nothing less than simply this process of commingling.

Walk-alongs are an essential "part of an attempt to take the study of eyesight" – as well as hearing, touch, movement, and balance – "back where it belongs, out of doors" (Ingold 2005, 97). Touched by weather, our perception of the world, while outdoors, "is invariably multisensory" (Ingold 2005, 97). We don't feel the weather, we feel *in* weather, Ingold (2005) observes. To wish that the weather would stop bothering us is to wish for the cessation of our hearing, seeing, touching, and feeling altogether. It is to wish that the transcribed text of an interview would show up on our desk without us having to get our feet wet and our hands cold. It is to wish that the walk-along interview would be more about the interview than the walking, the still pictures rather than the moving ones.

To recap my argument, the practice of filming a walk-along has a great potential for teaching us how to sense the lifeworld and how to relate to a human being along whom we walk. Cinema – a medium which focuses on movement – is capable of apprehending kinesthetic practices such as walking in a way that writing and photography cannot match. But for cinema to generate useful knowledge that is sensorially rich, it must be edited, shared, and shown.

Cinema, moreover, has the enormous potential to enliven what is essentially unique about life in the open: weather. Still photographic representations and soundless writing cannot animate weather in the same way that cinema does. A more sensuous understanding of the walk-along than the one that seems to currently dominate within the social sciences would treat weather as an inseparable component of the embodied and emplaced experience of walking rather than a limitation of this method, and would actively generate cinematic tales of video-recorded walks rather than turn them into still and muted moments that are frozen in time.

WALKING BEYOND METHOD

April Vannini

A Glance at the Map

We are here, in the Scottish Highlands, to walk. Not to execute a component of our research design. Not to conduct a walk-along interview. Not to systematically engage in data collection. No; much more simply, we are here to get to know Chris and explore with him the Cairngorms National Park. The act of walking is not the problem with the so-called "walk-along." The problem with the walk-along lies in treating walking as an instrumental methodological procedure.

To avoid this problem, following the inspiration of Truman and Springgay (2016), I want to ask: what if we referred to walk-alongs as an "event activity" rather than a method, interview technique, or means of data collection? In treating walking as a means to gather data in the traditional sense the act of walking becomes detached from both body and place, and this reduces walking to a set of overly-planned instrumental protocols and procedures.

The reduction of walk-alongs to an instrumental method is not an uncommon phenomenon in the social sciences. McCormack (2008, 4), for example, observes:

> Admittedly, as a set of disciplinary associations straddling the natural and social sciences, much of geography has striven to conduct research according to a set of protocols – objectivity, detachment, disembodied distance – designed to reduce as much as possible the influence of body, affect, emotion, and feeling on the clarity and acuity of thought. Yet as has been extensively demonstrated, the practice and craft of geographical thinking is sustained by a range of corporeal, perceptual, and affective processes, including walking, seeing, and touching.

I agree with McCormack (2008). To be fair, my polemics is fueled by nothing but my personal preference for embodied ways of knowing that authentically and boldly push the boundaries of innovation. Examples of these more-than-representational ways of knowing have accumulated in the art world over many years, as I will describe shortly. Inspired by this growing tradition my arguments here are hopeful and positive. I, in other words, wish to continue seeing and hearing walk-alongs. But I want to see and hear walk-alongs that are more kinesthetic, more vivid, more sensuous, and more entangled with the material world than they currently are. If my critique is too personal, too radical, too ambitious, perhaps too indulgent, I am guilty as charged. Yet, I believe, there is tremendous value in developing and practicing embodied ways of knowing that do more than pay lip service to a set of ideals.

With this short critique I want to imagine ways of knowing that unfold as more than just opportunistic ways of squeezing interview data out of research participants' minds. Without pretending to have found ideal solutions, and without arrogantly attempting to teach my readers on the basis of nothing but the little and barely adequate walking that I have practiced in the Scottish Highlands, I write this chapter as a tentative outing, an inspired meandering, a fearless adventure of sorts. However, mine is not just a writing. Too much of go-along research methodology is encoded into nothing but words. Rather than just a written trace therefore I present you also with a cartographic evocation of our journey, the map displayed at the beginning of this chapter.

This map is not a realist representation of our walk. It is a memory map punctuated by landmarks and bodily traces that a single day out in the mountains will leave impressed upon the land and upon walking bodies. A map, not unlike a walk, that is shaped as a rhythmic sequence of steps marked by different speeds and changing terrain, by the curves of a trail, and by the weaving together of multiple walkers' movements. Rather than a linear and realist cartographic representation this map has all the characteristics of a wild walk out in the open, a walk that feels more like wayfaring than a kind of pre-planned transition from point A to point B (see Ingold 2010). A walk that feels more like an event, and less of a method for getting somewhere that is determined in advance. It is a map for a wild walk marked by embodied characteristics such as fatigue, pain from blisters, moments of feeling lost, exposure to meteorological events, and fear of falling and getting hurt.

Meeting Fellow Walkers Along the Trail

Before we get too comfortable in our initial steps, it behooves us to realize the trail we want to follow has been opened a long time before we have attempted to walk on it. At times it might appear from the social scientific literature that walking as mode of inquiry is a recent idea. Nothing could be farther from the truth. Walking as a way of knowing is something that has been practiced by indigenous peoples for centuries. As Careri (2009, 44) states: "the histories of the origins of man [*sic*] is a history of walking, of migrations of people and cultural and religious exchanges that took place along intercontinental trajectories." For instance, Australian aboriginal cultural stories are traced in the landscape through a system of routes that are mapped throughout the entire continent. Extensive knowledge of the land and the cultural stories and traditions has been created there through an intricate system of "path-stories":

> Every mountain, river, and spring belongs to a complex system of *path-stories – song-lines –* that continuously interweave to form a single "history of Dream Time," the stories of the origins of mankind [*sic*]. Each of these paths are connected to a song, and each song is connected to one or more mythological tales set in the territory.
>
> (Careri 2009, 44)

For Careri (2009) walking is even at the roots of architecture, since the first construction of space began with human beings wandering in the Palaeolithic landscape, following traces and leaving trails.

Ethnographers, mobile or otherwise, have not even been the first career intellectuals to utilize walking as a means to generate new knowledge. Walking as a way to form new thoughts, to gather ideas, and engage in the creation and sharing of knowledge is a very old tradition in philosophy. Nietzsche, for example, often wrote and reflected on walking and on movement as a writing practice. In *The Gay Science* (1974, 322) he famously wrote:

> We do not belong to those who have ideas only among books, when stimulated by books. It is our habit to think outdoors – walking, leaping, climbing, dancing, preferably on lovely mountains or near the sea where even the trails become thoughtful.

Elsewhere he also put in more concise and memorable terms: "All truly great thoughts are conceived by walking" (1889, Aphorism 34). Similarly, Jean-Jacques Rousseau once "claimed to be incapable of thinking properly, of composing, creating or finding inspiration except *when walking*" (see Gros 2014, 65). And how could we forget about Martin Heidegger, who thought of his notorious forest hikes as a mode of thinking and often reflected in writing on the very idea of thinking by drawing upon walking metaphors (Sharr 2007).

Crossing a Bridge

Arts-based practices such as creative writing, performance, and visual arts have often explored walking as a mode of inquiry as well. One of the most prominent aesthetic walking practices was initiated by the psychogeography avant-garde group known as the Situationist International (SI): a collective made famous by Guy Debord (O'Rourke 2013; Smith 2013; Wark 2011). Intended as a game, Debord devised an urban walking technique called the "drift" or "dérive" whereby participants would gain sensuous knowledge about a whole city or a single neighborhood. This was a type of exploration intended to create counter-cultural forms of mapping. Mapping, as a form of resistance, was thought to be capable of reconfiguring the social and political geographies of the sites that one visited and in turn to provoke new forms of engagement with cityscapes. Such "drifts" could also give life to a deeper recognition of the psychogeographical properties of place, thus allowing one to connect with invisible and intangible connections between spaces. As Smith (2013, 106) recognizes, the SI inspiration has had a lasting impact on artists and urban explorers, "particularly their idea of 'psychogeography': the pseudo-scientific intuiting of the city's atmospheres and driving ambiences." Often nowadays artists use newly available locative technologies to create maps based on the practice of a drift, as in Conor McGarrigle's 2012 project *Walkspace: Beirut–Venice* (see Evans 2012; Richardson 2015).

Now, if meeting other walkers along the trail has perhaps inspired you to cross the bridge into the art world, then do take a quick glance at David Evans's (2012) edited book on how walking has been used in contemporary art and you will soon realize there are myriad ways in which peripatetic practices are being used as imaginative modes of inquiry. From Jeremy Deller, Hamish

Fulton, Richard Long, and Marina Abramović and Ulay, to Janet Cardiff, Fiona Robinson, and Francis Alÿs. This is not only a practice taken up by prolific artists. Many artists, groups, and collectives are working with perambulatory practices to engage communities and experiment with walking practices, such as Toronto-based artists, the *Department of Biological Flow* (DOBF). DOBF artists Sean Smith and Barbara Fornssler use walking, performance, and video in projects like *Gait Surfing 1* (2008) and *Kino-Gait Study No. 3* (2009)[4] as a means to create and experiment with walking as an aesthetic, non-representational practice and in order to experience walking in different ways. More and more artists are crowding streets and paths in an effort to engage in walking as an open-ended and fluid mode of inquiry. Within the social sciences, there are also a few scholars who have begun to pay attention to this art world (see *Visual Studies* 2010).

Finding More Walking Partners Along the Way

Artist Hamish Fulton has deeply influenced many of the styles of contemporary art walking. Fulton carried out his first aesthetic walk in 1967, a unique practice characterized by his reticence to leave traces other than footprints. Fulton believes that art is in the walk itself (see Smith 2013, 108). He does not consider himself a writer, a photographer, or a land artist (Fulton 2010). He clarifies his stance thus: "a walk has a life of its own and does not need to be materialized into a work of art" (Schneider 2013, n.p.), "my artform is the short journey – made by walking the landscape" (Wilson 2002, 21). Fulton's website (www.hamish-fulton.com), dedicated to his unique ambulatory art practice, shows how Fulton lives his art through his feet since for him "an object (artwork) cannot compete with an experience" (Enjalran 2015, 17).

In writing about Hamish Fulton's artistic practice Enjalran (2015) draws from the work of John Dewey in order to make sense of Fulton's understanding and perception of walking as an embodied practice and aesthetic experience that is distinct from artwork intended as object. Enjalran (2015, 17) writes:

> This tension between the incommunicability of experience and the deep desire to communicate it is what drives this "walking artist," who believes art is only valid if it can be experienced and activated by viewers [and that] "without external embodiment, an experience remains incomplete."

Over the years Fulton refined his artistic walking practice by defining his process as *pure experience*:

> only art resulting from the experience of individual walks./Only = Not a generalized response to nature./art resulting from = First the walk second the artwork./the experience of = A walk must be experienced it cannot be imagined./ individual walks = Each walk has a beginning and an end.
>
> (In Wilson 2002, 21)

Fulton's walking practice reminds us of the walking experiences of our newly made friend Chris Townsend. Both have walked the Cairngorms, both have used their practice as a way to raise political and environmental awareness, both are keen on seeking out wild spaces. Hamish and Chris also have similar perspectives on the significance of walking. There is no doubt that walking is more than a hobby for both of them. Chris writes books about the landscape and long-distance walks he pursues, he writes about the places he encounters, the people he meets, and he provides knowledgeable guidance for others wanting to explore wild spaces. His knowledge is gathered through his practice, through his feet.

Fulton's walking practice is embodied in his experiences of over 300 art walks in 20 countries including: Tibet, Bolivia, Nepal, Japan, England, Iceland, Austria, Canada, Peru, United States, and Australia. As for Chris Townsend, for Hamish Fulton walking is about transforming one's state of mind:

> I see walking as my form of meditation. If we were going into the mountains and there was no trail, then we wouldn't be able to think very much, because we would be paying attention to not breaking an ankle or falling over. Then walking becomes meditative. You stop the endless thinking mind. And that's a good thing – because every now and then you want to stop going down the same neural pathways. Then you have other perceptions.
>
> (Cited in Sooke 2012)

Fulton's artistic walking practice is fully emergent and only predetermined by points of departure and arrival. As is the case for Chris's, Fulton's photography is used – very sparingly – as a means to remember the walk but not as a representation or archive of a walk. What we can see from his walks in a gallery are just a few photographs with the addition of brief words. According to Enjalran (2015, 18) "by adding words to these images, he soon undermines their representative and contemplative purpose. The text then becomes the image's equal, not in order not to represent but rather to reconstruct, allowing the viewer to connect with the walk." The words and descriptions of his walk come directly from his journal: a raw evocation of impressions, encounters, observations, and factual information. As Enjalran (2015, 17) explains:

> It is then the natural environment that influences and determines the course of events. Dates and numbers have a certain importance. They are found everywhere in his photos, wall paintings and books. They structure the artist's relationship with time and space in his work. They give a sense of the walk, its rhythm. Because walking is also experiencing time _walk equals time_, and duration, and what better medium than photography to reconstruct this experience?

A Brief Pause Inside a Bothy

Listening to Chris reflect on his walking practice and his encounters with wild spaces, we soon realize that his practice is a mode of inquiry similarly to open-ended and emergent ethnographic fieldwork. Chris walks to learn about places.

Feeling Lost: Are We Going in the Right Direction?

As I write about walk-alongs as a method, I cannot help but feeling like an imposter. Though I am a walker and I have enjoyed both long-distance and short walks, walking as a mode of inquiry is something that Chris does far better than I do – enduring longer distances, undergoing deeper contemplation, and engaging in freer reflection thanks to his tremendous amount of experience with walking in a much broader and less-restricted field. Chris is indeed the walking "methodologist," not I.

Phillip and I are simply tag-a-longers. We – despite our good intentions – are still overly preoccupied with producing an outcome: a filmic evocation of our encounter. This is especially the case for Phillip, whose presence behind the camera is making him virtually absent on the trail. Chris is the one who is truly walking.

Taking a Final Break

As I near the conclusion of our walk, I would like to return to the idea that walk-alongs should not be considered a method of gathering data but rather something that unfolds as a sensorial event. Reducing walk-alongs to a method of data collection fails to fulfill the learning potential of this mode of inquiry because it predetermines the type and quality of understanding that may take place as walking organically unfolds. This predetermination is antithetical to qualitative inquiry since this way of knowing is meant to be an emergent process.

By treating walking and walk-alongs as a "method" we limit the sensory potential of this mode of inquiry even before the walk begins. The notion of "method" implies a systematic and instrumental way of collecting data subservient to a well-defined research question and scope. It objectifies those with whom we walk as research participants, and it turns our own walking bodies into research instruments subservient to the need to collect data and reach a conclusion. I agree with Truman and Springgay (2016) who suggest that walking as a mode of inquiry should be considered a propositional act. Following the work of Erin Manning and Brian Massumi, Truman and Springgay (2016, 266) suggest that:

> Walking as propositions triggers conditions of emergence activating self-organizing potential that invents its own parameters (Manning 2013). Methodologically, this is quite different from giving directions, collecting

data, or establishing pre-determined methods. Walking propositionally demands that we conceive of research happening in the now. Research thus becomes "an occasion for experience holds [that] [*sic*] within its potential the dynamics of singularity" (Manning 2008, 6).[5] Walking sets in motion a variety of bodily movements, intensities, and affects that unfold and extend new variations.

To sum it up, I believe we should be wary of engaging in walk-alongs as acts of walking-and-interviewing. What we should strive for is something much broader and deeper than an "interview on the go." We should rather go somewhere to feel a place, sense a landscape and its weather, and encounter a human being with whom we choose to walk. To think of walking as just a novel technique for conducting an interview is simply the easiest way to forget about walking as the aesthetic and exploratory practice – the wild practice – that it really is.

Notes

1 The video referenced in the following pages can be seen at https://vimeo.com/ 129221257.
2 The Munros are the nearly 300 Scottish mountains of 3,000 feet or more. "Munro-bagging" refers to the leisure practice of climbing them all.
3 Within phenomenological traditions "lifeworld" refers to a universe that houses subjects' experiences. As opposed to the more generic idea of "world," the notion of "lifeworld" underscores a horizon of unfolding feeling, sensation, consciousness, and perception.
4 www.departmentofbiologicalflow.net/gait-surfing-i; www.departmentofbiologicalflow. net/kino-gait.
5 This quote should read: "an occasion for experience [that] holds within its potential the dynamics of singularity." It appears that the original sentence was improperly corrected by the quoting writers.

References

Büscher, Monika, John Urry, and Katian Witchger. 2010. *Mobile Methods*. London: Routledge.
Careri, Francesco. 2009. *Walkscapes: Walking as an Aesthetic Practice*. Barcelona: Editorial Gustavo Gili.
Carpiano, Richard. 2009. "Come Take a Walk with Me: The Go-Along Interview as a Novel Method for Studying the Implications of Place for Health and Well-Being." *Health and Place*, 15: 263–272.
Edensor, Tim. 2010. "Walking in Rhythms: Place, Regulation, Style, and the Flow of Experience." *Visual Studies*, 25: 69–79.
Enjalran, Muriel. 2015. "The Value of Experience." In *Canto di Strata*, 17–23. Nuoro: MAN.
Evans, David. 2012. *The Art of Walking: A Field Guide*. London: Black Dog Publishing.
Evans, James and Phil Jones. 2011. "The Walking Interview: Methodology, Mobility, and Place." *Applied Geography*, 31: 849–858.

Feld, Stephen and Keith Basso. 1996. *Senses of Place*. Santa Fe, NM: School of American Research.

Fulton, Hamish. 2010. *Mountain Time, Human Time*. Milan: Charta.

Garcia, Carolyn, Marla Eisenberg, Ellen Frerich, Kate Lechner, and Katherine Lust. 2012. "Conducting Go-Along Interviews to Understand Context and Promote Health." *Qualitative Health Research*, 22: 1395–1403.

Gros, Frederic. 2014. *A Philosophy of Walking*. London: Verso.

Ingold, Tim. 2005. "The Eye of the Storm: Visual Perception and the Weather." *Visual Studies*, 20: 97–104.

Ingold, Tim. 2010. *Being Alive*. London: Routledge.

Jones, Phil, Griff Bunce, James Evans, Hannah Gibbs, and Jane Ricketts Hein. 2008. "Exploring Space and Place with Walking Interviews." *Journal of Research Practice*, 4: 1–9.

Lorimer, Hayden and Katrin Lund. 2008. "A Collectable Topography: Walking, Remembering, and Recording Mountains." In *Ways of Walking*, edited by Tim Ingold and Jo Lee Vergunst, 185–199. Farnham: Ashgate.

MacFarlane, Robert. 2008. *The Wild Places*. London: Penguin.

MacFarlane, Robert. 2009. *Mountains of the Mind*. New York: Vintage.

McCormack, Derek. 2008. Thinking-Spaces for Research-Creation. *INFLeXions*, May, www.inflexions.org/n1_mccormackhtml.html.

Merleau-Ponty, Maurice. 1962. *Phenomenology of Perception*. London: Routledge and Kegan Paul.

Nietzsche, Friedrich. 1974. *Gay Science*. Toronto, ON: Random House.

Nietzsche, Friedrich. 1889. *Twilight of the Idols, or How to Philosophize With a Hammer*. Leipzig, Germany: Verlag von C. G. Naumann.

O'Rourke, Karen. 2013. *Walking and Mapping: Artist as Cartographers*. London: MIT Press.

Pink, Sarah. 2007. "Walking with Video." *Visual Studies*, 22: 240–252.

Pink, Sarah. 2008a. "Mobilising Visual Ethnography: Making Routes, Making Place, and Making Images." *Forum: Qualitative Social Research*, 9: 1–18.

Pink, Sarah. 2008b. "An Urban Tour: The Sensory Sociality of Ethnographic Place-Making." *Ethnography*, 9: 175–196.

Richardson, Tina. 2015. *Walking Inside Out: Contemporary British Psychogeography*. London: Rowman & Littlefield.

Sooke, A. (2012). Hamish Fulton Wanders the Neural Pathways. *Telegraph*, www.telegraph.co.uk/culture/art/art-features/9014354/Hamish-Fulton-wanders-the-neural-pathways.html.

Sharr, Adam. 2007. *Heidegger for Architects*. London: Routledge.

Smith, Phil. 2013. "Walking-Based Arts: A Resource for the Guided Tour?" *Scandinavian Journal of Hospitality and Tourism*, 13: 103–114.

Schneider, Carrie Marie. 2013. "The Ten List: Walk as Art," *Glass Tire: Texas Visual Art*, http://glasstire.com/2012/11/23/the-ten-list-walk-as-art.

Truman, Sarah E. and Stephanie Springgay. 2016. "Propositions for Walking Research." In *Routledge Handbook of Intercultural Research*, edited by Pamela Burnard, Elizabeth Mackinlay, and Kimberly Powell, 259–267. New York: Routledge.

Vannini, Phillip and April Vannini. 2016. *Wilderness*. London: Routledge.

Vergunst, Jo Lee. 2008. "Taking a Trip and Taking Care in Everyday Life." In *Ways of Walking*, edited by Tim   Ingold and Jo Lee Vergunst, 105–121. Farnham: Ashgate.

Wark, McKenzie. 2011. *The Beach beneath the Streets: The Everyday Life and Glorious Times of the Situationist International*. London: Verso.

Wilson, A. 2002. "'The Blue Mountains are Constantly Walking' – On the Art of Hamish Fulton." In *Hamish Fulton: Walking Journey*, edited by B. Tufnell and A. Wilson, 20–31. London: Tate Publishing, Tate Gallery.

Witmore, Christopher. 2004. "Four Archaeological Engagements with Place Mediating Bodily Experience through Peripatetic Video." *Visual Anthropology Review*, 20: 57–71.

Yi'En, Cheng. 2014. "Telling Stories of the City: Walking Ethnography, Affective Materialities, and Mobile Encounters." *Space and Culture*, 17: 211–223.

Landscapes of Luxury.
Source: Caroline Knowles.

Walking W8 in Manolos[1]

Caroline Knowles

In mediating the sensory footwork of dwelling,[2] in connecting us with the ground on which our lives are lived-in-motion, appropriate shoes are needed. Few would countenance leaving home without shoes when embarking on the mundane journeys of everyday life: and this underscores their central, if rarely explored, function in mobility. Shoes need to fit the walker *and* the territory. Flip-flops,[3] the world's cheapest shoes, are for the beach, and for the poor in the global south who can't afford other shoes. Manolos are London W8. If postcodes could be shoes, W8 would be a fabulous pair of high-heeled Manolos, suitably elegant, appropriately expensive. Plutocratic shoes: suitable for navigating one of London's über wealthy neighbourhoods, shoes for delicately stepping around the tensions between the concealment and exposure of wealth and erring on the side of exposure in an expensive pair of shoes. Shoes both express and co-compose urban social morphology and social distinction.

Walking serves many of the same social functions: it endlessly, unconsciously repeats learned behaviour, bodily apprenticeships shaped by class and culture,[4] emerging urban dispositions. W8 calls forth a gait shaped by a sense of entitlement. Walking is a mode of mobile urban occupation, a way of inhabiting the streets, of wrapping them around the feet of a body-in-motion on the routines of everyday life. The inhabitation of the streets co-composes them, so walking produces urban form[5] as well as urban subjectivities, ways of being in the world. Walking is also a sensory method of urban knowing: we know the streets as we feel them, experience them, beneath our feet; their fleeting ephemerality and their regulated forms revealed in our constant circulation of them.[6] Where we can and cannot walk[7] where streets have been sequestered as exclusive enclaves of privilege and exclusion is infused with urban politics. W8 summons the leisured outsider status of the *flâneur*[8] observing bourgeois urban life, just as Benjamin through his famous *Arcades Project* did in Paris. Walking is no innocent by-product of urban life; it is both constitutive of it and a way of knowing about it at the same time.

W8 is part of the *alpha territories*. This refers to a spatially calibrated estimate of wealth based on the mosaic classification of people from a range of big data sources. The four most prestigious of which are collectively called the *alpha territories*: 'groups of people with substantial wealth who live in the most sought after neighbourhoods in the UK'.[9] Average house (and flat) prices in W8 are in excess of £3 million. It houses one of the highest intensities of high-net-worth individuals (HNIs) – with investible assets of over £1 million – and ultra-HNIs – with investible assets of more than £20 million – on the planet.[10] In 2015 there were 80 individuals with wealth of more than £1 billion resident in London, more than in any other city in the world. London attracts plutocratic capital[11] and W8 is one of the places where it is consumed and parked, with res-idential property operating as a safe store of value.

The royal borough of Kensington and Chelsea's library, just off its main com-mercial artery, Kensington High Street, is the best place to begin walking W8. Cities are inevitably work-in-progress and the library archives its past. Here we learn that the W8 of today arises from a Victorian imagination and numerous forays into land speculation by wealthier builders. It was created on land occu-pied by the great country houses; part of the fashionable world gathered around the court of William and Mary at Kensington Palace in the late seventeenth century, and some distance from the city. Transformed by Victorian builders, developers like James Freak who built Onslow Square (1845–1865) and urban designers like Thomas Wood, it was intended for 'persons of good worth and quality'.[12] It exhibited the benefits of the practical application of arts and sci-ences with a mid-nineteenth-century imperialist confidence. Nearby on the banks of the Serpentine stood Crystal Palace (1851) exhibiting the best in raw mater-ials, decorative arts, machinery and jewellery as city spectacle, in the Great Exhibition. Extending and grounding this display of mastery and expertise, the Victorian and Albert Museum opened nearby (1852); the Royal Albert Hall (1871) followed where the Royal Geographical Society (1830) was already dis-seminating the benefits of the exploration on which empire was founded. From the 1840s the canals and railways connecting it to London ended its status as a fashionable suburb. The extension of the underground to South Kensington and Kensington High Street (1865–1869) and the emergence of the great department stores such as Harrods (1861) and Harvey Nichols (1850s) and a cluster lining Kensington High Street, made it what it is today. Cities it seems are as restless as the (mobile) populations co-composing them.

From the library we pick our way along the streets to the north of Kensington High Street, along Phillimore Gardens. Victorian (and earlier) versions of what much later became W8 linger in the biographies of long-term residents. Harriet, who first moved into the neighbourhood in 1952, was presented as a debutante at court; she 'did the season', the royal enclosure at Ascot, the rounds of dinners, balls, luncheons and coffee mornings young women did at that time. For several years now she has been selling off the lower floors of her house and moving up until she now lives, in comfortable if rather cramped conditions, on the floor below the attic in which she stores much of the contents of her former house. Houses on her street now sell for around £10 or £11 million and new kinds of über wealthy neighbours are moving in. She knows that the banks dominate the neighbourhood; they rent properties for their executives, often Americans, or French families wanting to be close to the Lycée. It is not that many of them are foreigners; but that they are rich changes the casual convivialities of the street, she thinks. People who can afford staff don't need to lean on the reciprocities of the neighbourhood. And so it becomes a different kind of place.

Crossing over Kensington High Street and walking gracefully along Wrights Lane and Marlow Street heading south, past ox-blood coloured purpose built mansion blocks built at the turn of the century. We walk past the new serving class: nannies pushing small charges in prams; young women cleaning windows and polishing front door knobs; a cacophony of brown feet passing through London, navigating routes through their own lives. There are deliveries and pick-ups; elaborate forms of domestic management hold sway, overseen by the wives of English, French and American bankers, who may once have been bankers themselves. The occasional hedge fund manager with flexible working hours steers a little girl in a traditional 1950s style private school uniform struggling with a violin and bulging school bag. A young woman tripping along in rival Manolos relives last nights' cocktails in a loud phone conversation with her friend: 'I was sooooo tharsty ...'.

Turning east, we walk along Launceston Road. Pillars and beautifully groomed window boxes frame its well-appointed early nineteenth-century four-storey stucco houses with impressive steps up to the front door. A relative of the Queen lives on this street when he's in London, and royalty has long been part of this neighbourhood. Residents can tell you how long it takes to walk from here to Kensington Palace, thus making it part of the neighbourhood. An ex-premier league footballer and his family moved in and then moved out again.

Walking just off Victoria Road, high-end bistros that were once pubs reveal the delicate morsels tackled by ladies who lunch. A smattering of art shops and estate agents fill in the gaps created by rising real estate values and the rents that reflect them. Corner shops, places where it was once possible to buy milk and newspapers have disappeared; even resilient Asian grocers have moved on to avoid the rising costs of trading.

The renovation of elegant period properties is the most relentless activity of these streets: the sounds and the debris of building, the disruption to parking from the skips now mark these otherwise quiet back streets. London housing is now valued by the square footage. Whether they are needed or not, basements were dug three storeys down until recently when the royal borough stepped in and limited basements to one story; games rooms, swimming pools and spa areas were slipped into the gaping caverns builders and mining engineers created. While the historical character of the area is carefully stewarded in protecting with regulation the appearance of the outside of these houses, their interiors are another matter. Highly skilled craftsmen, often at a cost in excess of a million pounds, carefully recreate these in high quality materials and finishes. Housing is a store of wealth as well as a key avenue of consumption and the financialisation of living space deepens.

On rounding the corner into Victoria Road we walk straight into an invisible block on the building ambitions of the neighbourhood's house owners in the form of the Kensington Society, which one of the long-term residents describes as 'the essence of Kensington'. Its remit is the preservation of the historical character and aesthetic appearance of the area. Under its influence the Victoria Road Residents' Association upholds the character of the block of streets around it. As part of its federal structure, each street has a representative. It is well organised and scrutinises planning applications, changes to parking caused by building work and other developments in the area like the potential sighting of hotels. It monitors the empty properties – part of the buy-to-leave schemes of absentee investors who are interested in capital returns not neighbourhood conviviality. In parallel, the Friends of Holland Park try to prevent it from being turned into an events space rather than a public park for everyone to use: valuable land is the most difficult to protect from commodification.

From the south end of Victoria road we wind through further period elegance until we hit the rush of the Cromwell Road and the feel of the area changes abruptly as we run up against the W8/SW7 borderlands of Earl's Court. Earl's Court is not appropriately navigated in Manolos, it needs a different kind of shoe entirely; a more serviceable workaday shoe is called for in order to traverse the fraying and encroaching edges of plutocratic London. Trainers perhaps?

Notes

1 This chapter is inspired by an ESRC funded investigation of London's super wealthy called *The Alpha Territory*. The author was a member of the research team.

2 Tim Ingold (2004) 'Culture on the Ground: The World Perceived through Feet', *Material Culture*, 9(3): 315–340.

3 Caroline Knowles (2014) *Flip-flop: A Journey through Globalisation's Backroads*, London: Pluto.

4 Marcel Mauss (1934) 'Techniques of the Body', cited in Edward Tenner (2003) *Our Own Devices*, New York: Knopf, Random House, pp. 8–12.

5 Michel de Certeau (1988) *The Practice of Everyday Life*, Berkeley: University of California Press; Henri Lefebvre (1996) *The Production of Space*, Oxford: Blackwell.

6 Alexandra Boutros and Will Straw (2010) 'Introduction', in A. Boutros and W. Straw (eds), *Circulation and the City*, London and Kingston: McGill-Queen's University Press.

7 Anna Minton (2012) *Ground Control*, London: Penguin; Raja Shehadeh (2007) *Palestinian Walks: Notes on a Vanishing Landscape*, London: Profile Books.

8 Walter Benjamin (2002) *The Arcades Project*, Cambridge, MA: Harvard University Press.

9 Richard Webber and Roger Burrows (2016) 'Life in an *Alpha Territory*: Discontinuities and Conflicts in an Elite London "Village"', *Urban Studies*, 53(15): 3139–3154.

10 Roger Burrows (2017) 'The Plutocratic City: Elite Formation, Power and Space in Contemporary London', using the 2015 World Wealth Reports produced by Capgemini and RBC Wealth Management for the financial sector states that globally there are 14.6 million HNIs, over half a million of whom are in the UK and concentrated in London and the south-east, *Theory, Culture and Society*, forthcoming.

11 This comes from the Sunday Times Rich List 2015, cited in Roger Burrows, 'The Plutocratic City: Elite Formation, Power and Space in Contemporary London' (forthcoming) *Theory, Culture and Society*, 2017, forthcoming.

12 Annabel Walker with Peter Jackson (1987) *Kensington and Chelsea: A Social and Architectural History*, London: Antler Books.

Index

Page numbers in **bold** denote figures.

Printed in Great Britain
by Amazon